Dear Tony

Inspired by the Story of a Neglected Girl

Fighting to Survive a Predator

M. Alexis

**Dear Tony: Inspired by the Story of a
Neglected Girl Fighting to Survive a Predator**
Copyright © 2023 M. Alexis

Produced and printed by Stillwater River Publications.
All rights reserved. Written and produced in the
United States of America. This book may not be reproduced
or sold in any form without the expressed, written
permission of the author(s) and publisher.

Visit our website at
www.StillwaterPress.com
for more information.

First Stillwater River Publications Edition

ISBN: 978-1-960505-51-4

1 2 3 4 5 6 7 8 9 10
Written by M. Alexis.
Cover design by Elisha Gillette.
Interior book design by Matthew St. Jean.
Published by Stillwater River Publications,
West Warwick, RI, USA.

Names: Alexis, M., 1994- author.
Title: Dear Tony : inspired by the story of a neglected
girl fighting to survive a predator / M. Alexis.
Description: First Stillwater River Publications Edition. |
West Warwick, RI, USA : Stillwater River Publications, [2023]
Identifiers: ISBN: 978-1-960505-51-4 (paperback)
Subjects: LCSH: Alexis, M., 1994- | Abused children--
United States--Biography. | Child abuse. | Mother
and child. | LCGFT: Autobiographies.
Classification: LCC: HV6626.52 .A44 2023 |
DDC: 362.76092--dc23

*The views and opinions expressed in this book
are solely those of the author(s) and do not necessarily
reflect the views and opinions of the publisher.*

*I dedicate this book to my beautiful sisters.
We made it through the rain.*

*Every word in this book is true on the account
of my perception of life.*

Contents

Acknowledgments vii

1. Run 1
2. Growing Up Rough 16
3. The Move 28
4. A Knock at the Door 45
5. La Familia 61
6. The Secret 74
7. Man of God 90
8. Hostage 111
9. Summer Camp 124
10. Green Cup 144
11. The Things He Said to Me 161
12. Outside 175
13. Cluster C 181
14. Enrollment 195
15. Birthday Wishes 209
16. In Plain Sight 219
17. Suffering in Silence 227
18. It's Just a Shirt 238
19. The Moving Finger Writes 250
20. New Beginning 269

Acknowledgments

I would like to thank my family and friends who supported me through the journey of writing my truth into a book.

I appreciate the hard work and talent that went into my publishing team.

CHAPTER 1

Run

Summer of 1997, my family and I recently moved to a trailer park in Von Ormy, Texas. My mother, Regina, has had a hard life. Growing up, she has endured abuse and neglect. While in her teens, she became a struggling teen mom. Regina is currently a mother of three children. She struggles with money and shelter to provide for her family. She believes that Von Ormy, Texas is a place where she can have a fresh start. Regina, 25, sits on the wooden steps outside the trailer door. Regina has fair skin. Her blonde hair is twisted up with a brown clip. She is wearing a t-shirt and high-waisted jean shorts. I watch Regina from my poorly homemade sandbox that was here when we moved in. My name is Maria and I am three years old. I use my shovel to dig into the dark brown sand as I glance upon Regina. Regina adjusts her thin, wired framed glasses that sit gently upon her freckled cheeks. She speaks to me while shuffling through a stack of mail.

"Are there any fire ants today, Maria?" Regina asks.

"No ants," I reply.

Days ago, my sandbox became infested with an infamous Texas insect: Red Fire Ants. They swarmed my legs, biting me, because I was shoveling their nest. Suddenly, Regina's icy blue eyes shift from calm into angry while she opens an envelope. Frantically reading, she rants aloud.

"Your father is a real asshole," Regina yells. She then ponders while taking deep puffs of her cigarette. I look out into the grassy meadow. I spy my older siblings approaching. Shannon is seven years old, James is eight years old.

"You are a Tonto!" Shannon shoves James on the back. Tonto means idiot in Spanish. They both like to explore the trailer park together. The rules are they must never split up nor ever go into someone else's home.

"Mom! James burned a piece of my hair off!" Shannon holds up her long brown hair with a few front pieces.

Regina stands to her feet and approaches the situation. "Why would you do that?" Regina questions.

James has pale skin, blonde hair, and blue eyes. "The older neighborhood kids gave me a lighter and Shannon's hair *accidentally* got in the way," James whines.

"Not accidentally!" Shannon folds her arms.

"Let me see your tongue and check for lie bumps." Regina points at James. 'Lie bumps' is a tactic Regina uses to catch us in an obvious lie. James presses his lips together. He slowly reveals his tongue. "Look at all those bumps." Regina acts shocked.

James pulls his face away, "I am going inside."

Regina continues to smoke her cigarette. "Don't worry, it is not noticeable." She pats Shannon on the back. Regina blows smoke up in the air and sits back down.

"Sissy!" I wave from my sandbox. "Play with me," I demand. Shannon approaches me. She sits on the edge of the sand box. Shannon takes her index finger and draws in the sand. 'S' for Shannon. 'M' for Maria. I watch her, amazed. I point to the letter. "M," I sound out. Shannon smiles.

"Let's go to the payphone!" Regina calls. She picks me up from the sandbox. James comes out of the house with popsicles in his hand. "Sorry for burning your hair." James gives one to Shannon. Then he passes more out to Regina and me. We begin our travel to the payphone, enjoying our cold snack. The freeway with the phone is in the middle of nowhere. The road has worn down concrete and open forest on both sides. The sky turns dark purple with an orange horizon. We live in the days when technology is a luxury, not a necessity. The streetlights come on and it helps light our path. The payphone pole is cemented into a patch of gravel pebbles. We stand underneath the fluorescent lamp. "Don't go in the road," Regina demands. She picks up the black phone with a blue plug lining and metal wire. 'Plunk, plunk.' The quarters fall into the machine.

"Girls, don't scream if you see a coyote," James teases us. Shannon rolls her eyes while picking me up. She places me on her back and then begins to spin me around.

"Woohoo!" I shout with enjoyment.

"Mom!" Regina freaks over the phone. "Do not get mad but I need you to help fly us back home," Regina explains. "...because I got a notice from the state of Connecticut," she adds. "Apparently, Julian hired a private investigator to spy on me?" Regina explains. "This investigator is bullshit! They are claiming to have photos of us in Texas. Photos of Maria and Shannon being chased by wild turkeys in the woods," Regina shouts. "How can the court believe these lies? Now I have to go back because Julian wants to fight for custody of Shannon," she continues to explain. "I bet that Star is helping Julian," Regina says, holding the phone under her chin. She begins to light a cigarette.

"Star?" Shannon whispers. She tunes into Regina's phone conversation. "Why are you talking about Star?" Shannon asks. I clutch onto Shannon's shoulders as she continues to hold me.

"Shannon, not now." Regina shoos her away.

"It's just a question," Shannon mumbles and continues to play with me.

Suddenly, Shannon trips over where the cement and the pebbles meet. I fall backwards. Shannon falls face first into the ground.

"Mom, hold on... Do not hang up!" Regina lets the payphone dangle from the metal wire.

Shannon smiles as small drops of blood, slowly, drip down her forehead. "I am alright," she says.

"There is a pebble stuck in your forehead!" James points.

"I don't feel it," Shannon laughs.

Regina pulls out her lighter from her pocket. She takes the end of the lighter and pops the pebble from Shannon's head. A small, bloody imprint remains on her skin. "Can't you guys just stay still for a second?" Regina scoffs and picks up the payphone's dangling phone wire. "Mom, I promise I will pay you back," Regina begs. "Thank you, I love you!"

She sighs with relief and hangs the phone up. "Let's start walking back," she directs us.

"Did you speak to Star on the phone?" Shannon asks while we walk.

"No, it was Grandma Leona," Regina answers. "Don't go asking all your questions, I am already stressed out," Regina states.

"I will race you home!" James challenges us.

"Not if I beat you there." Regina begins to run down the empty freeway. They both run ahead while Shannon bends to scoop me up on her back once more.

"Go, sissy!" I chant while holding onto her shoulders. My hair blows as Shannon runs with me. The race is on.

"I can run faster than you!" Shannon yells.

"No, I am a mighty fast runner!" James shouts back. I feel so happy and free with my family. Our giggles linger among us. We make it back to the trailer. Living away from light pollution, the night sky shines bright.

"Look at the stars!" Shannon points up.

Still clinging on Shannon's back, I admire the twinkling stars. I whisper "Run."

Run. Running away. This is what Regina has done for so many years. Running from her past. Running with hope to a new place, for a new start. Regina struggles to provide a stable home. She walks around, unhealed from her past. She yearns for romance yet can't escape never-ending cycles of toxic relationships. My family and I have lived in many different places before Texas. Sometimes we would live together, other times separately. Before I was born, Regina, Shannon, and James once moved all the way to Kansas. Evidently, running to Texas isn't working out.

In a blink of an eye, we return back to our hometown, Danbury, CT. Danbury is a small city known as 'Hat City.' Back in the old days, Danbury was rich within the hat trade. The small city is mostly made of middle class families. However, it has a fast growing rate of poverty. My family lives on food stamps and state housing. We walk or take the public bus. Danbury residents look down upon families like ours. The city has an underlying issue of out-casting certain streets and hangout spots.

At the Danbury airport, we walk through the gate with nothing but a few bags of clothing. Regina holds me on her hip while she scans the airport crowd.

"Grandma Leona!" James throws his hands in the air. A blonde woman with fair skin approaches us. Leona is wearing blue jeans, brown boots and a purple blouse.

"Hi, how is my sweet boy?" Leona strokes James' face.

"Hi, Mom." Regina smiles and greets her with a kiss on the cheek.

Grandma Leona is Italian, her roots are from Potenza, Italy. Leona and Regina have a love-hate relationship. Since childhood, Leona always pressured her to be as well put together as her other daughter, Sophia. Regina dates outside of her race and has dealt with homelessness. This deemed her as the black sheep within her family.

"Well, everyone follow me to the car." Leona smiles. "We need to get to the court house in time for the hearing." Leona rushes. We pack our things in Grandma Leona's car and continue our journey.

At the court house, James, Shannon, and I sit with Leona in the members of the public wooden benches. Regina sits with a public defender lawyer. The courtroom is styled with late 70's wood decor. The ceilings are high and curved. It has a mimic of the Sistine Chapel ceiling.

"Papi!" I smile as I see my father with his lawyer. Julian looks over at me with a serious face. He has dark brown skin, thick short hair, big muscles and a stone-cold face.

"Shh, Maria," Leona says.

Regina states to the judge her reason why she is a better fit parent for Shannon.

"Your honor, she is a liar!" Julian snaps. The judge bangs his gavel. "You kidnapped my daughter and took her to Texas," Julian points at Regina.

"Kidnap?" Regina snaps.

"Control your clients!" the judge shouts to the lawyers. The adults talk back and forth and come up with a final verdict. "I grant Regina DeWitt full custody of Shannon. Julian Colon must report to city hall to set up a child support plan." The judge bangs his gavel once more.

Julian is furious. "Both of you can get on your knees and suck me off!" Julian scoffs.

"See, he is a nasty man!" Regina shouts.

Julian stares at us. "I'm not paying for that one!" He points at me. "How do I even know that Maria is mine?!" he asks.

"Ignore him, let's just keep walking." Grandma Leona pulls Regina along.

In the parking lot, a woman calls out "Regina, Regina!"

Leona looks and rolls her eyes with annoyance. "Oh god, what is *she* doing here?" she scoffs.

"Look, it is Star!" Shannon's face lights up. Star has fair skin, dark red pixie-cut hair, acrylics nails, and strong perfume. Shannon wraps her arms around Star.

"Well, look who it is," Leona says plainly. "The crazy woman who started all of this bullshit," she adds.

"I didn't start anything, honey." Star rolls her eyes. Star is an Italian woman originally from Brooklyn, New York. Star has been in our life since we were born. She isn't blood related, but she is like a grandmother to us. Star and Regina met when Grandma Leona kicked Regina out of the house for being pregnant. Star's daughter was friends with Regina at the time. Her daughter asked Star if they could help Regina. Since then, Star has become a recurring babysitter and safety net for our family. Although, throughout the years, Star spoke against Regina, calling out Regina's toxic traits as a mother. Thus creating the never ending frenemy feud between them.

Leona shakes her head at Star. Leona and Star's feud stems from unknown places. They despise each other. "If you didn't start this, why are you here?" Leona asks.

"I am here to be sure the girls have someone to fall back on when shit hits the fan," Star says fiercely in her Brooklyn accent.

"You are the last person I would call." Leona rolls her eyes.

"I would reconsider." Star laughs and looks directly at Regina. We stand between cars in the lot.

Regina takes a deep breath revealing her secret. "I called Star."

Leona gasps, "Regina! You gave Shannon to this woman then had to lie about going to Disney to get her back!" Leona yells. "Then I paid for all of you to go to Texas," Leona adds. "Now, I helped you come back because your kids' father is a nutcase!" Leona lists her frustrations.

"Star always takes good care of the girls," Regina sighs.

"So do I!" Leona defends herself.

"Honey, you only step in to care when James seems to be at risk," Star snaps at her. Leona shakes her head with anger. "You don't care about the girls," Star adds.

"Take a hike, lady!" Leona flips Star off.

This time around, Leona is done with Regina's toxic parenting cycle. "You are a fool!" Leona scoffs. She grabs hold of James' hand and heads to her car.

Regina looks down at Shannon. "You are going to go stay with Star again," Regina explains.

"Really?!" Shannon's face lights up and she runs over to Star.

"I will call you soon." Regina smiles at Shannon.

"Wait, what about Maria?" Shannon asks.

"Oh honey, you will see her again." Star smiles. "She will visit and sleep over," she adds. Regina places my feet on the floor. Shannon and I hug goodbye.

"Her clothes are in the car." Regina states. "Oh please, I have brand new ones for her at the house," Star states.

"Can I play my Gameboy when we get home?" Shannon asks Star.

"Yes, it is at the house waiting for you." Star smiles and guides Shannon into her old-fashion blue car.

Regina and I approach Leona's car. James is in the back seat. "Come on out, James." Regina opens the back door.

"He just got in the car..." Leona snaps.

"I want to walk to the shelter, it is around the corner," Regina says.

Leona scoffs. "James stay in the car!" Leona demands, aggressively.

"Another shelter, Regina?" Leona questions. "You can't take care of all these children yourself!" Leona shouts. "Let me at least save one of them," she adds.

"I pick James," Leona states.

"Take Maria, figure out what you are going to do for your future,"

Leona says. "Maybe your kids will come back to you once you are more stable," she adds.

"Fine," Regina says plainly.

Leona pops the trunk. Regina takes out a small bag of my clothing and a backpack of hers. She leans into the backseat. "See you later, James." Regina gives him a kiss on the forehead. "I will come visit you soon," she adds.

"Love you, mom." James half smiles.

"We will call you soon," Leona assures him.

Regina shakes her head and slams the car door shut.

As we walk, Regina rambles to me about Leona and her current troubles. We stop to rest at the front of the library. We sit on the stone benches. "These bags are heavy." Regina places our belongings next to me.

A man approaches us. "Regina?" he asks.

"Miguel!" Regina smiles and throws her hands around him. Miguel is a Puerto Rican man. He has tan skin and short curly hair. He and Regina have had a fling in the past.

"Did you just get back into town?" Miguel asks with his hands around her hips.

"Yeah, I am on my way to a shelter so I can figure out shit," Regina sighs.

"With the baby?" he says looking at me. "Come stay with me." He smiles. "I am staying in a room at my cousin's, Lucito's, house," he explains.

"I don't want to intrude on your cousin's household," Regina states.

"It will be fine, he is barely at the house anyway," he explains. "I have Lucito's car," he explains. "I am parking over there." Miguel points to the street parking. "Let's catch up," he adds.

A month after catching up with Miguel. Regina ditched the Shelter plan. She and I have been staying with him. Regina placed me in the YMCA's Head Start program. Life consists of watching TV, going to school, and playing with friends. I love preschool. I get to be creative and learn. Recently, I was in the Danbury News Times paper. In the local news, my preschool had a small article about how YMCA's Head Start is successfully giving low-income children high quality learning. My photograph was pictured at circle time on the carpet. I sat on the carpet in one of my only outfits. Blue jean overalls with Minnie and Mickey mouse on the front.

"Oh, Maria!" Star smiles as she places the article and my newspaper picture on the refrigerator. "You look so cute sitting at school." She pinches my cheeks. I smile and give her a hug. Star always makes me feel special.

"Too bad they didn't interview me," Regina says as she eats. Star made homemade Lasagna.

"Why would they do that, Regina?" Star asks.

"I am a low-income mother, I have a story too," Regina states.

"Anyway, I have a job opportunity," Regina smiles.

"Oh do you?" Star sips on a cup of fresh coffee.

"I was in a poetry shop when I met a couple from Boston," Regina says. "The husband wants me to assist his wife. She has Multiple Sclerosis," she explains

"Oh, nursing can be a good career path," Star encourages.

"Yes, I signed up for Nursing school," Regina reveals.

"Danbury has decent nursing opportunities," Star states.

"Well, I am moving to Boston," Regina smiles.

Star jolts her head back. "Boston?" Star questions.

Regina laughs, "I just told you the couple is from Boston. They live in a penthouse."

"What about Maria?" Star asks.

"I am taking Maria with me." Regina stands to her feet. She places her plate in the sink. "I will get a job in Boston. I am here to let you know," Regina says.

"What about that boyfriend you have?" Star asks.

Regina rolls her eyes, "Miguel," Regina says. "He says he is going to call me every day." She smiles.

Living in Boston with Regina has been simple and quiet. The place where we live is in a fancy penthouse apartment building. The couple, Michael and Ester, have antique decor. I am just not allowed to touch anything. Regina and I live in a room. In the early morning, Regina helps the sickly woman get ready for the day. Since the woman doesn't need 24/7 care, Regina has free time. She takes me to preschool and goes to her Bagel Shop job. After work, she picks me up from school, then we head back to the penthouse. In the evenings, Regina assists the woman while doing light cleaning and studying for her nursing exam. The woman is old and thin. She can be nice at times. Usually, she is overly demanding. I enjoy when she plays her music on her record player. The sound of the needle scratching while music plays is calming to my creative mind.

It is a regular morning. Regina and I stand by the crosswalk in downtown Boston. I need to be dropped off at daycare. I step forward to cross the street. Suddenly, a man on a bicycle cycles past me. He is trying to drink his coffee and ride his bike. While he juggles this task, he knocks me over. His back tire runs over my small arm.

"You ran over my daughter, you asshole!" Regina screams.

She helps me out of the road. The surrounding public watches the scene. Regina frantically runs with me in her arms. We hop on the next bus to the hospital. People stare at me while I sob over the pain of my arm. Regina is a friendly person, she explains to people what happened. "Then he just kept cycling on his bike," Regina tells fellow bus-takers.

At the hospital, the results reveal my arm is dislocated. I am put in a sling. The bike incident did not just hurt me. It hurt Regina as well. Since I had to go to the hospital, Regina was late for her bagel shop job. They fired her. The sickly woman's husband isn't too happy about the news.

"I have two more weeks left for my nursing program, can't we just stay here until then?" Regina begs the husband. The man is standing in the door frame from the hallway. He is in a fancy gray suit. He has dark hair and fair skin.

"What will you do about food?" he asks. "You are here rent free while you help my wife," he reminds her. "I will give you two weeks and then you need to leave," he states. "I have found Ester an OFFICIAL nurse, anyway," he scoffs.

"That is fine, I take my exam soon," Regina assures the man.

Regina passes her nursing exam. She tried to find an apartment around Boston. However, due to the expenses, Regina and I head back to Danbury. This time, James remains living with Leona. Shannon remains living a routined life with Star. Regina warns Star that, once she has a stable job, she will be back to pick Shannon up. As for Little Maria, I ping pong between Regina's care and Star's babysitting. The bright side is that I get to see Shannon often. I grow up vulnerable and stuck in-between everyone's life.

Maria and Shannon

The newspaper article of Maria sitting at school. Star put this on her fridge.

Shannon and Maria playing at Star's house

CHAPTER 2

Growing Up Rough

Fall of October, 2000. We live in Waterbury, CT. Waterbury is one of the poorest cities in Connecticut. It is infamous for its 'Holy Land,' which has structures from the Bible made with recycled material. There is a big metal cross on top of a mountain overlooking the city. Recently, Shannon has re-joined the family. She is getting used to living with us again. I have been loving that Shannon is back home. However, Regina uses her to cook, clean, and help take care of our new baby sister, Karina. Karina was born a year ago on May 9th, 1999. Miguel is the father of Karina. Miguel and Regina have been dating steadily for the past few years.

At first, Miguel ran from the news of actually becoming a father, again, since he has another daughter with a different woman. While he was running from his fatherly duties, Miguel was out in the streets. He likes to hustle and have fun with his friends, which landed him incarcerated for a month. However, as soon as Regina got news he was released from jail, she took me on a car ride to find him. We drove around town in her used, beat-up car. When we found Miguel, Regina rolled down my window and directed me to scream 'fuck you' out of the window. We both gave him the middle fingers. Soon after, Miguel came back. He promises he will help raise Karina. Miguel treats me like his daughter. Now that I am six years old, he has taught me how to ride a bike. I have watched him steal sweet treats from the grocery store. Sometimes I copy him. The only one Miguel dislikes is Shannon. They have a conflicting relationship. Shannon sees the way Miguel truly treats our family.

All five of us live in a one-bedroom apartment. The project complex is nicknamed 'Brick City.' The gag is that 'Brick City' is known for being a hub for bricks of drugs. The complex begins with a stone tunnel full of graffiti artwork within its walls. The tunnel leads to the inner courtyard and gravel parking lot. The courtyard has green, grassy patches grown between the concrete pathways. Scattered around are black T shaped poles for drying laundry. 2000 is a simple time of living, especially when growing up in the projects. No social media, no luxury needs. Most projects I have lived in hold a class of mixed cultures. Latino, Black, Asian, and Indian. Regina is friendly with everyone, that is until a problem arises. She also has a habit of dropping her children off with anyone interested in babysitting us. Either she will work long hours as a nurse or go out to party with her friends. Either way, I always find it interesting to see how other people live within their walls.

On the very top story is our apartment. Shannon and I play outside the apartment door. Below, I hear the busy projects buzz with people chatting and bumping reggaeton music. Shannon and I play a classic game called 'Lemonade Stand.' Our stand consists of a children's plastic yellow table with a milk crate flipped over as a seat. Shannon sits on the crate mixing the lemonade powder with water. She is wearing her black jacket, unzipped, with her favorite shirt. A sage green shirt with a Japanese dragon on it. The shirt is a gift from our father, Julian. Her long brown hair is in a low ponytail with two strands of hair pulled out as bangs. I am wearing my $10 gray Champion sweatsuit and my hair is in pigtails. I stand near the neighbors' apartment door pretending to be in a ballet class.

I point my old, dirty sneaker out, lift my leg up, and spin. I have been obsessed with ballet ever since I heard on MTV that Britney Spears once did ballet.

"Maria!" Shannon points. "Watch out!" She runs over to me and pulls me back.

"What?" I look behind me. On the black metal grate floor, there is a pile of wood.

"That pile has rusty nails," she alerts me. I examine the large rusty nails poking through the wood. Seems like broken wooden furniture.

Miguel appears at the top of the metal stairs and approaches the apartment door. "Yo, where is Regina at?" he asks. Miguel is wearing baggy pants and his slick black jacket. Lately, he has been very different. Sometimes he can be very sweet. Other times, he is scary. Miguel stares at us. He has dark circles under his eyes.

"She is inside with Karina," Shannon answers him. Miguel goes inside the apartment. "He is so dumb, just open the door and go look," Shannon mumbles. "Anyway, Maria...come taste the lemonade," she tells me. I watch her pick up a mug and pour lemonade in it. "I have a good feeling about today," she states. "I am wearing my lucky shirt Papi gave me when we visited him." She smiles. "With this luck I want to make real money!" Shannon exclaims looking over the railing. "Lemonade for sale!!!" Shannon shouts from the 5th floor.

"I don't think anyone can hear you," I inform her. "Let's go downstairs and sell our lemonade!" I suggest.

"I really want to!" Shannon perks up. "...But Mommy says we can't go downstairs today. Remember, she said a man got stabbed yesterday," she informs me.

I roll my eyes, "but...we never get caught when we don't listen to the rules," I remind her.

"Mommy and Miguel were fighting last night... And Miguel just came home..." she explains. Shannon can already foresee a recipe of disaster. As the older sister, she is more aware than I am about the chaos within our home. She knows when we can or can't push our limits. I always take her advice into consideration when she warns me about things.

"Then you pretend to be the customer," I suggest. Shannon's face lights up. We love to play pretend together.

"I will be someone from New York City! Like the woman from Star's black and white movies!" She smiles. "Hey, doll face," Shannon smirks. She speaks with an old fashion New York City accent. "Lemme get a lemonade on the rocks, if ya know what I mean," she says with a wink. "I will pay with coins." She slams down pebbles as fake money.

"Rocks?" I questioned. Shannon turns around dramatically. She pretends to smoke a cigarette while looking over the railing. I scoop up the pebbles and place them into her mug. "Lemonade with rocks!" I shout. I finish pouring her drink.

In character, Shannon takes a sip of the mug but quickly gasps. "What the hell?" Shannon exclaims. She pours the cup upside down. The yellow liquid flows through the metal grate flooring. The pebbles 'ping' as they meet the metal floor. "MARIA!" she shouts. "That hit my tooth!" Shannon yells.

"You said you wanted rocks," I state, raising my eyebrows.

Suddenly, the apartment door flings open. "Get the fuck outta here!" Regina shouts. "I have no money for you." Regina pushes Miguel out of the door. "You look like you haven't slept in days," she scoffs.

Shannon pulls me close to her.

Miguel stands and reaches for the cigarette that sits behind his ear. "I need a few dollars. Just a few dollars," Miguel begs.

"Why, so you can go shoot up more?" Regina asks. "You haven't been home. Where have you been?" She demands answers. Miguel is silent.

"I will tell you, just let me inside." Miguel walks up to her.

Regina holds him back. "What is on your hip?" She points. Miguel has a new beeper on his baggy jeans.

"My beeper," Miguel states. "My homeboys gave me it so they can reach me easier," Miguel explains.

"How about you page one of them to come pick you up," Regina scoffs. "You are a joke, you don't live here anymore." She steps inside the house. The door slams shut.

Miguel shakes his head and looks at us. He chuckles and lights a cigarette. "Listen girls, we've all been here before," Miguel speaks as he balances the cigarette between his naturally dark outlined lips. "She is mad for a few hours then comes and finds me," he chuckles. "Then, I am back in the apartment and we are a happy family." He smiles.

Shannon shakes her head, "You are no family to me," she states.

"You think you're tough?" He laughs.

"Yeah, I'm tough," Shannon states confidently. Miguel walks closer, towering over us.

"Well, I am tougher than you will ever be." He points his finger in her face. Miguel pulls a beeper out from his pocket. He shuts the vibration off. "I'll be back," he states. He walks down the stairs with a cocky chuckle.

Inside the one-bedroom apartment, Shannon and I share the only bedroom. We have an old wooden bunk-bed set. Regina and Karina sleep in the living room on a dingy royal blue couch that folds out into a bed. I step into the living room and see Regina crying. She is writing on a piece of paper.

"Mommy, are you alright?" I ask softly.

"Maria, get the fuck away from me right now. I am too pissed off," she states. She begins to shake her leg. When she is this upset, it is best to leave her alone. However, I don't like seeing my mother cry.

Sometimes I forget that she likes her space. I pat her arm. "Don't touch me," she snaps. I sigh and look over my shoulder. Karina watches us from the floor. I take her by the hand and lead her out of the room. Karina has beautiful, almond-brown eyes. They always sparkle with joy. Her short curls bounce as she walks. "Tell Shannon to serve dinner, it is on the stove," Regina yells to me.

Karina and I enter the bedroom. Shannon lays on the bottom bunk. She likes to write poems. She is writing in her kitten journal. "Mommy said dinner is ready and you have to help us get it," I relay the message. Shannon hides her writing tools under her pillow. When she leaves, I quickly lift up the pillow to be nosey. "Shannon's blue kitten journal," I tell Karina, showing her the cover that has kittens on it. "I like reading it. It's interesting," I say as I skim through a page. Karina is kind of like my partner in crime. She usually watches the experiments I do around the house, like the time I showed her all of the cooking spices and cried when I poured a big scoop of cinnamon in my mouth. Now, I sit on the floor beside the bed. Karina sits next to me. We explore the journal together. "This drawing looks like a perfume spray," I point out to Karina. In the drawing, water sprays out of the bottle and then there is a heart with the name Kevin on it. "Ke-vun," I sound out the name. "OO she loves a boy!" I chuckle as I translate the gossip to Karina.

The passage in her journal reads:

I have a crush on Kevin. He likes me. At recess, I put on my Love perfume. He asked me what the smell was. I told him my love perfume. He smiled. I never felt this way!

The next morning, I get ready for school. I put my navy uniform jumper on with thick navy-blue stockings. Waterbury public schools require each student to wear uniforms. As I gather my backpack, I see Shannon roll something on her neck. "What is that?" I ask.

"My perfume," she says kindly. "I got it from going to the mall with Star," she brags, holding up a perfume sample.

"You love a boy and want to smell like perfume," I giggle.

Shannon's smile quickly disappears. "I told you to stop reading my journal, loser!" Shannon stares at me with anger. She shoves me as she leaves the room.

"Bye, Britney." I wave to my oversized Britney Spears poster. Miguel got me this poster for my birthday that recently past. It has become one of my best friends. I admire seeing Britney Spears on my TV screen while she dances in her music videos.

At the bus stop, Shannon and I stand next to a girl, Danielle. Danielle has fair skin, blonde hair and dark brown chunky highlights. She once told us she is a witch. I believe her because when she came over to the house, we were painting and dipped the paint brushes in a plastic bottle of water. Danielle said she put 'wish magic' in the paint water. If I drink it, all my wishes will come true. So, I drank the water wishing I could go to dance class.

"You smell good today," Danielle says to Shannon.

"The love perfume is going to work today!" Shannon smiles.

"It is a full moon!" Danielle adds.

"Love Perfume?" I question. I remember Shannon putting something on her neck and then in her journal she drew a bottle that sprays. Slowly, I look up at Shannon. Danielle has made my sister into a witch.

At recess, I am told to stand on the yellow line for not completing my homework. I rarely do homework because no one at home helps. So, I face the consequence of standing on the yellow line while watching all the other kids play. The teachers are huddled together in the middle of the playground.

"SISSY!" I spot Shannon walking nearby the yellow line.

"I told you don't call me that in public," Shannon stops to speak with me.

"Come on," Danielle says. "He is over there." She points. I look where Danielle points. It is a boy with a faded haircut and curly hair on top. He is waving in our direction. "We have to go." Danielle laughs and tugs Shannon along. I watch them walk away.

I am bored standing and doing nothing. I begin talking to the other kids on the line. I hype them up with a plan for all of us to run off the line at the same time. "3...2...1...RUN!!" I shout. We all run. I look behind me and see teachers begin to freak out. I cackle and run off to the side of the playground by a tree. I turn the corner to a secret hiding spot at the edge of the building. A teacher catches me hiding. I am surely going to get a phone call home for my behavior, again.

After school, Shannon and I step off the bus. We decide to hang out on the neighborhood's 'trampoline.' The trampoline is actually just two random king size mattresses stacked on top of each other near a small tree. I jump on the trampoline. Shannon and Danielle hang out nearby. They talk and look at Danielle's cool poster magazine.

"Look, it is Mr. MacDonald," Danielle points.

Mr. MacDonald is a man that lives in the bottom floor of the building. He has no legs and rides in an electric wheelchair. "Maria, go see if you can catch a ride home from him." Shannon points to Mr. MacDonald.

"No," I state.

"Danielle and I want to hang out alone," she tells me.

I roll my eyes. I know Shannon will argue with me until she wins. So, I hop on the ground. "Alright." I sigh. "Hey, Mr. MacDonald can I have a ride!" I shout.

"Sure thing, Maria, hop on," he states. I ride on the back of the electric wheelchair as we enter the tunnel.

"You look like Santa Claus," I tell him as I stare at his long, white beard. Mr. MacDonald laughs. I walk up the sidewalk to the black metal stairs.

Regina sits at the round kitchen table, her forehead rests upon her palm. Miguel towers over her as I fully enter the doorway. My mother sniffles, "Hi, Ria."

Miguel stands tall and stern with a scrunched face. I toss my backpack on the floor. Miguel points at me. "I have been waiting for you to get home," he scoffs. I feel scared as he approaches me. "Why did the school call us?" he barks.

"I-I-I... I don't know." I shrug, my chest tightens.

"You always make trouble at school," he states.

"No, I don't," I cry.

"Regina, this is why you need to get your shit together." He turns and yells at her. "Your kids are disrespectful," he adds.

"Miguel just leave her alone." Regina says.

"You need to learn some fucking respect!" he yells in my face.

"I am sorry," I beg. He grabs my arm and pulls me close. I gain a clearer perspective of his face. His eyes are glazed over with dark circles.

"Do you hear me?" Miguel shouts in my face. I stay silent. Sometimes I go mute when I do not know what to say or do.

"I am gonna make you hear me," he says, walking into my bedroom. Miguel returns with my Britney Spears poster. "You see this poster, it was a gift!" he shouts. "I can take it back at any time."

"No, please!" I beg.

"You have to learn your lesson." He pulls me by my hand. Miguel takes the keys and lifts me up.

"I just got the car fixed, don't fuck with it," Regina warns him.

"I need to go and give this poster to another little girl who behaves," Miguel teases.

"No, please, it is mine!" I shout. Regina follows us with Karina on her hip.

"Are you insane?" she screams. I am stuffed in the back seat, scared. Regina opens the passenger door. "You aren't leaving with her," Regina shouts. Miguel begins to reverse the car. The open passenger's door pushes on Regina. "Hey! I have Karina in my arms!!" she shouts. Miguel hits the breaks,

"Get in the car if you are coming." Regina sits in the passenger's seat with Karina on her lap. He drives out of the complex on the road. "Let's find a new home for this poster." He laughs.

"No, please don't do that!" I cry.

"Miguel, come on, stop teasing her," Regina states, rubbing his arm in an attempt to calm him down. He pulls his arm away from her.

The daytime sky turns into a cool blue. Miguel drives in silence. He lights a cigarette. "It is going to get dark soon, let's go home," Regina suggests.

"Look, the graveyard," Miguel points out to the other side of the road. There is a graveyard across from a blue and white gas station. Miguel steps on the gas and does a reckless U-turn. "This will teach you to be respectful," Miguel says. He parks near the graveyard's wooden fencing. Miguel grabs the poster.

"No no!" I scream and try to grab it.

"Maria, get in this car!" Regina shouts. I sit in the middle of the back seats and watch him through the front windshield. Miguel stands by the graveyard's wooden fence.

"Mommy, go get my poster," I cry. I hear Regina lock the car doors. I begin to cry loudly.

"Maria, stop it. You are going to make him even more angry," she states. "All you have to do is just fucking behave," she scoffs and rolls her eyes.

Miguel looks at us in the car. He holds the poster in the air and waves 'goodbye.' I watch, heartbroken, as he smashes the poster into the wooden fence. Glass shatters onto the ground. The black frame cracks and breaks off. He tosses it in the grass.

"NOO!!" I cry reaching out in front of me. Miguel returns to the car. He puts it in reverse. I rush to the back window and watch my poster disappear in the distance. Miguel drives us back to Brick City. He parks the car.

"I am going to search the house for the money you are hiding." He opens the car door and heads up the stairs to the apartment. Regina quickly follows him with Karina still in her arms.

"There is no hidden money!" she shouts. I follow behind them as fast as my small feet can climb the black metal stairs.

"AHHHHH!" I hear a horrid shriek. I reach the top of the stairs and watch Regina laying down on the metal flooring. Miguel is looking down at her. He is holding a long, familiar wooden plank. Instantly, I recognize the plank is from the broken furniture with the rusty nails Shannon told me to watch out for.

"MOMMY!" I scream. Regina's eyes are shut. Karina is on the floor, crying. Miguel drops the plank. He turns and runs away, disappearing into the night.

"HELP!!" I scream.

"Maria?!" Shannon shouts in terror from behind me. She is returning from hanging out with Danielle.

"Miguel hurt mommy," I cry. I look at Regina, unconscious. I see blood in her blonde hair.

"HELP US!!" Shannon and I scream. Shannon bangs on apartment doors. A lady by the name of Lis opens her apartment door. Lis babysat us a few times. She is acquaintances with Regina.

"Oh Dios mío!" Lis cries, seeing Regina still on the floor. "Stay there, mi amors," she says. I hear Lis speaking in Spanish and the sound of phone buttons being dialed. An elderly woman comes to the door. She looks at Regina and back at us.

"Ven aquí," she tells us. She gestures her hand inside the house. "Entra, estás a salvo." She assures us it is safe to come inside. Lis gives us each a bowl of rice and beans with steak. Soon the police and ambulance come. They take Regina away on a stretcher.

Shannon assures Lis that she is able to bring Karina and I back to our apartment. She thanks Lis for the help and dinner. When I walk through the apartment door, my eyes instantly look at the kitchen table. Just hours ago, that is where Regina was sitting when I came home from school.

"I am going to get Karina ready for bed," Shannon tells me. "Get ready for sleep," she adds.

"Alright," I say softly. I get myself ready for bed and lay on the top bunk. Karina and Shannon are snuggled on the bottom bunk. Through the dark, I hear Shannon's feet walk on the tile floor. The phone dials from the kitchen.

"Star, it is Shannon," she cries. She tells Star the events of this evening. I roll over in bed. I keep having flashbacks. The memory of Regina tumbling down the stairs. The memory of Miguel smashing my Britney Spears poster. It haunts me.

CHAPTER 3

The Move

Regina has been resting after spending a day in the hospital. She came home with a few staples on the top of her head, as well as the paperwork of a positive pregnancy blood test. Shannon and I sit in the kitchen with a worker from the Department of Child Services. Shannon and I have assured her that we feel safe at home. "We haven't seen Miguel in a while," Shannon tells the lady. The woman writes on her notepad.

"Here is my number if he does come back." The lady gives Shannon a card. "The police are still looking for him," she adds. I look at Shannon while she thanks the woman. I stay silent with fear. No matter, what I understand is that I must never let any social worker know the truth about my household. Regina makes it very clear that we can be taken away by the worker and never see each other again.

After the worker checks in with Regina, she leaves. Regina shuts the apartment door with a smile on her face. "Good job, girls." She smiles and sits at the kitchen table. Regina dials numbers on the landline phone. Shannon and I play in our bedroom. We can hear the echo of Regina's phone crusade. She has called all her friends and family to update them on her injuries. During this time, an incoming call brings her good news. State Housing contacted her about being approved for an apartment with three bedrooms. With this news, Regina feels like this apartment is a new start. Regina has packed up half of the house in large black trash bags. The new baby and apartment has distracted her from the incident with Miguel. It feels as if it never happened.

I wake up to start my day. I climb down the bunk bed ladder. I see Shannon organizing belongings on her bed.

"What are you doing?" I ask Shannon.

"Mommy said we are moving into a bigger apartment," Shannon explains. "You better put everything you want to keep on your bed," she adds. I rub my eyes and try to understand what Shannon is saying.

"Why?" I ask.

"Mommy said that she will be throwing things out. Save what you want to keep and put it on your bed," she explains.

I nod my head and look around the room. I begin grabbing small items and putting them on my top bunk. Having to quickly decide what to keep is nothing new to me. I am used to quick, chaotic life changes. I know exactly what I want to keep.

"Star is on her way." Regina peeks her head inside the bedroom.

"Star?" I question.

"She is taking you girls for the weekend so I can move everything to the new apartment," Regina explains.

"Maria, go take a bath," Shannon demands. "We don't want to keep Star waiting when she arrives," she adds.

I sit in the tub and wash my hair. I am excited to see Star. My belly is hungry and usually she feeds us really yummy food. Regina barges into the bathroom holding a magazine. She's wearing sweats and a tank-top. She places the magazine on the sink. "Can you believe they shaved my fucking head?" She examines her hair in the mirror.

"Why?" I ask.

"To put these damn staples in," she groans. I nod my head with understanding. My brain flashes back to the moment when I finally had the guts to look at the staples in her head. Regina has a bald spot. It was pretty gross to look at. "I think I might cut off all my hair," Regina states. "What do you think of this kind of haircut?" She holds up the magazine to a page with a woman on it. I see a woman with short hair.

"Pretty, Mommy." I smile at her.

"You think so?" She smiles at herself in the mirror. Regina begins to groom her 90's thin eyebrows. I finish my bath and go to my room to get dressed. As I put on jeans and a shirt, I continue gathering my items that I want to keep for the next apartment.

Shannon and I walk down the metal stairs with our overnight bags in hand. We see Star's 1994 Buick LeSabre. Star steps out of her car with sunglasses on and a purple shirt that is bedazzled on the shoulders. She has dark red, blown-out, pixie-cut hair. I watch her hug Shannon. "How are you, my darling?" Star smiles. "Oh honey don't cry." She wipes Shannon's tears. I greet Star with a smile and hug. Her pretty perfume hits my nose before she fully hugs me.

Shannon and I hustle into the front seat. The coolest thing about Star's Buick LeSabre car is that a third person can sit in the front seat. The driver, the passenger and the middle place between them. The seats are blue velvet with a brown, laminated wooden dashboard. I miss being in this car, it always smells like mints. It feels like old times when Star would babysit us. We would jam out and watch Star sing to her Elvis Presley music. "Whew girls, I am so glad you guys are moving out of this place. It is dirty and ghetto." Star shakes her head, referring to Brick City. I shrug my shoulders, she says that about all the places we live.

"Where are we going, Star?" I ask.

I watch her drive while I sit in the middle front seat.

"We are going to my granddaughter, Kristi's, birthday party at Fun Station," Star explains.

"Wooo hoo!" I throw my hands in the air. "I love Fun Station." I smile.

"Maria, you need to be on your BEST behavior," Star demands.

"I know." I smile. Fun Station is an arcade and roller rink in Danbury. It has everything from a rollerblading rink, ball pit, and laser tag. We continue on the highway from Waterbury to Danbury.

"Star, can you put on that Ronnie Spector song?" Shannon asks.

Star chuckles. "What song? Be my Baby?" Star asks. Shannon nods her head. 'Be my Baby' by the Ronettes. Star loves Ronnie's music. Back in the early 90s, Star was the nanny for Ronnie Spector. I remember meeting Ronnie and her sons when Star babysat us. Ronnie once told me my eyes sparkle with light.

As we hop out of the Buick, Star gives us a warning. "Girls, your grandmother Camila is here with your cousins," she tells us. Camila is our father's mother.

"Is Papi here?" I ask with hope.

"He should be, Camila invited him… She told him you girls would be coming." Star smiles. She applies her dark red lipstick as we walk inside of the building. The best thing about Star is that she is friends with Julian's mother, Camila. Since Regina rarely communicates with our father's side of the family, Shannon and I get to bond with Julian's family because of Star's connection. It is such a pity that both sides of my family have a division within them.

At Fun Station, we gather in a large party room. There is a viewing window to the roller skating rink. Star's Italian family is always going the extra mile for parties. They invite everyone's children, aunts, uncles, grandparents, and family friends. They bring extra folding tables just for the catered Italian food. Different types of pasta, rice, chicken, cupcakes, etc. Pink birthday party decor lingers all around the jam-packed room. Star's family is happy to see Shannon and me. We greet everyone with hugs and kisses on each cheek.

"Hey Shannon," Simone greets us. Simone is one of our cousins from Julian's side of the family. She has dark, tan skin and light blue eyes. Her light brown, tightly curled hair is slick back in a ponytail. "You wanna go on the rink?" Simone asks Shannon.

"Yeah, let's go get skates," Shannon smiles. I sigh as Shannon leaves me. I scan around the room to figure out what to do. I hear my other cousin, Matias, speak.

"Your Papi is here." He smiles. Matias has dark skin. He is wearing baggy 90's styled clothing with a black durag and red cap on backwards.

"How do you know that he is here?" I ask him.

"Because, him and I just played an arcade game together," he chuckles. I follow Matias out of the party room. He leads me to a brown table full of adults.

"Uncle Julian, Maria is looking for you," Matias says. Julian looks down at me. He has dark brown skin, brown eyes and he has a slight scar on the right side of his face. Julian is wearing a black shirt with a red plaid button-up. Papi gives me a kiss on the cheek and holds me in the air. He smells good like his favorite lotion, cocoa butter. When he holds me, I take a sniff of his scent. It makes me feel safe that I am in my father's arms. I giggle as I am risen. He would always do this thing where he would pick me up high, he even would pick Shannon and I up at the same time.

"Hello gorgeous daughter," he says.

"Can we go skating?" I ask him.

"First say hello to your grandmother," he says. Papi puts me down and I look at the table full of adults.

Grandma Camila is Puerto Rican. She has light olive skin, high cheek bones, pointy eyebrows, thick red lips, and brown eyes.

"Hi grandma." I smile and give her a hug.

"Hola, Maria." She gives me a kiss on the cheek. I sit next to her.

"I will be right back," Papi whispers in my ear. I look around the table and see other adults I recognize.

"Hey you," a man sitting at the table says to me. I look over at the voice and see a familiar man.

"Do I know you?" I ask.

The man is tall with a pop out stomach. He is wearing jeans and a polo shirt. His hair is jet black with loads of gel in it. "I am Star's friend, Tony." The man smiles.

"Tony?" I question.

"I used to be Star's roommate," he explains. "When you were younger, you would visit her house," he adds. I nod my head, trying to remember the man.

"Oh…" I say, confused.

"Remember, I go to church with Star too," he adds. I smile to hide the fact I do not remember the man.

"Let's go, precious," Julian returns. I hold Julian's hand and follow him. I look up at Julian as we walk. I like to remember small moments of what it is like to stand next to my father.

Papi and I head to the benches. Looking down, I see Papi is about to put blue Velcro baby skates on me. He leans down and grabs my foot. I yank it back. "What is wrong?" he asks. I fold my arms,

"Those skates are for babies!" I scoff. "I want skates like the big girls," I demand.

Papi rolls his eyes, "Okay, drop the attitude," he states, holding up his hand. He looks annoyed. "I will be right back." He aggressively collects the blue skates and walks away. He is reacting like other adults do when I am particular about what I want or need. He returns with a small pair of blades.

"Can you fix the red line on my sock?" I ask. I am wearing white classic 90's socks. For me to be comfortable, I need the red line to be perfectly aligned with my toes. I smile, watching him place the blades on my feet. We roll onto the rink.

"Keep your knees bent," he reminds me. I will always remember this day I enjoyed with my father. As we skate side by side, he talks to me about how to give someone a good 'one, two boxing punch' and that he has been on a meditation journey.

The next day is Sunday. Star dresses us up for church. Shannon and I wear our fancy dresses with church hats. Slowly, Star drives down a long hill that leads to the parking lot. This church is run by a woman named 'Pastor Mary.' Pastor Mary has big, silky black hair. She always wears elaborate, bejeweled dress suits. She reminds me of a dark hair version of Dolly Parton. Star loves her preachings. Due to our recent situation with Miguel, Star is bringing us to church to have Pastor Mary pray protection over us. When Pastor Mary prays over people, they usually always fall to the floor because the 'Holy Ghost' is healing them. I am scared and hope that doesn't happen to me. After the sermon and being prayed over, my favorite part of church begins: when we eat cake. I follow Star out of the sanctuary doors and stand in the lobby. The adults always have fellowship time with each other after service. They bring homemade pastries and baked goods. The smell of yummy homemade sweets fills my nose.

"Maria, there it is!" Shannon whispers in my ear. "The table of the best chocolate cake we ever had." She smiles. We rush over to the table. An elderly woman with silver hair smiles at us. She sticks a fork in the cake and hands us each a plate.

"Thank you!" I smile at her.

At Star's house, we sit in the kitchen enjoying Star's family recipe of pasta with meatballs. Tony and Missy, Star's friends, sit at her round, wooden table. They chat and gossip about life.

"Can I go watch 'I love Lucy' and eat my food?" Shannon asks.

Star sips her coffee and points one eyebrow up, "Yes, but only sit on the floor and eat. You know how expensive my couches are," she adds.

Shannon grabs her plate and heads into the living room. "Hey, I want to go with her," I say.

"Oh no no, you eat like a crazy girl," she says. "You will have sauce all over my carpet," she adds.

"Shannon gets to do everything." I stab my meatball with my fork.

"Excuse me." Star taps her acrylic nail on the table three times. "My Shannon is responsible," Star states. "When you are at home, your mother lets you do whatever you want," she adds. I purse my lips and roll my eyes.

"Oh my god," Missy shakes her head. "Star, what a little attitude this one has," Missy states.

Tony eats his food and listens. He looks at me and rolls his eyes in a funny way. I flash a quick smile. "What has Regina been up to anyway?" Missy asks. "Are they here for a reason?" she questions. The adults begin to talk about Regina. "Well, now she is leaving her latest apartment moving to another ghetto slum," Star explains our new life update to her friends.

"Is she still staying in Waterbury?" Missy asks.

"Yes, what is it called? Umm…" Star thinks. "Oh, Gilyard Court," Star says.

"I never heard of it." Missy says and sips her coffee.

"Yup, she is moving and pregnant, again." Star sighs.

"Another baby?" Tony questions. Star presses her lips together while nodding her head. I sit at the table, eating. I am actively listening to the adult conversation. I am used to being updated about my household through the gossip of my family. "Oh, sorry," Tony says and looks at me.

"Its fine, anything said here isn't new," she states with her NY accent.

"These kids have seen and heard it all before," Star adds.

From across the table, I look at Tony. He winks at me.

"It's a real shame," Missy states.

Shannon shouts from the living room, "Mommy is here!"

Missy and Star glance at each other. "Speak of the Devil," Star laughs to Missy. Regina turns the corner from the living room. Shannon follows. Regina carries Karina and looks super different.

"Mommy, you look so beautiful!" I shout with glee. Regina runs her hands through the side of her new, short pixie-blonde hair.

"It suits you," Star compliments her new haircut.

"Thank you." Regina smiles, handing Karina to Star.

"Oh look at your little chunky cheeks." Star hugs Karina in a highchair and begins to feed her.

Regina looks around the table. "Hey Tony, how have you been?" Regina asks while having a seat at the table.

"I am doing well," he says. "I am living in New York now," he adds. "However, I am always in the area because my office job is in Greenwich, Connecticut," Tony explains.

"And he needs to come and see his best friend," Star smiles.

"Well, I only truly stop by for the pasta," Tony jokes. The adults chuckle. Regina nods her head attentively.

"Cookie, woo woo," Karina whines. She points to the Italian pastry Shannon is eating while standing next to the highchair. "Woo woo, cookie!" she shouts.

Regina, Shannon, and I simultaneously gasp. We glance at each other in excitement. "Mom, she said woo woo," Shannon smiles. We all laugh.

"Why is that funny?" Star asks.

"Miguel calls Karina, 'Woo Woo,'" Shannon states.

"Yeah, he pretends he is a train and then lifts his hand up and yells, 'Woo Woo,'" I explain. "Then he will let out a fart." I giggle.

Star rolls her eyes, "How charming."

Changing the subject, Star looks at Regina. "Did you move everything into the new apartment?" Star asks.

Regina nods her head, "Yup, one of Miguel's friends offered to build the girls' bunkbed for me," Regina explains.

"Miguel?" Star questions.

"I haven't spoken to him," Regina states. "I only asked one of his friends to help me," she adds.

Star and Missy glance at each other. "They are attending the same school?" Missy asks.

"No, they start their new school tomorrow," Regina says.

Shannon and I look at each other.

Star shakes her head, "Oh they are going to a new school, I didn't know that," Star states.

Shannon slams her palm on the table. "I didn't get to say goodbye to any of my friends, again!" she shouts.

"Shannon, you knew we were moving," Regina replies. Regina stands up and gets a wet paper towel. She cleans Karina's face and hands. "Get your bags, we have to go home," she demands.

Shannon wipes her tears as she leans on Star for support.

"It will be alright," Star whispers to Shannon.

Regina picks Karina up. "Well, Star thank you for watching them," Regina states.

"Of course, anytime," Star says.

In the car, the ride is silent. I am used to always moving, I am not bothered. Shannon is more aware of what it is like to have a stable routine. Moving away from the friends she just got to know is tough for her.

"We are here," Regina says, turning the steering wheel. In the headlights, I see a big concrete sign with maroon letters that say 'Gilyard Court.' As we drive down the long driveway, I see long rectangle apartments with sidewalk spaced between each one. A few people are gathered around here and there. Regina drives to the end of the complex.

"Look Shannon, there is a basketball court!" I shout.

"I don't care," Shannon snaps. We hop out of the car and follow Regina. The back of the complex looks slightly larger than the front. Between two of the rectangle apartment blocks is a large plot of grass.

"This is our door," Regina says. We stand in front of a red metal door. "A few doors down is Jenna's apartment." Regina unlocks the door. Jenna is Regina's best friend from years ago. Coincidentally,

Jenna will be three doors down from us. She is also pregnant with twins. "It will be nice for us to be near each other when our babies are born." Regina opens the door.

The fluorescent lights are on in the apartment. We enter our new kitchen. The aroma of recently cooked food fills the air. Regina has been moving everything while we were with Star for the weekend. "Take a look around, girls," Regina says, placing Karina on the floor.

Shannon and I scan the kitchen. The kitchen table is in the middle with black garbage bags on top of it. "Shannon, that bag is your clothes." Regina points to a garbage bag. I walk into the living room. To my surprise, Miguel is sitting on the dingy, royal blue couch. He is eating a plate of food.

"Hey, Ria." He smiles.

"Woo woo!" Miguel smiles and puts his plate beside him. Miguel picks Karina up and gives her a kiss.

"She said, 'Woo woo' today," I tell Miguel. Regina enters the living room and sits beside Miguel on the couch. Shannon drags her garbage bag of clothes into the living room.

"Mom, where do I take my clothes?" she asks. Looking up from the bag, she gasps at the sight of Miguel. "What is he doing here!" Shannon questions.

"He helped moved your bunkbeds," Regina answers.

"So?...he made you go to the hospital!" Shannon shouts. Regina rolls her eyes.

"I am okay and he said sorry. So mind your fucking business, Shannon," Regina snaps. "You should be thankful he helped moved your bed," she adds.

Miguel perks up as a cynical smile comes across his face. "Actually, the beds will be finished in a few days," he states.

"Tomorrow?" Regina asks.

"Well, maybe." Miguel shrugs his shoulders. He uses the remote and turns the TV volume up.

Regina scoffs. "I told you they were sleeping in the room tonight," Regina states.

"They can still sleep on the mattresses. Just push them together," Miguel suggests.

"Girls, push the mattresses together." Regina instructs.

"No, Maria wets the bed!" Shannon whines.

"Then figure it out, I don't know what you want me to do about it." Regina rolls her eyes and leans on Miguel's shoulder. "Your bedroom is the last room at the end of the hallway," Regina explains. Miguel and Regina cuddle on the couch.

"I am so happy to have you back in the house, Papi," Regina smiles, "Te amo." She kisses Miguel.

"Gross." Shannon rolls her eyes. I shake my head as I cringe. Shannon and I hate it when Regina tries to speak in Spanish. Regina acts like the classic woman who dates Latino men. This type of woman tends to mimic the culture of their man. It's an odd characteristic of Regina. However, Regina makes 'being Spanish' her thing. She always laughs and tries to correct us when we attempt to speak it.

"Maria, can you help me take this upstairs?" Shannon asks. She slides her garbage bag of clothing across the tile flooring. We both lift the bag and carry it up each step. The hallway is small, and the walls are a dirty, musty white. We enter the room and push the garbage bag inside. A bunch of wood from the deconstructed bunkbed is tossed around the room. With the instruction of Shannon, we push the two mattresses together in the corner of the room. I snuggle up next to my older sissy.

"Well, this is our new life," Shannon says softly. "I cannot believe she is back together with Miguel," she rants. I nod my head in agreement. Last time I saw Miguel, he broke my Britney Spears poster then slammed a plank with a nail through my mother's head.

"Maybe, he will be nice this time," I state. I understand Miguel is wrong. However, I am young. The only solution I can come up with is wishing my family can be normal and loving. My innocent mind believes in giving people endless chances. Shannon rolls her brown eyes.

"You are still a baby, one day you will realize how fucked up everything is." Shannon shakes her head.

"I am not a baby," I pout.

"Yes you are, you do not realize how evil people can be." Shannon rolls over in bed.

Later that night, the house is dark and quiet. I wiggle my way off my mattress. On my tippy toes, I move through the night. I have a habit of being awake when everyone else is asleep. I like to walk around the dark house and play in my imagination. Tonight, I am roaming the house so I can map it out in my head. I like to learn where each room is and what it looks like. In the kitchen, the stove light is left on. On the counter, I see the house phone is lit up blue. I smile. We moved enough times for me to know that if the house phone is plugged in, then Regina is currently paying for cable. Usually, the cable only lasts one or two bill cycles before they turn it off for unmade payments. I race into the living room. I turn the TV volume on low and sit on the couch. I flip through the channels to find Cartoon Network. I catch the ending of the Powerpuff Girls.

Suddenly, I hear foot steps coming down the stairs. I try to rush to turn off the TV. "Maria?" I hear Shannon question. The TV shuts off, the room becomes dark.

"Yeah?" I say.

"I thought you were in the bathroom. Go back to sleep," she tells me. I pass Shannon through the dark.

"Goodnight," I whisper. I pretend to walk up the stairs. However, I stay behind and spy on Shannon. I wonder why she is up as late as I am. Peeking around the stairs, I see her walk into the kitchen. I hear Shannon dial on the house phone.

"Star..." Shannon says. I tiptoe closer to the kitchen. "I am alright..."

Shannon whispers over the phone. "I just hate living here. Our beds aren't even built," Shannon cries. "Miguel is living here again!" she adds. "I want to live with you," she sniffles. I hang my head low. I don't like when Shannon is sad. "Yes, I promise I will look out for Maria," Shannon adds. "I love you so much, Star." She ends the conversation. I quickly tip toe up the stairs and into the bedroom. I toss myself on the mattress. I begin to think of a beautiful place I once saw in a book at school. A grassy meadow with a treehouse in the middle. As I imagine, I transition into sleep.

Star, Shannon, and Maria at Fun Station

Shannon and Maria at Fun Station

Shannon and Maria at Star's house, ready to go to church

Maria and Star

Shannon and Maria at Star's house wearing matching outfits

CHAPTER 4

A Knock at the Door

The apartment is decorated for Christmas. Tis the season when Regina pulls out the two containers full of Christmas decorations. Regina holds these decorations near and dear to her heart. So much so that if the house were on fire, she would save the containers first. Her children, second. Lately, I have a habit of paying attention to people's actions. Shannon has been telling me it is time to grow up. She can't keep looking out for me. It is time for me to look out for myself. With this advice, I have begun to observe people when they are doing a simple task. I am sure to make notes of who is around whatever environment I am in. This new skill has come in handy because I have been able to recognize when the energy in my house is about to get scary. For example, when Miguel is around I keep an eye on him. I examine his facial gestures and tone of voice. There are different types of Miguels. He can quickly go from being in a good mood and helping me with math homework, to a raging, angry man. Or he will be quiet, slow paced and a certain type of silly.

"It is time to decorate the tree!" Regina smiles as she stands in front of the fresh evergreen tree. The tree scent makes it feel like

Christmas cheer is in our house. I sit on the couch with Miguel, Shannon, and Karina. The evergreen tree stands in the corner of our small living room. Regina pops open the two containers of decorations. "This year, the lights of the tree will be colorful!" She smiles and rubs her baby bump.

"RAINBOW LIGHTS!" I shout with glee and look over at Miguel. His eyes are a bit squinted.

"Woo Woo!" He tickles Karina while she sits on his lap. Karina smiles, admiring her father. Regina twirls the lights around the tree. We all begin hooking ornaments on the branches.

"Come on, Miguel, help out," Regina demands. Miguel slowly stands up. Regina hands him an ornament. Miguel smiles with his squinted eyes. He slowly tries to balance the metal hook on a tree branch. We all watch him completely miss the tree. The glass jingle ball falls and breaks on the floor. Regina sighs, "Ugh, what the hell."

Miguel claps his hands and laughs. "Oops," he says and licks his lower lip. I am too young to understand that he is high off heroin.

"Just sit back down, you dummy." Regina rolls her eyes and applies pressure to Miguel's shoulder. Miguel falls back and lands on the couch.

"Time to put the angel on top of the tree!" Regina smiles. She pulls out a red, unopened box with a clear plastic covering. "We are going to use the new angel Grandma Leona gave me at Thanksgiving," Regina tells us as she flips open the top of the box. The angel has a long, green and red velvet dress with a porcelain face. Regina stares at the tree. Perhaps the reason why Regina loves Christmas is because it holds a special time when she was younger and living with her family. Now, the only time she sees her family is around the holidays or celebrations. We are the black sheep of her family. Nevertheless, Christmas is where Regina shines. She loves to gift bomb us to make up for how we struggle throughout the year. Most of our gifts that we get are from Regina signing our family up for donations. Other than that, she will ask us what is one thing we really want. This year, Shannon wants a bike and I want a Britney Spears barbie doll.

In the morning, I stand in the living room waiting for Shannon to come downstairs so we can walk to the bus stop. It is our last day of school before Christmas break. I am wearing my school uniform, donated winter coat and carrying my backpack on my shoulders. I admire our Christmas tree and sing 'Where are you Christmas' from the remake of *The Grinch*. As I sing I believe that Santa is going to come and make Christmas great this year.

"Come on, Ria." Shannon walks past with her backpack on her shoulder. I follow her outside. "Be careful, it looks slippery out," Shannon warns me. I stand on the sidewalk with my black sparkle boots. We walk closer and closer to the bus stop. I begin to get a nervous feeling in my stomach.

"Shannon, I don't want to go on the bus," I state.

"Why?" She asks.

"Isabella!" I say, flustered, revealing my school bully. Isabella is a 4th grader who sits in the front of the bus. "She tells everyone I smell like caca!" I whine. "I just wanted to be her friend. I think she has cool hairstyles," I explain. "...but her aunt is the bus driver, so she never gets in trouble." I roll my eyes. I see Isabella waiting for the bus. I pucker my lower lip at Shannon. "Can you beat her up for me?" I ask nicely. I have seen Shannon fight before. She is good at it.

"Maria, you are in 1st grade now. You have to start fighting your own battles," she informs me.

I roll my eyes. "You never help me anymore!" I shout. I try to avoid Isabella while waiting for the bus. I lean against the concrete sign at the beginning of the complex. It says, 'Gilyard Court.' I begin to act like I am a Spy Kid on a mission. Recently at our neighbor's house, I watched a movie called 'Spy Kids.' It is about two kid siblings finding out their parents are secret spies. As I lean on the wall, I act like the character Carmen. Carmen is a tough girl who finds out information before she attacks the evil villain. Acting like this person helps me face Isabella with tough skin.

In my classroom at Gilmurry school, I am in the 1st grade. The teacher's name is Ms. Oats. She is a fun teacher. I quickly learned she does not like being called 'Ms. Oatmeal.' Ms. Oats has curly brown hair. She always wears long blouses and dress pants. At my new school, I have made a few friends like Rachele, Remi, and Lanyia. They think I am funny. We play double-dutch, hopscotch, and pretend secret agent adventures at recess. School for me is an escape from home, though the schoolwork has become hard. I would rather crack jokes than listen to the teacher. I would rather go on adventures in the hallway than sit in my desk. Today, my mind is stuck on the fact that Isabella likes to bully me on the bus. I think about Shannon's words, 'you have to start fighting your own battles.' Ms. Oats begins her first lesson of the day. I pull out a pencil and paper. I begin to draw a rectangle. This is when my revenge against Isabella comes into motion. The rectangle reminds me of the 'Gilyard' sign. I remember she walks behind the sign to get to her apartment. A slight grin comes across my face. I smile with a plan.

At dismissal, I quickly rush out of my classroom to do my daily freak out in the hallway. I have an irrational fear that I will not be able to find Shannon and I will miss my bus. "SISSY!!" I scream with fear and a lisp. I walk against the crowd heading to the school's main entrance. "SHANNON!" I scream. I push past kids. Usually, Shannon waits for me by the cafeteria doors. She isn't here today. Dramatically, I drop to my knees. My oversized backpack weighs me down. "SISSY, WHERE ARE YOU!" I throw my hands in the air.

"Get the hell up," I hear Shannon's voice from behind me. I turn and look at her with a smile. "People are looking at you." She grabs me by my arm. I hug her.

"I thought you left on the bus without me." I follow Shannon through the crowd. We step onto the bus, and I make eye contact with Isabella. She sits in her normal spot.

"*My sissy, where is she?*" Isabella mimics me as I sit in the front row. I roll my eyes. I am embarrassed. Isabella and her friends must watch me in the hallway. I stay silent with my plan of revenge.

We approach our bus stop. I rush out of my seat, down the steps and quickly through some snow. I crouch behind the 'Welcome to Gilyard' sign. Isabella gives the bus driver, her aunt, a hug. I wait to attack her. I hear her feet approaching in the snow. "BITCH!!" I scream. Extending my body. I hop and throw my fist up in the air. I upper cut Isabella's lip. "One, two!" I shout out with my hands in a boxing formation that my father taught me. She steps back and slips in the snow. I stand with pride and fists up, ready to fight.

"Ow!" Isabella cries holding her lip. Shannon runs over to me.

"Look who is crying, don't mess with Maria!" Shannon shouts in her face. I growl like a dog and show my teeth. Kids around us laugh at Isabella. I like the attention. We hear a woman shout in Spanish. I look over my shoulder and see Isabella's grandmother running towards us. She is wearing black boots, a bata de casa gown and a long sweater.

"Maria, run!" Shannon shouts. Shannon and I run away to the back of the complex. Hopping through the snow, I can feel snow slipping into my boots, causing my socks to become soaked.

The next day, apparently, my revenge towards Isabella is what every grade is talking about. In the hallway, I wait against the wall in a line. We are waiting for the older grades to finish exiting the cafeteria for lunch. Classmates chatter as I stand with everyone. A blonde-haired girl, Hannah, looks at me. "I bet you didn't beat up a 4th grader," she whines.

I roll my eyes. "Well, I did," I state. Hannah and I both see life differently. There is a 1% of wealthy people within Waterbury. Hannah's family is one of them. Her family donates to the school and her mother is in charge of the Girl Scouts program. Her mother fought hard to get me thrown out of Girl Scouts due to Regina always picking me up late after meetings. I have been warned from past issues with Hannah to not speak to her because we cannot get along.

"You're not that tough," she giggles. A few kids giggle with her.

"Yes, I am." I squint. I look over at Ms. Oats, she is talking to another teacher in their classroom doorway.

"If you are tough, then I double dog dare you to bite me," Hannah snickers and holds out her hand. I dig my front teeth into the top layer of her skin. "GRR!" I growl as I bite her.

"OWW!" Hannah cries.

"What is going on?" Ms. Oats turns and looks at us in line.

"Maria bit me!" Hannah wines, holding up her hand.

Ms. Oat's rolls her eyes. "Go to the office, now!" she demands.

"...but she told me to bite her!" I argue.

"Go to the office!" Ms. Oats repeats.

I sigh and begin walking down the hallway. I become distracted by the colorful tiles of the hallway flooring. In my mind, I begin to pretend I am on a Spy Kids mission. The floor is lava and my mission is not to get caught by evil minions. As I play in the hallway, I find myself near Shannon's classroom. Slowly, I creep and peek into her classroom doorway. The room is empty and the lights are shut off. She must be coming back with her class soon. I spot Shannon's backpack near a desk. I tiptoe inside.

Suddenly, I hear voices come from down the hall. "Everyone, please go sit at your desk and pull out a pencil for your spelling quiz," a woman says in the hallway. A group of kids are approaching. I panic. My small feet don't know where to run. I pause and scan the room. I see a table with a blue checkered tablecloth on top of it. Running between desks, I slide underneath the table. Kids begin to enter the room. "Okay, pull out your list and review it quickly," the teacher says. I lift the cloth slightly to peek at the classroom. I see Shannon sitting at her desk.

The school intercom bleeps, "Maria, please report to the main office... Maria, please report to the main office." A female voice announces.

Uh oh, I tell myself. Shannon shakes her head, and I can see her leg shaking. We inherited this anxious trait from our mother. Whenever I am in trouble, they always get Shannon. She must be wondering why they are calling me on the loudspeaker. The class begins the quiz. "Psst Sissy," I whisper with my lisp.

"Dude, did you hear that?" a boy says.

"Shh! This is a quiz," the teachers states.

I lift the tablecloth again, "Psst Sissy!!" I make eye contact with a boy siting the closest to the table.

"There is a little girl under the table." He points at me. The whole class begins to chatter. I hide back under the cloth. I hear heels clicking, coming close and closer. The cloth is risen.

"Hey," I smile and bat my eyelashes.

"Out from underneath the table please," the teacher demands. I slide out from the table and stand up. The whole 5th grade class is staring at me.

"Oh my god," I hear Shannon say.

"Hi sissy!" I smile and wave. The class begins to laugh.

"What is your name?" the teacher asks me.

"Maria and that is my sissy, Shannon!" I state. My lisp embarrasses her even more.

"Please bring your sister to the main office," the teacher demands. Shannon stands up and I follow her.

At the main office, the principal pulls us into her office right away. Principal Sanchez has thin brown hair. She is wearing a fancy pants suit. Shannon and I sit on chairs in front of Principal Sanchez's desk. "Maria, where have you been?" Principal Sanchez asks. She folds her hands together on her desk. Looking at me, she continuously blinks her brown eyes. She has a blinking tic that I am not aware of. I lower my eyebrows at her with curiosity as to why she blinks so much.

I lean over to Shannon. "Why she be blinking her eyes like that?" I whisper.

"Maria!" Shannon says with frustration. I am the type of kid to always say what is on my mind.

"Excuse me, but why do you..." I begin to speak. I feel Shannon slap her hand over my mouth.

"Girls!" Principal Sanchez looking up from a pile of papers. "Maria, I am going to have to call your mother," she states.

"No, please don't do that," I beg.

"You bit a classmate and disappeared on school grounds," Principal Sanchez states. She shakes her head. "We almost called the police. We thought you left the school!" she adds. I stay silent. She has not mentioned anything about me punching Isabella, so I would rather just get in trouble for this. Principal Sanchez picks up the office phone.

"Regina, you will need to come pick her up. She is suspended and cannot return to school for three days." Principal Sanchez argues with Regina on the phone.

At home, Regina is angry at me. "You are not allowed to watch TV or play with your Barbies," she informs me as we enter the apartment. I sit at the kitchen table, I look down and see my name on a piece of mail.

"I have a letter!" I smile and open the envelope. It is just a bunch of words and numbers. "Who sent this to me?" I question. Shannon rolls her eyes and pulls out her homework.

"Give me that, it is the cable bill." Regina snaps. I am too young to figure out that bills have already been made with my name. This is a common trend for Regina to use our names on bills.

"You can set all of that right here, my man," Miguel says, coming into the apartment. A man with big muscles, light skin, and almond-shaped eyes follows him in. They are lifting a long wooden dresser. "Regina, you know Big Chino," Miguel states. Shannon and I watch the adults interact.

"What is going on?" Regina asks.

"Yo, I thought you said everything was cool?" Big Chino snaps his head back.

Regina stands there with her hand on her hip. "Is this stolen shit?" she questions.

"Aye, Mamí," Big Chino gasps.

"Regina, act right," Miguel demands. "Make us some food," Miguel demands.

"I am cooking pasta for tonight," Regina says.

"Nah, I am not eating pasta," Big Chino laughs.

"Make us rice and beans," Miguel demands.

"No, the pasta is almost finished boiling," Regina states. "There is only rice and beans left for a few days. My food stamps aren't refilled until the 1st," Regina adds.

"Just cook the food." Miguel smiles and leads Big Chino to the living room. Shannon continues her homework as Regina cooks. I sneak and follow Miguel into the living room. I watch the men from the doorway.

When Regina is at work, Miguel usually has friends over. I always find his friends interesting to watch how they hang out. To me, I see them as a group of grown men gathered with excitement over a new toy or music video with half naked girls. "I got some good shit right here." Big Chino pulls out a ziplock bag of brownish green powder. The powder is heroin, though I am too young to understand what is in the ziplock.

"Yo!" Miguel's eyes rises. "This is for later." Miguel looks around and pats Big Chino on the back. "Maria, shouldn't you be grounded in your room?" Miguel notices me. "Go upstairs and don't play with anything," he demands. I do as I am told. I stomp my way up the stairs. In my bedroom, I pull out a few toys and begin to play.

As I play, time flies by. It is dark outside. I am hungry. I begin to hear the echoes of the sound of a movie starting. I head downstairs and see Shannon, Regina, and Karina sitting on the couch with bowls of pasta in their hands. "Dinner is ready?" I ask.

"Oh, Maria, I forgot to call you," Regina laughs. "Go get a bowl," she states. I join my family and sit on the floor, next to the small couch. We are watching a Christmas Movie on my mother's favorite TV channel, LifeTime. Regina sits by the arm of the couch, her favorite spot. She rubs her pregnant belly while enjoying her bowl of pasta and a cold glass of milk. Big Chino and Miguel walk by the living room doorway. "What are you guys doing?" Regina shouts.

"Nothing," Miguel says.

"He needs the broom!" Big Chino screams. Shannon looks at Regina.

"Why is he yelling?" Shannon laughs.

Regina gets up from the couch to check on them. "Get back in the house!" Regina shouts. Shannon and I race over to the kitchen. We see Big Chino holding the broom. I notice the men are moving and talking slower than usual.

"I need to go sweep the basketball court," Big Chino smiles.

"You guys are high as hell." Regina snatches the broom from his hand. "Both of you, upstairs," Regina demands. Regina escorts the men upstairs. As she returns there is a knock at the door. "Ugh, what now?" Regina scoffs.

Regina walks over to the door. "Oh, hi," Regina says, shocked.

"Who is that?" I ask Shannon.

"I am not sure, mommy is in the way," Shannon says. Regina holds the door close to her hip, we can hear a man's voice from the outside.

"Alright, thank you… Talk to you soon," Regina says and shuts the door.

"Who was that?" Shannon asks.

"Mind your business, Shannon."

The next morning, Shannon leaves for school. I stay home due to my suspension. I sit at the kitchen table reading a book called, *Green*

Eggs and Ham by Dr. Seuss. I like how the book rhymes and plays off the meaning of other words. It can keep my mind occupied. Regina comes down in her robe and slippers. She sits at the table and drinks her morning coffee. "I guess you being suspended from school helps mommy get the good night shifts." Regina smiles.

"You work tonight?" I ask.

"Yes, I work tonight." She smiles and picks up the cordless phone. I watch Regina pull out a piece of paper.

"Who are you calling, mommy?" I ask.

She waves her hand around, "Ugh, Maria, hush." I look at my book and listen to Regina speak on the phone.

"Hey, this is Regina." She smiles as she speaks into the phone. She stands to her feet to pace the kitchen while she talks. Her slippers drag on the tile flooring. "It was perfect timing because I do not think Miguel can continue to babysit the girls," Regina sighs. "Yes, I would love that," she adds. "Maria is home from school, Shannon gets home at 3pm," she explains while she rubs her pregnant belly. "That would be great! Shannon loves anything to do with her Game Boy, books, or comics," she says. "And Maria..." she says looking over to me. "She loves just about everything, her favorite thing in the world is Britney Spears," she states. "Perfect." She hangs up the phone.

"Who were you talking to? Why do they need to know I like Britney Spears?" I question.

I wait for Shannon to get home. I sit on her bed and dig under her pillow. I read her latest journal entry. It reads:

Dear God, I hate Maria, she is a brat and bitch. Miguel got her McDonalds and not me.

"Get out of my bed!" Shannon shouts. She tosses her backpack on the floor.

"Yikes," I say, shoving her journal under her pillow. I scurry up the bunkbed ladder.

Shannon follows me up and holds me down, "You want me to give you a swirly?" she threatens. "The devil lives in the toilet and will grab your face." She laughs.

"No please!" I cry. "I am sorry," I plead. She laughs and lets me go. "You wrote you hate me." I fold my arms.

"You are mean to me sometimes, Maria!" she yells.

"When?" I ask.

"You called me fat for not fitting behind the dresser when my Gameboy fell behind it," Shannon explains.

"I am sorry," I say.

"Girls, get your shoes on and come downstairs!" Regina shouts from the hallway. Shannon and I look at each other confused. We come downstairs and see Regina dressed in her nursing scrubs. "I have to go to work," Regina states. "Karina is next door at Jenna's house," she says. "You are going to Burger King with your new babysitter," Regina informs us. "You will stay with the babysitter until Miguel gets home," she adds. "Babysitter?" Shannon questions. "Also, if DCF speaks to you at school or anything... Tell them you have a babysitter." She smiles. Shannon and I look at each other, confused. We head into the kitchen and see Tony standing near the front door.

"Surprise!" He smiles. "TONY!" Shannon runs over and gives him a hug.

Tony is wearing a light, black jacket and blue jeans. His hair is black, he has a goatee, slick back hair, and his nose is red from the cold. "Hi Maria." He waves to me. "Shanny, you got so big from the last time I saw you," Tony tells her. I remember him, however, I do not know him like Shannon does. Tony used to be Star's roommate back when Shannon lived with Star.

"Hi," I smile. "Maria, you also have gotten so big." He smiles.

"Bye, mom!" Shannon opens the front door. Tony leads us to his car. It is a black, shiny Chrysler sports car. Even in the snow, his car looks clean and brand new.

"Wow, nice car!" I tell him. The car has only two doors and seats that fold down for someone to get into the back.

Tony folds down his driver's seat. "Hop in." He smiles kindly.

At Burger King, Shannon and I sit at a table while Tony orders us food. "I want a crown!" I demand.

Shannon walks over to a countertop and takes two fake golden crowns. Tony approaches us with a tray of food. "Bon appétit!" he says while placing the tray on the table. Shannon and I begin to eat. Tony flips open his black and yellow Nextel cell phone. He dials a number. "Hello." Tony smiles. "Guess who I have with me?" he tells the person on the other line. Tony hands the phone to Shannon.

"Hi Star!!" Shannon shouts. "There is a gift from you?" Shannon says. I watch as Tony stands up from the table.

"I will be right back." He winks at me. I nod my head and rip the crispy skin off my chicken nugget. Moments later, he comes back with a few gifts wrapped in blue, shiny wrapping paper. "This one is from Star." Tony smiles. He hands us a gift. I unwrap my round-looking gift. It is a small, pink purse. I look over to Shannon. She has new Gameboy games.

"Thank you, Star!" Shannon says into the phone.

"Tell her I said thank you!" I say.

"Maria says thank you!" she shouts into the phone. Tony ends the phone call.

"Now girls, these next gifts are from me," Tony says. "You can open them now, or on Christmas." He gives us a choice.

"Now," Shannon and I simultaneously say. Tony hands us the gifts. My gift is shaped like a rectangle. I rip it open.

"Britney Spears!" I shout as I see her face on a VCR tape box. A few families having dinner around us begin to eyeball us.

"Shhh," Tony says lowering his hand down. "In music, this gesture means take it down a notch," he says. I nod my head.

"You got me a Britney Spears video tape!" I say in a low excited whisper. He smiles. I stand up and give Tony the biggest hug. "You are the best babysitter. I love you," I say. Tony pulls me up onto his lap. I feel him place his hand on my lower back. He begins to rub his hand in a circular motion.

"Open your gift, Shanny," Tony says. Shannon rips open the blue paper.

She asks, "What is this?" Tony and I look at her. She is holding a round thing made of black material.

"It is a carrying case for your Gameboy and all the games," Tony explains.

"Ohh!" Shannon states as she un-zippers the case. "I love it!" She smiles.

"Alright, girls," Tony says tapping me on my thigh. "Lets see if Miguel is home," he states. "I gave him an extra 20 minutes." He chuckles. We clean up our gift wrappings and food.

In the car, Tony plays music. He plops in a cassette tape. It plays a fun, bubbly pop song called, 'Honey.' Instantly, I am amazed by the woman singing. Her voice sounds light and sweet like an angel. "Is this Britney Spears?" I shout over the music.

"No, even better," he says with his New York accent. "Mariah Carey," he states. Tony reaches behind the seat and hands me a cassette tape case. There is a woman on it dressed up in a golden belly shirt and she has a butterfly near the tip of her finger. We make our way home. Tony drops us off, although this time he does not come to our front door. "Your mother said I am not allowed near the house when Miguel is home," Tony informs us. "Is it alright if I babysit you girls again?" he asks us. I nod my head with a smile. "Yes!" Shannon gives him a hug. Tony gives me a hug and kiss on the cheek. We walk to the front door. Miguel opens the door for us. Shannon turns around and gives Tony a thumbs up to ensure Miguel is home.

Entering the house, I quickly rush to the TV.

"Hey hey, I am watching that!" Miguel shouts.

I look up at him and begin to fake cry. He hates when I cry. "Tony got me this Britney Spears video for Christmas, I want to watch it!" I pretend to whine.

"Alright," Miguel sighs. "I am tired anyway. Wait who is Tony?" Miguel back tracks.

Shannon sits on the couch. "Our new babysitter, guess you are out of a job," Shannon laughs.

"I am going to sleep," Miguel states. "Ain't no way, you and her are staying down here alone. Ya'll will be fighting as soon as I get into a good sleep," he adds.

Shannon rolls her eyes. I see her tuck her gifts under her jacket so Miguel doesn't see. Shannon doesn't like it when Miguel and Regina know Star gave her a fancy gadget. They like to use it as a threat to punish her. I bet she is going to go play her new video games on low volume. "Maria, just don't leave the house," Miguel warns. He heads upstairs.

"Goodnight, Ria." Shannon walks over to me as I push the video tape in the VCR. I look up,

"Night, Sissy!" I smile. "Have fun playing your games," I whisper. She winks at me.

I pop my VCR tape into the TV. I lower the volume as the screen lights up with Britney Spears walking down a hallway. I am amazed at how when she talks, she stares right at the camera. As if she is having a conversation with me. The video follows her around the recording studio and NYC. I see her hopping into cabs and the big city behind her. The tape ends with the behind-the-scenes footage of her music video, 'Oops I did it again.' I see the cameras and directors on the set. It sends excitement through my mind. I have seen the music video so many times on MTV. It amazes me at what it takes to be backstage and create a video. The camera, the directors, and a group of people doing Britney's hair. It's all so interesting to learn about. "I am excited to be working on this video project," Britney says with the set behind her. She had her hair and makeup done while wearing a red body suit.

"Video project," I repeat to myself. That's when it hit me, all music videos I watch are simply video projects.

CHAPTER 5

La Familia

By the springtime, Regina gives birth to another baby girl, Selena. She is born on May 9th, 2001. Coincidentally, Selena is born on the same day Karina was. They are exactly two years apart. Selena is precious when she comes home from the hospital. She has tan skin and perky lips, just like Miguel's. In Regina's room, Selena lays on the bed while Regina does my hair. I sit crisscrossed on the bed as Regina parts my hair with a fork. "Remember Maria, do not tell mommy's business to your father or his family," Regina states.

"Alright, mommy," I say.

"Your father doesn't have a car. Tony is going to pick you and Shannon up, then drop you off with Julian," Regina explains.

"I love Tony, maybe he will buy us McDonalds." I smile. Regina finishes my hair. I have pigtails on each side of my head and one in the back. "Thanks, mommy!" I shout. I head into the hallway.

I walk on my tippy toes and gently sway my head back and forth. I love when the curled ends of my pigtails bounce around. Ready for the day, I sit at the kitchen table and begin to read my 'Green eggs and Ham' book. Suddenly, I hear Regina scream from the stairway.

"Shannon, you are not wearing that skirt!" she yells. I look up from my book. "You look like a slut in that," she adds. I hop off of the kitchen chair and peek my head into the hallway.

"Star gave this to me, I am wearing it!" Shannon shouts.

"I don't fucking care, Star isn't your mother!" Regina yells. I see Regina on the edge of the last step. She is carrying Selena in one arm and lifting her hand with the other.

"Let go of me!!" Shannon shouts. Regina's foot slips off the step. Her back taps the wall, catching her fall with the baby in her arms.

"GODDAMN IT!!" Miguel barges in the hallway. "GO CHANGE THE FUCKING SKIRT!" he shouts, getting in Shannon's face.

"Miguel, I am sorry," Regina says softy.

"Fuck all of you!" Shannon shouts and runs to the front door. I look out of the doorway. Shannon runs to Tony's black, shiny sports car.

Tony has been babysitting us for a few months now. He is a part of our daily life. Most times we go out to have dinner, to the park, or to shop at Walmart. Other times he likes to show up to our house to stock our refrigerator with food and snacks. I shut the door behind me. "Hey Tony!" I shout as I approach his car. Shannon sits in the front seat of the car, pouting. Tony picks me up. He has his dark shades covering his eyes. He hugs me. Tony and I have gotten very close. He has developed a secret game. Tony tells me he is in love with me like a father loves a daughter.

"How is my daughter doing?" Tony whispers into my ear.

I place my hand on his face. "Hi Dad." I smile. Tony likes it when I play the game. He gives me a kiss on the cheek and places my feet on the floor. I hop in the backseat, ready to go and see my Papi.

In Danbury, we park in front of the Danbury Ice Rink, which is the spot where Papi told us to meet him. "Girls, do you see your father?" Tony asks. He pulls his shades down. We scan the area from the car.

"Oh, there he is! That is my Papi!" I shout. I unbuckle my seat belt and reach in between the two front seats. I press on the horn.

"Maria, be careful." Tony moves my hand away. Shannon rolls down her window as Papi approaches us.

"Hello, my beautiful daughters." Papi smiles wide, he bends over to look at us through the window.

"Hey, my man," Tony says, reaching over Shannon. Papi and Tony shake hands,

"Hello, Tony from New York." Papi smiles. They know each other from gathering events. "Well, thank you for bringing my girls to me," he states and opens the car door. Shannon and I step out.

"Anytime. Regina couldn't bring them due to car issues," Tony states. "Good thing the girls have me around." He smirks as he tilts his black shades at the tip of his nose.

"My daughters know that they can call me when they need me." Papi rolls his eyes and opens the passenger door.

"Ha, yeah, I am sure they do," Tony says. We hop out of the car and watch Tony zoom off around the corner.

"Well girls, let's venture forward on our walk to Abuela's house," Papi states. We follow him, walking on the sidewalk to the next block over.

"We should have had Tony just drop us off there." Shannon rolls her eyes.

"Listen, I chose the Ice Rink because it gives us a nice distance to walk and catch up." Papi smiles. He stops walking, Shannon and I stop and look at him. "Do my beautiful girls not want to spend quality time with their father?" he asks. Suddenly, he lifts us both up. I am in his left arm and Shannon in his right. He rocks us. "Do they not want to hang out with me?" He laughs.

Shannon and I look at each other as we are lifted high. Shannon rolls her eyes, "We do." She laughs.

"Yeah, we want to hang out with you and your stinky armpits," I laugh and look down at my Papi's visible hairy pits.

"Listen, that smell is weed," he says proudly.

"Papi!" Shannon gasps. "I tell her it is your armpits," she whispers to him.

"It is fine, I have a nice herbal smell." He laughs. Papi places us safely back down on the ground.

We turn onto Main Street, a small main road in Greater Danbury. It has restaurants and small shops. "We need to turn on the corner of Nicko's restaurant and the library," Papi tells us as we walk. Walking with Papi always feels like an adventure. He likes to update us on his life. Currently, he is boxing at a gym, working at a restaurant and mediating. He has a girlfriend who we can't meet because he doesn't want her to know he has children. We turn the corner and enter Abuela's street. The houses are lined up on each side, with a clean sidewalk and small cherry blossom trees. At the corner of the street is Abuela's apartment. The bottom half of the apartment is red brick with white house siding panels on top. I can see the window on top where Abuela's kitchen is.

We walk up the back stairway, the stairs have dark red wine carpeting. "It smells like her cooking." Shannon smiles.

"I love when she puts the tiny hotdogs in the yellow rice," I exclaim. My mind can visualize her big chef pot on the stove filled with warm yellow rice. At the top of the steps is the front door of the apartment.

"Wait." Papi says. He dips his fingers in a small water bowl hanging on the door frame. "Never forget the cleansing Holy water," he states. Before stepping into Abuela's house, one must cleanse and bless their energy with Abuela's homemade holy water. Papi flicks the holy water at us. "Get back, you demons!" he jokes.

"I'm melting!" Shannon cries mimicking the voice of the wicked witch from *The Wizard of Oz*. The door flings open,

"Julian, you know better." Abuela shakes her head with disapproval. I smile, locking eyes with Abuela. My Great-Abuela, Felictica. She is the mother of Grandma Camila, as well as a professional chef.

Abuela has round glasses that sit on the bridge of her button nose. Her hair is short with thick brown curls. She is wearing a flowery bata de casa. A bata de casa, translates as a house dress. A bata de casa, the ultimate multipurpose dress for cleaning, cooking, babysitting grandkids, and resting on the couch watching a telenovela. Abuela shakes her head and dips her fingertips into the holy water. She is very spiritual. Abuela correctly flicks her holy water at us. She believes in church views but also believes that energy can be good or evil. Abuela always tells us there is energy all around. Some of us can feel it more than others. Some of the things she teaches, I have never learned in church. "Hola, Abuela!" We greet her with hugs.

Entering the living room, I look around the room. I always feel so comfortable at her house. There is a beige couch and a large, thick screen TV in the corner. A glass coffee table, Puerto Rican island patio decor and vibrant vine plants growing around the room. The walls are painted with Caribbean blue paint and a gray carpet. The TV always plays one of two channels, Telenovelas or Nasa Car races. Today, it is a Nasa Car race. Tio Pablo, Grandma Camila's brother, sits on the couch drinking a can of beer. He has olive skin, big brown eyes, dark hair and a very thick mustache. He wears bleached blue jeans, shiny black loafers and smells like he bathes in fancy cologne. Papi follows Abuela in the kitchen. I look around. I am comfortable in this room.

However, sometimes, I see the man who no one else can see. Sometimes I see a vintage old Puerto Rican man sitting on the couch. His skin is tan and has wrinkles. He always wears a button-up polo island shirt. He never speaks but he watches everyone with a faint smile on his face. He isn't scary. I do get frustrated when I try to talk about him to my family. They look at me like I am crazy. Besides Abuela, she winks at me when I mention the man. No one can see him except for me. I do not see the man today.

Shannon sits down on the couch. I instantly follow her. "Hola, Tio Pablo." Shannon smiles.

"How are you, girls?" Pablo asks.

"We are good," Shannon answers.

"Can I play with the toys?" I ask him pointing to the space behind the couch.

"Yeah, go ahead, just don't kick me." He laughs, leaning forward. I climb the couch and peek over. There are a bunch of toys between the wall and couch. I grab the blue bag of race cars. "So, Shannon..." Tio Pablo says after taking a sip of his beer. "Nasa Car racing isn't just about racing, it is about controlling the speed." Tio Pablo begins his usual rant on how to gamble on car racing.

I stand on the carpet near the glass coffee table. Flipping over the open bag, a stream of cars rush out and make a loud noise. "Wepa!" Tio shouts as he watches what I am doing. I begin to play and pretend the cars are in traffic on the floor. "Those cars use to be your fathers," Tio Pablo tells me.

I smile kindly, "Really?"

"Yeah, he was obsessed with them," he adds. I play while Shannon enjoys her time with Tio Pablo. Time passes.

"Maria and Shannon, come eat!" Papi calls from the kitchen. Shannon and I walk deeper into Abuela's house. It feels like a tight hug as the hallway is decorated with objects she has collected through her life. We begin to race for the best seat in the kitchen. The seat near the kitchen window.

"I GOT IT!" I shout as I toss myself ahead of Shannon.

"Aye, cuidado!" Abuela shouts. She tosses her cooking rag over her shoulder. I stick my tongue out at Shannon in victory.

The reason we love this seat so much is because squirrels like to come to Abuela's window for food. If a squirrel comes by, the person sitting near the window gets to feed it. "Abuela..." I call. I begin speaking in random fake Spanish. Abuela's face drops, she looks confused.

"Julian what is she saying to me?" she asks with her Spanish accent.

"She is speaking Spanish." He winks. I place my hand under my chin and smile.

"I can speak Spanish, Abuela." I say.

"Julian, you need to teach them real Spanish." Abuela shakes her head. "None of this blah blah words." She rolls her eyes. Julian nods his head while he fills up two bowls of rice.

"Tiny hotdogs!" I shout receiving my bowl.

"You need to bring them around here more often, Julian," Abuela says. She snaps her cooking towel at him.

"Ow!" he yelps. Shannon and I laugh.

As we eat Abuela pulls out an egg and a glass of water. She pours salt into the water, "limpia de huevo," she tells us, which means egg cleansing in Spanish. We watch Papi hold out his arms as Abuela rubs the egg along his frame. She cracks the eggs into the glass of salty water. The yellow yolk sits at the bottom while pieces to the white yolk spiked upward. "No bueno," she says holding the side of the glass close to her face. She is reading his energy through the egg yolk.

"What does it say?" Julian asks.

"Lots of dark energy, Mal de Ojo," which translate to 'Evil Eye.' Julian looks at the glass.

"Hola, Mama." Grandma Camila enters while holding a small baby in her arms. She greats Abuela with a hug. "Who's that for?" Grandma Camila points to Papi's Limpa de Huevo.

"Me," Julian says. Grandma Camila rolls her eyes and pours the egg reading down the sink.

"Aye!" Abuela yelps. Grandma Camila doesn't like when Abuela talks about her spirituality.

"Mama, Jesus is the only truth and light," Grandma Camila says sternly.

"Let me see Nani!" Abuela smiles and takes the baby from Camila's arms. Nani has thick hair, dark skin and wide brown eyes. Grandma Camila rescued Nani from the hospital. Nani is the daughter of Uncle Thomas. In the early 90's Thomas witnessed his brother, Uncle Edwin, get decapitated in a car crash. This crash changed Thomas' life. He isn't able to take care of Nani, nor is Nani's mother. The mother left baby Nani in the hospital after she was born. Now, Camila is raising her.

"Hi, girls." Grandma Camila turns to us. I smile and gaze upon her. Grandma Camila's dark hair is pulled back into a low bun. Her bangs are blown out, and her lips are lined in dark red. She wears a black 90's flared leather jacket and golden, small hoops. Grandma Camila walks over to the small, silver TV with two metal antennas sticking out of the back. The TV sits upon a stack of cookbooks on Abuela's counter. She turns the channel to a telenovela. Camila sits next to Shannon at the kitchen table. We all sit and enjoy the telenovela.

"Hola, Michie!" Abuela says from the stove. Michie is Pablo's older daughter. Michie has tan skin, pretty, wavy long black hair and is dressed in jeans with a striped pink and white v neck shirt.

"You look so pretty!" I smile at her. I always love seeing Michie, she dresses the way I wanted to when I grow up.

I watch her pull out her Nokia cell phone with a string and charm of Winnie the Pooh holding a pink heart. "Wow, is that a hit clip?" I ask.

She chuckles, "No, it is a cell phone." She clicks the buttons. Her nails have French tips.

"Hi, China," Esten, Pablo's son, says. He steps into the room. He has tan skin, a shaved head and is wearing a basketball jersey and headphones. Esten has autism and a connecting bond with Shannon. She once read him a book about Traveling the World: China Edition. Ever since creating a fun reading moment, he calls her China. Esten holds his CD player. "Listen to this new mix." Esten immediately places his headphones on my head. He plays, 'Hyperballad' by Björk. "This singer's name is Björk." Esten says loudly holding a thumbs up. I listen to the beats of the music and the uniqueness of Björk's voice.

"Well, well, well…" Pablo says stepping into the small, cramped kitchen. "This is what I like to see, the whole family together." He smiles. I look around the room and see my family. I wish I got to see this side of my family more often. I love being around and the cookouts we have.

"Do you girls like your new school? I heard you moved again," Camila asks.

"I guess," Shannon answers.

"Your mom's boyfriend, he still lives with you guys?" she asks.

Shannon shrugs her shoulders. "Sometimes," she answers. This is exactly what Regina was talking about. When we get questioned about life at home, we must not give too much information away.

"And you have a babysitter?" she asks.

"Tony? Star's friend?" Grandma adds. "Yeah, he watches us," Shannon answers.

"And, we have a new little sister!" I tell them with excitement. "Little baby Selena." I smile, cradling my arms as if I was holding a baby.

"I don't like that man, Tony," Julian scoffs.

"Why?" Camila asks.

"He has a cocky attitude." He shakes his head.

"Well, he is friends with Star… all her friends are stuck up," Camila explains. "I know, I am looking at one," Julian laughs. Camila chuckles. "I think he is a nice man." Camila states.

"He is nice, he likes to bring us to Friendly's and has money to buy the expense ice cream!" I state.

"See, he flashes his money around." Julian shakes his head.

By the end of the night, we are gathered around the living room TV watching a telenovela. "Alright, Julian, it's time," Tito Pablo says from the couch. Shannon and I look up at Papi. He is leaning against the hallway wall watching TV and holding a beer can.

"Alright girls, it is time to go home," he says. I stand up and wrap my arms around Papi's waist. He picks me up.

"How are we getting home?" Shannon asks.

"Tito Pablo offered to drive you girls home," he answers.

"Are you coming?" I ask him.

"No, Grandma Camila is gonna give me a ride home," Julian explains. "I will see you girls on the next visit," he states.

I feel my eyes water up, "I don't wanna say goodbye to my Papi." I burst out in tears. I feel Papi hug me.

Grandma Camila walks over to me. "Shhh. Shhh, María," she says my name in Spanish. "You will see your dad soon," she tells me. I listen to her words as I feel tears continue to flow. "Next time, you guys will do fun things together, just like today." She smiles. Her eyes are gentle and kind. I wipe my tears with the back of my hand and sniffle my nose. Shannon and I hug everyone goodbye. We follow Pablo and his kids out of the apartment door. I look back and see Papi in the doorway, waving goodbye to us.

In the car, Michie sits in the front seat. Esten, Shannon and I squeeze in the back. Tito Pablo's car smells like his fancy cologne and cigars. As we ride, Esten puts his CD player on full volume. He holds it between us so we both can hear his Björk mix. We pull into the complex. "This is where you girls live?" Pablo asks. He drives slowly and looks around. There are people walking around, hanging out at night.

"Our apartment is in the back." Shannon tells him. The car comes to a stop.

"Bye, Tito Pablo!" I say. Shannon opens the back door, and the light comes on. Shannon rushes out of the car. I hop out and turn to shut the door.

Before I shut it, I hear Tio speak. "See, Michie, you need to be grateful for what I give you. You could live in a place like this," he explains.

I shut the door and Tio drives away. I look down at my feet. I always wonder what people mean when they comment on where my family lives. Tony and Star like to comment on this subject as well. "Maria, let's go," Shannon rushes me.

I follow Shannon down the concrete pathway to our apartment door. There is shouting coming from behind us. Shannon turns and looks. "Let's get inside, it looks like there is a fight about to happen on the basketball court," Shannon states. She opens the door. I turn around and look across to the court. I see a group of men gathered. Their harsh voices echo while they curse each other out. "Come on, Maria," Shannon says pulling me inside. The stove light lights up the kitchen. "Mommy must be asleep," Shannon whispers. Upstairs, Shannon and I get ready for bed. Suddenly, we hear a gunshot go off. I duck to the floor. I have heard gunshots before from living in Brick City. Shannon runs to the window. I creep next to her. There is smoke rising underneath the basketball court streetlight. Some men run away and others argue while we hear police sirens in the distance. We continue to watch as the police show up. Neighbors come out from their apartments to see what is going on. Police shout as they pull on men running.

"Why is everyone so mad at each other?" I ask Shannon. She closes the window.

Shannon tucks me into the bottom bunk. "I had a fun time seeing Papi," I tell her.

"Me too," she says, sitting on the edge of my bed. "I wish Papi cared more about us," she states.

I tilt my head confused. "He loves us," I tell her.

"If he truly loved us then he would visit and call us all of the time," Shannon explains.

"He doesn't have a car," I state. Shannon shakes her head. "You are too young to understand." She sighs. "He is just like mommy," she states.

"How?" I ask.

"He only cares about himself and his girlfriends," she states.

I think about her words. "How do you know all that information?" I ask her. Her words begin fogging up the image of my father.

"I don't wanna talk about it anymore, Maria," Shannon says. "You just need to pay attention to life more," she adds. Shannon climbs up to the top bunk. "Goodnight, Maria. I love you," Shannon says.

"I love you, Sissy," I say.

I roll over to the wall. Placing my hands under the side of my face. I stare into the abyss of dark space in front of me. I ponder on Shannon's advice on how to pay attention. My thoughts begin to link to another similar thought. Teachers tell me the same thing, 'Pay attention, Maria.' 'Use your listening ears.' Officially, I come to a conclusion. I need to use my eyes and ears at home. "Can you sing me the song?" I ask Shannon through the dark.

"What song?" she sighs from the top bunk.

"The angel song." I smile. "I am tired tonight, but I will sing it from my bed," she tells me. I smile and roll over facing the open space of the room. Shannon's softy high-pitch voice sings 'Angel' by Shaggy.

"Girl, you're my angel
You're my darling angel
Closer than my peeps you are to me, baby
Shorty, you're my angel
You're my darling angel
Girl, you're my friend
When I'm in need, lady"

I listen while I feel something within the dark. I see a blue sparkle flash from across the dark room. I gasp to myself. I am not sure what it is. Looks like something magical. Seeing it makes me feel safe. My eyes become heavy. I drift into a restful sleep.

In Loving Memory
Rest in Peace
Abuela Felictica

CHAPTER 6

The Secret

It is summer vacation. Gilyard Court has been active with cookouts and residents hanging out around the complex. Regina and Jenna often let their babies play together. I have become friends with Jenna's son, JJ. It is a hot summer day. Jenna is having a cookout in front of her apartment door. Adults are gathered around the small black grill, drinking and smoking while they have conversations. I watch the adults from the top of a green electrical box. I like to stand on it and pretend I am a pop-star on stage.

"Hey Maria, look what I just got from Ms. Florence," JJ tells me. Ms. Florence is an elderly woman who sells Kool-Aid Icy's. I look down at the grass and see JJ holding two red icy's. I jump down from the box and thank JJ. JJ has chunky cheeks, dark eyes and hair. He likes to play Spy Kids with me, as well as walk around the complex by my side. I feel safe around him because he is tough. I once witnessed JJ chase his father with a knife when they argued. I wouldn't want to get the kid mad.

Suddenly, there is a familiar beep from the parking lot.

"Tony!" Shannon races out of Jenna's apartment door. "Come

on Maria, grab your bag!" Shannon demands while handing me my backpack. I scan the adults for Regina. She is hanging out with Miguel by the grill.

"Mommy, Tony is here," I tell her.

"Alright, have a good time." She waves. I begin to follow Shannon. We walk towards the parking lot. Tony emerges from his sports car. He has his sunglasses on.

"Bye Maria!!" JJ runs after us. I give him a hug goodbye.

"Bye JJ, I will see you when I come home from New York," I tell him. I walk over to Tony and greet him with a hug.

"Who is this?" he asks while taking hold of my bag.

"My best friend, JJ," I say. Shannon gets in the front seat of the car.

"Do you and him kiss?" Tony asks me.

I scrunch my face, "Ew, no he is my friend," I state. I hustle to the back seat of the car.

Tony has steadily been our baby-sitter for months. He brings us to Friendly's or the public pool. Tony has grown trust with Regina. Since Regina has been having overnight shifts on the weekends, Tony has been taking us to his house in New York. This will be our third time going to Tony's house. So far, it has been fun. Tony takes us to the mall and church. We arrive in White Plains, New York. Tony takes us to a nail salon. Immediately, I recognize a daughter around my age out with her mother. They are getting pedicures. I sit at the nail desk as the nail tech begins to do my nails. Behind her is a wall of mirrors. I watch the mother and daughter sit next to each other as they get their pedicure. "Oh yup, it is our girls day." The lady laughs to the nail tech working on her feet. I wish my mother would take Shannon and I out to get pedicures. I get my nails painted, Barbie pink.

After the salon, Tony takes us shopping for new outfits. We have dinner at Sal's pizza, a classic Italian New York pizza parlor. Going around town is fun and different. Where Tony lives, the streets are cleaner, without potholes. Everyone around town has a smile on their face. They are friendly and dress as if they are going to a fancy party. I love seeing women walk around with heels and purses. I want to wear nice clothes like them when I am an adult. Behind Tony's back, Shannon and I call him fancy. He has a house with a backyard and lives in a suburban area. I love visiting New York because it is something different and new to me. Tony has been so nice to my family and me. The bond between us has trust and love.

The day turns into evening, and we head over to Tony's house. He lives in a house owned by his family. The house has two apartments. His brother lives upstairs, while Tony and his mother live on the main floor. Apparently, we are allowed to be over because his mother, Anna, isn't home this weekend. He says this every time we come over. In his apartment, there are three bedrooms. One bedroom is his mother's, one is a playroom for his mother's grandchildren. The last is an extra bedroom that Tony uses.

Shannon and are only allowed in the kitchen, living room and Tony's bedroom. I sit on the bed with Shannon as I observe Tony's room. The room is painted baby blue, and everything is made of wood. There are three wooden dressers, a wooden desk, wooden chair, and a bed.

Shannon puts on the small 80's wooden laminated TV that is on a tall dresser. Tony explained that this is the house he and his six other siblings grew up in. Apparently, this baby blue room used to be the bedroom of his sisters.

Shannon lays back and lounges on the bed. "I want to go to sleep," she yawns. Tony opens the long, wooden closet door. Every time he opens it, I like to watch. The closet is filled to the ceiling with objects. Tony pulls out a small yellow crib mattress. It has a pattern of teddy bears holding red balloons.

"Maria, your bed," he states, placing it on the floor in the middle of the room.

"But, I ain't tired," I state.

"Say, 'I am not,'" he corrects me. "Here in New York, you speak properly," he adds. "How about you watch a movie in the living room with me?" he says. "Come on, you are not going to stay up bothering your sister," Tony says pulling me by my hand. I pull my hand away from him.

"I need my pajamas," I say. Tony digs through my bag.

"You need anything, Shanny?" Tony asks.

Shannon yawns and shakes her head, "No, I am good." She smiles.

Tony shuts the door as he and I exit the room. "Go change." Tony opens the bathroom door. I step into the 80's pink tiled bathroom. "Do you need to use the bathroom?" he asks me.

"Yes," I say.

"Do you need to go number one or two?" he questions.

"One," I answer.

"If you need to do number two, let me know," he states. I nod my head and watch Tony leave the bathroom. He shuts the door, slightly. I have been over to Tony's house enough times to know that when I use the bathroom, Tony waits by the semi-closed door. If I pass a bowel movement, I must call for him. Tony claims he doesn't trust me enough to clean myself. I clean myself just fine when I am at home with Regina. I have learned when I am around Tony, I have rules.

I watch the door as I use the toilet. "All done," I whisper.

"Wait!" Tony swings the open. "Let me see that you only went pee," he demands. He shuts the door, pushes me back down and looks behind me. "Alright, you are good," he says. I look up at him while I stand to my feet. We walk down the hallway, and I see a collection of glass angels in a tall glass cabinet. We turn into the living room, and I hop on the couch. I look around the lit-up room. There are two green couches with a flowery pattern stitched into them. A wooden piano that has tons of picture frames of family members. The walls have pictures of Christian quotes and Jesus. Tony puts on the musical, *Annie*.

"I remember this, we watched it last time!" I smile pointing at the screen.

"My favorite character is Daddy Warbucks," Tony states.

"Yeah...you are like him!" I recall. "You take us to get our nails done and give us gifts!" I explain.

"You really think so?" Tony smiles, flattered by my comment.

"You are kind of like Annie," he says. Tony shuts the lights off. "You are hyper, loud and likes adventures," he explains while he cuddles up to me on the couch. "You also have a difficult time with receiving love from your parents," he comments.

I look up at Tony and tilt my head. "Huh?" I say.

"It is alright to agree with me, your mother and father do not know how to love you," he explains. Tony pulls me close to him. I reflect on what he has just said. He gives my feelings words and self-reflection. Tony kicks his feet up on the couch. I can see his face through the light shining from the TV. He leans in and kisses me on the lips. "I am always here for you." He smiles. I stay silent.

"Is it alright that I kissed you?" Tony asks me. Tony sighs, "Are you mad at me?" he asks. "You hate me, now?" he overly questions.

"No, I don't hate you," I say.

"Do you want to try and kiss again?" Tony asks me.

I stay silent once more. "No," I shake my head.

"See you are mad at me." Tony backs away from me. I am alarmed at making Tony upset.

"I am sorry." I place my hand on his arm. Tony looks at me and shrugs his shoulders.

"What are you going to do?" he asks me.

I look him in the eyes with the gut feeling that there is only one correct answer to his question. "We have to kiss," I state. Tony begins to kiss me once more.

Suddenly, Tony gasps.

"What is it?" I ask.

"Shhh," he hushes me. With the TV as a light source, I watch Tony slowly walk into the hallway. He disappears around the corner. I wait and look at the TV. The beginning of the movie has begun. "She is sleeping," Tony states, tiptoeing back into the living room. "Stand here."" He pulls on my hands. I stand in front of him. He places my hand on his black sweatpants. He begins whispering how I should touch him. With fear, I do as I am told. Seeing and touching his bare genitals has completely made me frozen on the inside. My mind feels detached. I feel like I can't hear my own thoughts. Suddenly, Tony begins pulling on my clothes. "Tell me that you want me," he demands pulling my bare body on top of his. I stay silent. He shifts my body around, "Come on, tell me," he demands. I do what he says. I look at his creepy smile, his face begins to feel like I do not know who he is. Tony yanks my body towards him as I feel his genitals pressing into mine.

"Ow, that hurts," I speak.

"Shh." Tony lowers his eyebrows at me. "You need to be quiet," he scoffs. Tony begins to move his genitals around. He lays his back on the couch while I remain on him. "Hump me," he demands. Unsure of what he means, I remain still. "Go like this," he pulls my hips. Tony forces my body to move in certain ways. I try to keep up with how he is pulling on me. I am overwhelmed and try to ignore an unknown feeling. He is causing my body to naturally react to the sexual situation he is forcing me into. Tony laughs, "You like that, don't you?" His chuckles linger. He begins to make an unsettling noise. Tony pushes my body beside him and pulls on the back of my head. "Put it in your mouth," he demands. I begin to gag on nasty liquid that comes out of him. Tony sits up and laughs. "Here, spit in here." He pulls off his t-shirt. I am grossed out by his hairy chest, fat stomach and ugly red genitals. Tony holds my mouth open and wipes my tongue.

"Get dressed." He places my PJ's on the couch. "I need to get a clean shirt," he states. Tony walks into the hallway and returns with a new t-shirt. I sit on the couch, staring at the TV. The movie is almost over. It is at the part where Annie is having fun visiting Mr. Warbuck's house. I began to wonder if Annie does the same thing I have just done with Tony. "Hey." Tony sits beside me. I instantly become attentive to him. "I am sorry," he says.

"Why?" I ask.

"I shouldn't have done that with you." He begins to cry. "I am sorry." He buries his face in his hands. "Now you are going to hate me forever," he whines. I feel bad that Tony is crying. I am six years old, I don't like to see people cry.

"It is alright," I whisper and lean on Tony's arm.

He hugs me. "Really?" he says.

I stand up and look Tony in the eyes. "Yes," I state.

"Can this be our secret? Promise me you won't tell anyone?" he asks.

"I promise," I state.

"I don't believe you," he says. "What if your mom asks you about it?" he asks. I stay silent. "Maria, if you want to go home, you have to promise me this is our secret," he states.

"I promise, I won't tell anybody," I assure him.

The next morning, I wake up on the small yellow crib mattress with the pattern of teddy bears holding red balloons. I can smell breakfast in the air. "Good morning, Ria," Shannon smiles from the hallway. Looking at her, I feel a deep shame. I feel guilty for what I did with Tony last night. I would feel embarrassed if Shannon ever knew. "Come on, Tony made breakfast." She smiles. I follow her into the kitchen. We sit at the small wooden table.

"Pancakes with chocolate chips!" Tony smiles placing plates in front of us. "Your favorite, Maria." Shannon smiles. I look up at Tony. "I made them just for you." He smiles and pats my back. I smile halfway. "Well today we are going to visit my sister's house." Tony explains. He leans his back on the counter edge. I watch him cut a piece of pancake with the side of a fork. "Then I will take you girls home," he adds. "I wish you girls could come to church with me tomorrow," Tony says while he chews. "Your mother said you can only stay over on Friday nights," he explains. It seems odd to simply get over what Tony did to me last night, though he doesn't seem bothered by it. Shannon has no idea. I am simply the only one aware of the situation. I feel alone. I don't want to keep thinking about it.

A week later, Regina has Tony pick us up for the weekend, again. Tony performs exactly what he did last weekend. We watch a movie when Shannon is sleeping. That is when Tony directs me to perform horrid acts with him in the living room. Each weekend I visit Tony's house, he does the same routine. When he is done, he always cries and begs me to promise never to tell anyone. By the end of the summer, Tony's routine becomes a normal recurrence within my life. I tend to not ponder about his actions. Especially when I am home with Regina. Out of sight out of mind. Though, I am always reminded as soon as it is nighttime at Tony's house.

The new school year begins. It is September 11th, 2001. The day is partly cloudy and humid due to a tropical storm that is on its way to us. I am excited to start 2nd grade. My teacher's name is Mrs. Larson. She looks exactly like one of the witches from Hocus Pocus. She has curly red-hair and big front teeth. My school year has been off to a very rough start. The principal warned Mrs. Larson that I am difficult to deal with. However, Mrs. Larson is a fun teacher. She always has me occupied with some type of project. She keeps my mind busy by giving me a composition notebook to create stories. I sit at my desk. Today, each of my classmates is trying to estimate how many giant marbles are in the glass jar. Mrs. Larson holds the jar up high at the front of the class.

Suddenly, the loudspeaker tunes in. "Today we will be having an early dismissal. All students must begin to collect their personal belongings," the loudspeaker announces.

Suddenly the classroom phone rings. Mrs. Larson runs over to pick it up. "Oh my!" Mrs. Larson's face drops with worry. "Class we need to remain calm." She hangs up the phone. "Pack your backpacks up with your items," she frantically demands. "There is an emergency, everyone needs to go home," she adds. The class chatters as we do what we are told.

We are immediately sent home due to the fall of the Twin Towers in New York City. I follow Shannon off the bus, everyone is in a panic. I hold Shannon's hand as she explains to me what is going on. "Teachers said America is under attack," she states. I gasp with anxiety. We enter the front door of our apartment, I see Miguel is sitting at the kitchen table eating. The aroma of fish sits in the air.

"The girls are home!" he shouts.

Regina turns and looks at us. She is in a light blue robe. She wipes her tears while holding Selena.

"Is this why we were sent home early?" Shannon asks. On the TV, it shows the fall of the Twin Towers. I put my backpack down on the kitchen floor.

"Why is mommy crying?" I ask Miguel.

"The government is saying America is under terrorist attack," he states, licking his lips in between bites of his meal. "...but I think it is only in New York City and maybe the pentagon," he calmly states with a half mouth full of food. "New York City." I gasp with fear and confusion.

I know that I live in America and it is scary to hear that we are under attack. I go find Shannon in the living room. Karina is laying on the couch drinking a bottle of milk. She is watching Regina and Shannon stand in front of the TV with their eyes glued to the screen. The news channel flashes clips of the tragic moments. "This is so horrible!" Regina cries.

Shannon wipes a tear from her eye. "People are jumping out of the buildings," she yells. I see a clip zooming into a burning building and bodies dropping down.

"Maria, don't watch anymore." Shannon pulls on me.

"Maria, go in the kitchen with Miguel," Regina demands.

As I walk away, I hear the news caster say, "This is a sad day for the American people." I walk into the kitchen.

"Hey, come here," Miguel says from the table. He pulls out a chair beside him. I climb on the chair and wipe my tears. I can see Miguel's plate is full of crab legs. "I went out to get my food before the stores begin to shut down," he explains. "I even got this." He smirks and holds up a box of Goya food. "Want to try some?" he asks.

"What is it?" I ask. "Pulpo." He smiles with a chuckle.

I watch him peel open the metal box. A fishy smell appears. "It is like a special type of chicken." He laughs.

"I love chicken!" I smile. He hands me a slither. It is slippery and dark pink. I toss it into my mouth, it is squishy and fishy. "Ahhh." I spit the food onto the kitchen table.

Miguel laughs. "Ha ha." He slams his fist on the table. "I got you! Pulpo is octopus!" he states. "Look, these are little octopus legs." He picks up another piece. I examine what he shows me. I can see little suction cups on the legs.

I laugh, "You got me!" I look into Miguel's eyes. It is at times like these when I enjoy his company. When Miguel looks like he got sleep. That is when he is kind, helpful, and silly.

Months pass. Since Miguel has been hanging around the house more often, Regina hasn't been using Tony as a babysitter on the weekends. When he does babysit us, it is during the week. Tony takes us to McDonald's, helps us with homework, then brings us back home when Regina is done with her day shifts. Drug addiction has slowly consumed Miguel. His kind and silly self has faded into a heroin addict. His eyes hang low with bags. He walks around like he is angry at the world. He takes his anger out on Regina and Shannon. When Regina is at work, Shannon takes care of the household. Cooking and cleaning. Also dealing with the waves of Miguel's madness. He makes it a point to show Shannon how much he doesn't care for or respect her. Miguel punishes her for odd things like forgetting to clean a certain cooking pot. Miguel will take me to get a Happy Meal at McDonalds. While he makes Shannon eat cereal with water for dinner, alone in the bedroom. In Shannon's journal, she writes about how much she hates living with Regina. I see the sadness she has in her eyes.

I am officially seven years old. It is 2 a.m. on October 9th. I am wide awake because the night before my birthday I can never sleep. I am too excited to be one more year older. I roam the halls and play in my imagination. I sneak downstairs and watch my Britney Spears video tape on low volume. My Britney tape makes me smile. I want to be like her one day. I want to visit New York City. I want to have fans and be pretty.

"Miguel stop!" I hear Regina shout coming down the steps. Miguel is chasing her. I run to the couch with my blanket so I can be hidden. I hear their foots steps walk into the kitchen.

"Yo, just give me the money and I will go," Miguel says.

"I don't have money," Regina tells him.

"I will come back, just give me some cash," he demands.

"Why, so you can go out in the streets feening to shoot up?" Regina shouts. "You turned into such a druggy, it disgusts me," she says.

"Wait, stop!" I hear Regina shout. I begin to hear her gasp.

"I will choke you the fuck out, bitch!" Miguel shouts. "Who are you to disrespect me," he growls.

Scared yet curious, I tiptoe to the kitchen doorway and peek my head into the kitchen. I see Miguel pinning Regina against the refrigerator. His hands are around her neck. She is slapping his arms while gasping for air. I have learned by now that shouting at Miguel to stop hurting my mother does not help. I run upstairs.

"Shannon, Miguel is hurting mommy." I shake Shannon awake. Shannon shoots up from her slumber. We race downstairs. We find Regina on the kitchen floor leaning against the kitchen cabinets. The door is left open with Miguel nowhere in sight.

"Shut the door," she points.

"Are you alright?" Shannon asks.

"I am fine!" Regina snaps. I notice her holding onto her neck. "Go back to sleep, worry about yourself Shannon," Regina demands. Shannon shakes her head and walks down the hallway. I follow her.

"Next time, don't wake me up!" Shannon shouts at me. I watch her get back into bed. I shut the door and climb up the bunk bed ladder.

"I am sorry," I whisper. I begin to softly sing to myself Shannon's and my favorite song, 'Angel,' by Shaggy.

In the morning, I walk downstairs ready for school. Shannon and Regina argue in the kitchen. I walk over to see what is happening. I observe that Regina is in her work scrubs. Jenna is standing in the open doorway while holding one of her twin babies.

"You can't throw notes like this outside the window!" Regina shouts.

"That was my letter to God!" Shannon screams.

"Well, your letter to is gonna get D.C.F called on me, again!" Regina snaps. "I am your mother and you will respect me." Regina throws her hands in Shannon's face.

"Regina, back up," Jenna says. Jenna sometimes hears Regina and Shannon fight. She comes over to delegate the situations.

"I can't waste my time on you, I need to get to work!" Regina shouts. She shoves Shannon on the shoulder. "Move, I need to get my cigarettes," Regina snaps and picks her cigarette pack up from the kitchen table. Shannon pushes Regina back.

"Fuck you and fuck what you want!" Shannon screams. She flicks Regina's cigarettes out of her hands. "Fuck you, you whore bitch!" Shannon runs past Jenna. She grabs her bike and goes on a ride.

"She is supposed to watch the girls today," Regina scoffs. "It is too late for me to call Tony," she adds. "Can you watch them?" Regina asks Jenna.

"Yeah that is fine," Jenna states. Regina grabs her purse for work. "Maria, you need to help me," Jenna says while walking into the kitchen. She prepares to get Selena and Karina from the living room. I help Jenna transfer Karina and Selena into her apartment. "Go back home and get ready for school," Jenna tells me. "I will cook you breakfast," she adds. "Hopefully your sister will come back home," Jenna mumbles as I leave her apartment door. Today is an interesting way to start my birthday.

I step into our kitchen. On the table I see the letter Regina was talking about. I take a peek and read Shannon's letter:

Dear God, Please send me an angel to help me and my little sisters. We need love. I don't want to live with my mother anymore. I want to live with Star again!

Love, Shannon

I place it back on the table and go upstairs to get ready for school.

After school, I get off the bus by myself. I have less anxiety about missing the bus. Mrs. Larson gave me a birthday certificate and two sparkly birthday pencils for my special day. As I walk to the back of the complex, I see Tony standing next to his black shiny Chrysler sports car.

"TONY!" I shout and run into the parking lot.

"Happy birthday!" He smiles and picks me up. I rest my head on his shoulder.

"I got a birthday pencil at school," I tell him.

"That is great." He smiles. "Well, I can't stay for too long." Tony smiles. "Come follow me to the trunk... I have your birthday gift," he states.

"Really?!" I smile. Tony takes out a wrapped rectangle box. He sits me on the closed trunk. I rip open the paper. "SPY KIDS SHOES!" I shout with excitement. My favorite movie of all time is *Spy Kids*.

"Yup, I got them in a half-size bigger than you are so you can use them longer," he states.

"I will always wear these when I go on missions!" I squeal. Tony pulls something out of his light weight black jacket. "Batteries?" I question.

"They are from Star, for Shannon," he tells me. "Give them to her in secret." He winks at me. "I promise, I will be back soon. Happy birthday." He smiles.

Later that night, I lay in bed. Shannon has been silently playing her Gameboy. She did say happy birthday to me when I gave her the batteries. Besides that, I am having a birthday party on the top bunk with my Barbies. I have the Barbies sitting in a circle with pretend food. In my mind, I make the Barbies have conversations with each other. Suddenly, I hear loud noises from downstairs. I fear Miguel is hurting Regina again. "Did you hear that?" I ask Shannon.

We hear a crash and rush downstairs. In the kitchen, Regina is having a mental breakdown. "Fuck him, he is not coming back into this house again!" She screams into the air.

"What happened?" Shannon asks. Regina begins pulling out plates from the cabinet and tossing them against the wall. "Mommy, stop it," Shannon tells her. I follow Shannon and stay close by her side.

"I am tired of living in this dirty, bug infested, apartment with cement walls!" she screams and tossing another plate. "I gave Miguel everything. He gives me nothing!" She flings small objects across the kitchen.

We have seen Regina have raging fits before. However, this time, her eyes look lost. "I think mommy is going insane." Shannon whispers to me.

"What should we do?" I ask her.

"Mommy, please don't be angry," I say.

"Don't be angry?" she screams at me. "I have the right to be angry!!!" she yells in my face. "I work to feed...ALL OF YOU MOTHERFUCKERS!!" she screams, kicking the fridge door.

"Mommy is going insane," Shannon begins to sing.

"SHUT UP," she yells.

"MOMMY IS GOING INSANE," Shannon sings louder with a grin on her face. Regina covers her ears. "Come on, sing it," Shannon elbows me. I join in.

"MOMMY IS GOING INSANE, MOMMY IS GOING INSANE." We sing in unison.. Regina runs underneath the kitchen table.

"I don't want you guys anymore, I want to be alone!" she cries. Shannon stops singing. "Nobody loves me!" Regina shouts.

Shannon's laughter turns frail. She freezes and looks under the table where Regina is. "...We love you, mommy," Shannon says gently.

"That's not enough," Regina cries and pulls her knees to her chest. "That's not enough," she repeats and slams her fist.

"Come on, Maria," Shannon pulls on my hand. "She doesn't want us," Shannon whispers.

I look at my mother underneath the table. "Mommy, I am sorry," I say.

I approach her, "Leave me alone! I hate you!" she screams at me. Tears rush down my face.

"YOU ARE SO MEAN!!" I scream at her.

"Just don't talk to her, Maria." Shannon pulls me away. "She is a bitch and doesn't know how to treat us," Shannon states with anger. We walk away, leaving Regina and her emotional breakdown alone. I hold my throat and look at Shannon. Everyone likes to demand and yell at me. I always stay silent in fear. I fear that if I respond to them, they will get mad or not understand me. However, this time around, I yelled back at my mother. I am angry that her actions show that she doesn't love us. We always want to make her happy and feel loved. We yearn for her to show us just a bit of affection and attention.

CHAPTER 7

Man of God

Entering 3rd grade hasn't been easy for me. Regina has relocated us, once again. We quickly fled Waterbury and moved to Naugatuck, Connecticut. Naugatuck is known for being a middle-class area with a good education system. When State Housing called Regina with the news that she won the lottery on a middle-class apartment, she got the large garbage bags out and packed us up. Goodbye cement walls and rat-infested cabinets. Hello, 70's wooden panelled walls and a backyard. In our new neighborhood it feels very suburban. Our house is a New England styled home with three apartments within it. There is tan vinyl siding with dark brown framing. A wooden porch leading to three doors for each apartment. Our apartment door is the middle. Inside, the layout has three bedrooms, an attic, laminated wooden wall panels and brown shaggy carpeting. The wooden panels are from when the house was refurbished in the 70's. There is a back door near the kitchen sink. It leads to a back wooden deck with stairs.

The deck overlooks the backyard that is shared with the other tenants. I love gazing at the yard. Of course, I have seen backyards and been around some. However, I had never personally had a backyard before. I always thought they were for the rich families. Shannon and I have been enjoying our time outside. I like to walk around, touch the big oak tree. I like to dig in nature, collect worms and flowers. The day turns into dusk. I sit crisscross on the back deck. Between the wooden railings, I gaze upon the orange sunset with purple clouds. This spot became my secret hiding place. I like to sing to myself because no one can hear me. It is just me and the open sky.

"MARIA!" Shannon yelps from behind me.

"AH!" I shout as she scares me. I guess my spot isn't so secret as I thought. "What?" I ask, annoyed. Shannon is disrupting my state of peace.

"The girls are talking to the ghost!" Shannon squeals. "Come look," she directs me.

Shannon and I believe there is a little ghost girl haunting the apartment. The proof is in the attic that is connected to our apartment only. In the attic, there is an old wooden toy rocking horse, an old fashion wooden bed set and dresser. The edging on the wood is painted pink. The bed is made as if someone is going to come sleep in it. Shannon watches a lot of ghost hunting shows. She explained to me that the bed is made for the ghost girl. She relaxes on the bed or must play with the rocking horse. She warned me never to touch anything in the attic, for it could make the ghost girl upset. That was all Shannon had to tell me. I do not even walk near the attic door after she showed me what is up there. Although, I do feel like something is lurking around.

I follow Shannon into the bathroom. "I was giving the girls a bath when they started talking to the blank space between them," Shannon explains. I look down at Karina and Selena in the bathtub.

"Who are you talking to?" I ask them. Shannon stares at me with excitement. She already knows the answer.

"The little girl," four-year-old Karina states. I look at Shannon.

"Have you ever seen her before?" Shannon asks Karina. Karina tilts her head and then looks at Selena.

"Yeah, she plays with us in our room," she adds.

I gasp, covering my mouth. "That is unbelievable," I tell Shannon.

"I knew there is a ghost living here." She smiles. Suddenly, the phone rings.

"I will get it," I tell Shannon. I walk into the living room and answer the cordless phone. "Hello?" I say.

"Hey, it is Tony," Tony states. Tony has been babysitting us, though Shannon and I haven't visited his house in months. He has become a daily part of my life. Tony likes to call and check in on us when Regina works the nightshift.

"Hi, Tony. I did all my homework," I state. I walk to the kitchen table. I look down at a pile of my school supplies. There is my math homework sheet and a composition notebook. I love writing. Currently, I am writing about how a bat is an unusual pet because it can suck your blood.

"Are you sure all your homework is done?" Tony asks over the phone. "I can call your school tomorrow to find out," he warns. I look down at my blank math sheet. Picking up my pencil, I begin to fill in random answers. "What is Shannon doing?" he asks.

"Giving the girls a bath," I answer.

"Has anyone been over to the house recently?" he asks.

"Mommy's new boyfriend," I state. "...and sometimes I see Miguel," I add.

Tony likes to ask a lot of questions. I have learned it is best to always give him the answer he is looking for. If not, when he picks us up to babysit, he will question me about why I disobey him when he isn't around. He has groomed me to fear his authority. "You should start brushing your teeth and get ready for bed," Tony demands.

"I ain't tired yet." I roll my eyes.

Tony sighs heavily on the phone. "What did I tell you about saying ain't?" he questions me. "You sound ignorant," he adds.

"I am sorry." I panic.

"You better go and get ready for bed," he demands.

"Alright," I sigh.

"Excuse me?" he questions. "I have taught you better manners than this attitude that you are giving me," he reprimands.

"Yes, sir. I will go get ready for bed," I state.

"Good, girl. I don't want to get a call from your mother telling me you are awake when she gets home at 1 a.m.," he explains. "Love you, goodnight."

I smile. "Night, love you."

Tony hangs the phone up. I collect my school supplies and place them back in my backpack. "Can I have a snack?" Karina asks Shannon while they are led out of the bathroom.

"I am so tired," Shannon sighs walking past me. She takes the phone off the kitchen table. From the living room, I hear her dial a number. "Hi Star," Shannon says. She always calls Star whenever Regina isn't home. They like to catch up. I walk into the bedroom to begin getting ready for bed.

A few weeks later, it is a Saturday night. I play around the house pretending I am on a secret mission. I noticed Shannon has not been in the house as I play. This has been a common thing the past few weekends. Then she will come home on a Sunday evening. Though, I remember seeing her a bit ago. I rush into our bedroom. Shannon's mattress is on the floor on the left side of the room. Mine is on the right. Both beds are empty. I begin to investigate Shannon's side of the room.

Looking around, I see movement outside the window between the beds. I look outside, underneath the streetlight. I see Shannon hugging Tony next to his black shiny sports car. I gasp and stomp into the living room. "Where is Shannon and Tony going?" I ask Regina.

Regina lounges on the couch with Karina and Selena. She is watching the Lifetime channel. "Momm!" I shout while she ignores me.

Regina scoffs. "She is going to New York, she will be back on Sunday," Regina states.

"What?!" I place my hand on my hip. "I want to go to New York. She is going to get her nails done and that is not fair!" I whine.

"Ugh, Maria you will go next weekend." Regina tosses her hand up. I take a deep breath. I am very jealous that Shannon gets to go with Tony. Tony takes us shopping and to restaurants. I do not want to miss out on the fun.

"I want to go now!" I stomp my foot. "Call him!" I shout standing in front of the TV.

"Oh my God!" Regina screams while picking up the phone next to her. "Tony, are you still outside?" Regina angrily asks. "Cause this one saw Shannon get in your car. Now, she wants to come," Regina explains. Regina hangs up the phone.

"He is turning around, go and pack some clothes," she demands. My face lights up. I jet to the bedroom, grab random clothing and stuff it into a bag. I race down the steps and see Tony's car waiting for me by the sidewalk. Tony folds the driver's seat down while I step inside to the back seat.

"Hi, Shannon." I smile. Shannon presses her lips together.

"There goes my peaceful weekend," she sighs. Shannon has been escaping to Tony's house as a break from the chores Regina makes her do. She wants to be free from all responsibility. Tony begins to drive the car.

"You saw us from the window?" Tony chuckles. He tilts the rear-view mirror at me.

"Yes, I was like I want to go to New York too!" I state. "Can I get my nails painted blue this time?" I ask.

Tony smiles and winks at me through the rear-view mirror. "Sure thing," he says and then flicks the mirror upward.

In New York, Tony, pulls onto his street and parks. The porch light is lit up, and we walk to the front door. Inside, the hallway has white, bumpy wallpaper with thin blue flowers as decor. The carpet is dark blue. "You have a dog?!" I gasp at the sight of a larger boxer dog.

"That is my brother's dog, Jenny," Tony explains. "My brother that lives upstairs." "His new girlfriend doesn't like the dog. Now, Jenny lives in the hallway," he states. I look at Jenny, she looks like a sad dog. My heart hurts looking in her eyes. Inside the apartment, we enter a small main hallway that has a big glass case with shelves of collectible porcelain angels. "Follow me to the extra bedroom." Tony states.

In the extra room, Shannon places her bag down. She gets comfortable, I can tell she is used to being around the room. She kicks her shoes off, places them near the wall. I copy her. Next, she turns on the small TV on one of the tall wooden dressers. I sit next to her and watch a show on Cartoon Network. It is about a brother and sister who go on adventures with the Grim Reaper. I lay on the mattress. Tony tells us it is time for bed. Shannon uses the bathroom to get ready to sleep. Afterwards, she lays in bed with the light off. She falls asleep to the TV playing on low volume. While Shannon dozes off in the twin sized bed, I spy a digital clock glowing red in the corner of the room. The time reads 9:30 p.m. Tony pulls out the small yellow crib mattress with the pattern of teddy bears holding red balloons.

"You are going to sleep on this," he whispers. I am wearing one of Tony's t-shirts. This is because when I packed my bag I didn't grab any PJ's. I lay down on a pillow and Tony covers me with a small blanket. "Goodnight." He smiles and walks out of the room.

I drift into a slumber when suddenly Tony is shaking me awake. The TV shines light into the room. I sit up and look at him. He is kneeling on the floor. I remain on the small crib mattress. "Are you awake?" he whispers.

"Yeah," I whisper back.

"Stand up," he demands. I do as I am told. Tony lays on the small crib mattress. I watch as the mattress sinks into the floor while he lays his head on the pillow. He pulls me on top of him. "I have missed you," he whispers. Suddenly, my mind floods with the memory of what Tony used to do, although, we used to do this in the living room. Tony places his hands underneath the t-shirt I wear. He begins to rub my bare body. I look up at Shannon. She is steadily asleep on the bed. "Don't worry, she won't wake up," he softly chuckles. Tony pulls down his pants and forces my body against his. I do as he says without question. I look up at the red digital clock, it reads, '2:00 a.m.' Tony pulls my clothing off and begins trying to penetrate my behind.

"Don't scream," he warns me. I feel his genitals pressed on my behind.

"Ow," I whine.

"It doesn't hurt," he softly scoffs. I look at him in pain.

"Yes it does!" I loudly whine.

Tony covers my mouth with his fat, thick hand. His eyes turn angry. "Listen, my mother is sleeping in the other bedroom," he states. "I swear if you wake her up or your sister... you will regret it," he threatens. I nod my head, he removes his hand from my face. "Now, do as I say," he states. Tony, forcefully, makes my genitals rub his, without penetration. Suddenly, he forces my head downwards. The TV light shines as I am face to face with his oddly red penis. Around his area, I see small little skin tags. Tony forces my mouth onto his genitals until he is finished. He places the t-shirt back on me. "Remember, this is our secret," he whispers into my ear. Tony kisses me on the lips. "Go to sleep," he whispers before standing up to fix his sweatpants. Tony leaves the room as I lay there scared. I want to scream and wake Shannon up. However, I am unsure on how to even speak to anyone about what just happened. What are the correct words to say? Will they believe me? What does Tony mean when he said I would regret it if I woke anyone up? These questions haunt my mind as I drift into slumber.

The next morning, Shannon and I sit at the small kitchen table. Tony was sure to get both of our favorite cereals. I have Fruity Pebbles and Shannon has POPS. Both of us stare at the games on the back of the cereal boxes while we eat. Tony prepares his coffee on the kitchen countertop.

"Good morning, Anna," Shannon says as a woman with long black hair and wrinkly skin approaches us.

"Hi, sweetie." Anna smiles.

"Mom, this is Maria. Shannon's little sister," Tony explains.

Anna fills a mug up with coffee. "Hello." She smiles. Anna has fair skin, dark eyes, and thick black Italian hair. "Are you girls going to church today?" Anna asks us.

"Yup!" Shannon smiles.

"Maria, you will get to see Tony play the keyboard." Anna smiles.

"Really?" I ask.

"Yes, he is in the church band. One day, he will be the lead singer," Anna adds.

"You can sing?" I giggle at picturing Tony on a stage. I wiggle in my seat laughing. I do not believe Tony could sing like a pop star. He has a fat, hairy belly and a manly face. He is not like Britney Spears. "That is funny," I laugh.

"She must be a handful," Anna scoffs. "Sit still, you don't wanna fall out of your seat," Anna reprimands. I tilt my head at her. I just met this lady and she is trying to boss me around.

"Ahh, I am falling." I toss my arms around as if I am about to fall off the chair.

I catch Shannon giving me the stink eye.

"What?" I sit up straight laughing.

"Have some respect," she demands. I look up at Anna. She shakes her head at me.

"Come on, Maria you need to take a bath before church," Tony directs me. I follow him into the bathroom. Tony shuts the door behind us. He towers over me while he starts pointing his finger around. "Who do you think you are?" he asks me. I shrug my shoulders and look around at the pink tiled walls. Tony grabs my chin, "Answer me."

"I am Maria," I tell him.

"You are nobody," he states. "So who are you to treat my mother that way?" he asks.

I shrug my shoulders, "I am sorry."

"You better keep your mouth shut when we go to church. I have a reputation to uphold, I am not going to let your disrespectful mouth tarnish it." He stands tall. "Are we clear?" he asks.

I nod my head. "Yes, sir," I state.

"Now, you use the bathroom," he demands. Tony stands there and watches me sit on the toilet. "Let me see…." He pushes my back down and looks. He begins the bath. As Tony bathes me, he claims that I do not know how to clean myself properly. He washes me with soap and water. He even washes my hair for me, all while grabbing and slowly rubbing my shoulders, sides and back.

At church, the lobby is fancy. The carpets are maroon with golden shapes. The marble green and brown welcome desk greets people who pass by. The workers behind the desk have name tags.

"Who are they?" I ask Tony.

"Those people are church helpers. If anyone has questions or needs prayer, they will stop by the welcome desk." Tony explains.

Tony is instantly greeted by the welcome desk. "Good morning, everyone!" Tony waves. "God is good!" he cheers with his fist in the air. "All the time!"

People respond. "Good morning, Tony!" A young woman smiles at him.

"Praise the Lord Tony, can wait to see you up there." A man waves to Tony. I notice just about everyone that we walk by is looking at us. I look over to Shannon. I have never seen her so smiley and girly. She is walking slowly with a tall posture and polite smile. Tony pulls open the sanctuary doors.

"Oh good morning Mrs. Patty," Tony holds the door for an elderly woman.

"Oh are those your goddaughters, you have been talking about?" She gazes at Shannon and me.

"They sure are." Tony smiles.

"Good morning," Shannon smiles and gracefully nods her head. It is funny to see this side of Shannon. Usually, I see her as a tough chick.

"They are so precious." The elderly woman smiles. I sure am enjoying the attention that comes with walking alongside Tony.

"Goddaughters?" I question.

"Yes, you guys are my goddaughters," Tony says.

He gestures for us to walk to the left. The whole sanctuary is a large, tall room with a mural and a maroon carpeted stage. "How does everyone know you?" I ask.

"I am in the church band," Tony states.

We follow him upstairs to the balcony part of the sanctuary. Way up high, I can oversee the whole room. The rows of maroon chairs are perfectly lined up facing the stage. The two big screens tower over the choir and band pit on each side of the stage. The mural is hand-painted, grassy hills and mountains with a dove soaring.

"Hi, Linda," Shannon says walking to the left of the balcony. There is a small workspace with a laptop. A woman, named Linda, sits behind the laptop. She has curly brown hair and thin blonde highlights.

"Hey, Shanny." Linda smiles and gives Shannon a hug.

"This is my sister, Maria," she says.

"Hi, I am Linda," Linda says.

"She is one of my good friends here at church," Tony tells me. "Try not to give her too much trouble, I can see you from down there," Tony warns while he points at the band pit. I watch Linda laugh with her round nose and thick dark lipstick.

"I am sure she will be fine," Linda laughs. "Oh, with this one

Linda....you need to watch out," he laughs pointing at me. I stay quiet and shrug my shoulders.

As church service progresses a short man by the name of Pastor Phil, stands on the stage. He has fair skin, gray hair and wears a fancy silver suit with shiny black shoes. Everyone claps for him. The congregation remains standing. Pastor Phil stretches out his hands towards us. He smiles dramatically. I look up at Shannon.

"Does he have superpowers?" I ask her.

Shannon giggles and shakes her head. "Shh," she holds her finger on her lips.

I examine Pastor Phil. He is different than the Pastor at Star's church. Star's pastor is a woman, normally she speaks into the mic and paces the stage. However, Pastor Phil is elaborate with his words and movements. He reminds me of a Ring Master like in a circus performance. "I spoke to God, he said everything is going to be alright," he states.

Everyone cheers for him. Suddenly, he begins to speak in a funny gibberish language. "Maria, stop laughing," Shannon whispers to me.

I have never seen anything like Pastor Phil before. "What is he saying?" I approach Linda near the laptop.

"He is speaking in tongues, which is God's language," she explains.

"Ohh," I nod my head.

Linda lifts me up and I sit on her lap. "Look, this computer helps me put the lyrics to the songs we are about to sing on the two big screens," she explains. When service is done, Tony comes upstairs to collect us. Shannon and I follow him through the lobby crowd of church goers. People thank him for being in the band. Tony introduces Shannon and I as his goddaughters. Being around Tony at church feels like we are celebrities. Everyone wants to talk with us and ask us who we are.

After church, Tony takes us to get our nails done. I got blue nail polish and Shannon got purple. "Alright girls, now it is time to drive you home," Tony says as Shannon and I buckle our seat belts. Tony stops at McDonald's on the way back to Connecticut. By now, I have completely forgotten what he did to me last night. It is as if a switch turns off. Out of sight, out of mind. Tony says goodbye to us at the front door of our apartment. Shannon walks inside ahead of me. "Hey, Maria," Tony says. I look up at him. "Did you have fun this weekend?" he asks.

"Yes," I tell him. "I love my nails." I hold up my blue polished nails.

"Good." He winks at me. "See you soon, and remember...I am always watching you," he tells me.

I look him up and down slowly. The way he said that with a smile on his face slightly creeps me out. "Meet me at your bedroom window," he tells me.

"Huh?" I ask.

"When you go inside, do not let anyone know... but look out of the window," he demands.

I nod my head, "Yes, sir." I enter the apartment and head straight for the bedroom window, like I was told. Tony is leaning against his car waving to me. He blows me a kiss. I blow him one back. Suddenly he points to his eyes and back at me to let me know that he is watching me. I give him a thumbs up.

At school the next day, I am a ball of energy. More than usual. Mrs. Lascoski, my third-grade teacher, has me seated by her desk. I cannot be trusted to sit behind anyone because I had a phase of poking people on the neck with my pencils. Mrs. Lascoski and I have a special relationship. By special, I can tell that she secretly hates me. I drive her crazy.

Mrs. Lascoski has fair skin, green eyes, glasses, and short curly brown hair. She has her glasses on the tip of her nose as she reads papers at her desk. I pull my lavender backpack with wheels through the row of desks. I sit in my seat. "Good morning, Maria," Mrs. Lascoski smiles.

"Hey." I glance at her and pull out my composition notebook. She hands me a paper.

"Recognize this?" she asks.

"That is the math quiz we took." I look up at her.

"Yes, but this is not your name." She points to the line where names go. I press my lips together to hold in my giggle. I forgot I pranked my teacher by writing my favorite actress' name on the quiz. "Who is Alexa Vega?" she asks. Alexa Vega plays my favorite character in the movie *Spy Kids*.

"That is my name." I shrug my shoulders at her.

Mrs. Lascoski, pulls the paper away and slams it on her desk. "Maria, take these lunch tickets to the cafeteria," she demands, holding out an orange envelope. I perk up in my seat. Mrs. Lascoski is always quick to send me out of the class. She will not leave the class unattended with me in the room anymore. This is because when she is gone, I like to stand in front of the class and read funny stories I wrote in my composition book. Also, to be fair, the last time she left us unattended, I stood up on the desks dancing and singing a Britney Spears song. Then I tossed her candy bowl in the air, making fellow students pick it up like piñata candy.

I take the envelope and begin walking down the hallway. I hop on the colorful tiles. "I am a spy kid," I tell myself. I stomp down the hallway in spy kids shoes that Tony gifted me a year ago. I enter the cafeteria, and it is full of the older kids. I see Shannon's teacher, Mrs. Frost.

"Mrs. Frost, is my sissy here?" I walk up to her. She is standing by the lunch microphone.

"Hello, Maria." She smiles. She has short brown bangs, a funky dark purple vest and khaki dress pants. "Yes, we are here for the D.A.R.E assembly," she states. "What's that you've got in your hands?" she questions me.

"Lunch tickets," I state.

"I can take those for you." She smiles. I hand her the envelope and look around the cafeteria.

"Can I say hi to my sissy?" I ask.

Mrs. Frost pulls the mic close to her face. "Shannon, please stand up," Mrs. Frost says.

"Ooooo," Students shout. Shannon stands up at a table. She looks confused. Mrs. Frost points the microphone at me.

"Hi, Sissy!" I shout and wave my hand high the air. "I love you!" I smile, I loved hearing my voice on the microphone. Shannon shakes her head and sits back down. Other kids begin to laugh.

"No, no, quiet down," Mrs. Frost demands over the mic. I bat my eyelashes as I get attention for doing something funny. Mrs. Frost moves on from the moment. She bends over to look in a box full of objects. I see a red marker on the cart she has nearby. I grin with the opportunity to be even more funny for everyone. I begin to draw on the back of Mrs. Frost pants. I draw a dot on each butt cheek and a smile across the bottom. Suddenly, I hear a group of kids laugh.

"Look at Mrs. Frost's butt!" A kid yells. I drop the marker and run out of another door in the cafeteria. I run down the hallway, thinking I am being chased. I rush into the older kids' bathroom. Feeling hidden, I look around at the tall, metal, tan stalls.

Today I am feeling like I have superpowers because I am wearing the Spy Kids shoes. "Time for a mission," I state aloud. I lock all of the stalls. Time passes by as I play around the bathroom. I climb under the locked handicap stall. Using the metal assistance bar, I climb over the first stall.

"Maria!" I hear Mrs. Lascoski's voice enter the bathroom. Making it over the wall, I use my hands to hold myself up. I pin my feet to each side of the stall. I feel like a super spy, hiding. "I know you are in here, all of the stalls are locked!" Mrs. Lascoski shakes on the doors. I gasp as one of my feet loses grip and lands in the toilet bowl. "There you are, come out from there…now." She pokes her head underneath the stall.

"Haha, you found me!" I laugh at her angry face. I step out from the stall with a soaked foot.

"I can't even trust you to do a classroom job," she rants while we walk. I pull my arm from her grip.

"Let go of me, big, fat Ms. Hannigan!" I shout, insulting her with a character from the musical, *Annie*. We reach the end of the main hallway. "Mrs. Lascoski!" I shout.

"What?!" She looks down at me.

"My foot is wet," I tell her.

Everything begins to move quickly. I am in the office of Principal Snow. Principal Snow has big brown eyes, fair skin and short black hair to her chin. Around the room, there are Snowflake trinkets. "Why is there snowflakes everywhere?" I ask her.

"Because, my last name is Snow and the teachers buy me snowflake as gifts," she states sternly.

"All these snowflakes are beautiful," I smile at her.

"Do not try to charm me with your cuteness," she warns. "You have been missing for over an hour," she explains. "Your mother and a man named Tony are on their way to come pick you up," she states.

My eyes widen. I rush over to the principal's side of the desk. I duck down and hide underneath her desk. The principal rolls her chair out.

"What are you doing?" she asks.

"Tell Tony I am sorry," I state.

"I think you need to apologize to Mrs. Frost," she explains.

"Tell her too," I add. I hug my knees towards my chest.

"Maria, you are going to be suspended from school for a few days," she explains. "Do you know what that means?" she asks.

"Yeah, I can't come to school," I answer. Suspension is not new to me.

"They have arrived to pick her up," the office assistant enters the room. Principal Snow pats my back.

"Come on, time to stand up," she says softly. I follow her instruction.

In the main office stand Regina and Tony. Regina looks annoyed. Tony has a smile on his face while they speak with the principal.

"Sorry it took long. She was hiding under my desk," Principal Snow giggles. "She may not return to school until she is seen by a behavioral doctor," Principal Snow adds.

"Wait but I have to work," Regina scoffs.

"It is school policy that after enough write-ups the student needs to be seen by a professional," Principal Snow explains.

Regina rolls her eyes, "Fine."

Tony thanks everyone in the office for their time. I follow Regina and Tony out of the school doors. "Tony, take her to New York," Regina demands. "I am so pissed off at you!" she shouts at me. "Now, you can't go to school until you have a doctor's appointment." Regina gets into her car, slams the door, and drives off.

I look up at Tony. His smile turns into a scary stare. "Get in the car now," he says, unlocking the black sports car. I sit in the back seat.

As Tony drives, he is silent. "Do you hate me?" I ask him.

"I am very disappointed in your behavior," he tells me. "You are a reflection of me," he says. Tony pulls the car over. He unclips his seat belt and faces me. "You have made a fool out of me," he screams. Tony grabs my face and squeezes it. "The school knows that I help your mother out," he says. "They know who I am. I even chaperoned your school trip!" he shouts. Letting go of my face, Tony begins to jab his finger on my head. "You are thick headed. If you ever pull a stunt like this again, I will be sure you will never see daylight, ever again!" he threatens me. My heart is pumping with fear.

"I am sorry!" I cry.

"Yeah, right," he says. "Your 'sorry' means nothing to me. You better start proving yourself," he yells. His voice echoes off the car walls. "You better hope the school doesn't call D.C.F. on your mother," he warns. "Then you will be taken away, never to see your family again." He shrugs his shoulders.

"No, no, I am sorry!" I cry. "Whatever happens, it is going to be all your fault," he squints at me. Tony turns in his seat and begins to drive. "You ghetto ass child, making me look like a fool," he rants angrily to himself. "I will show her where acting a fool gets you." He begins to drive fast and honk at everyone.

At Tony's house, it feels weird to be here without Shannon. Tony said that Anna will not be home tonight. Apparently, when she isn't home, she is visiting her daughter's house. He said that I am going to stay in the extra room without any TV and toys. I sit on the bed, in the room alone. The light is on and the room is silent. Tony has instructed me to ponder about my behavior. He wants me to make him believe that I am truly sorry. Without having a clue how to do that, I figure the only thing I could do is write him an apology letter. I dig in my backpack and pull out my composition book. I press the pen into the paper and begin to write.

Dear Tony,

I am sorry for being bad and making everyone mad at me. I am sorry for making you mad. I am sorry for everything I did wrong. I didn't mean to be bad. I will try to be very good. Please forgive me. I love you so much!

Love, Maria.

I fold the paper in half and draw a flower on the front. I take my letter and walk into the living room. Tony is watching TV sitting in a reclining chair.

"Yes?" he says, sitting with his bare feet crossed.

"This is for you." I hold out my letter. Tony looks me up and down. He takes the paper from my hand.

"Oh really?" he says while he reads the letter. "Go back to the room. I will speak to you when I am ready," he states.

"Yes, sir," I nod my head and walk back down the hallway. I sit on the bed in fear of touching anything. I simply wait for Tony. Suddenly, I hear the bedroom door's golden doorknob jiggle. Tony walks into the room and pulls the wooden desk chair in front of the bed.

"Do you think writing this letter would fix everything you have done?" he asks me.

"Yes," I state.

"Well, I forgive you," he says with a gentle smile. A sense of relief comes over me, I lean forward to hug him. "Wait, don't get too excited just yet." He holds his hands up to stop me from hugging him. I sit back, my smile fades. "Just because I forgive you doesn't mean I am going to forget how you acted," he tells me. "Jesus teaches us to forgive and forget," he explains. I nod my head as I listen. "God throws our sin into the sea of forgetfulness," he says. "Do you think this is what I should do?" he asks. "You committed a sin by not obeying the rules," he explains. I take a deep breath and nod my head,

"Yes, sir, I understand," I say.

As the night moves on, Tony allows me to watch TV. He cuddles with me on the bed. However, things quickly become more intense. He begins touching my body and pulling off my clothing. His hands become rougher than usual. "Pretend I am someone at your school," he whispers to me. "Maybe your blonde friend, Lauren?" he asks. "Remember, I met her on the field trip I chaperoned," he states. "And you wrote about her in your notebook," he states. I lower my eyebrows at him. I didn't think Tony read my notebook. That is my private journal. I shut my eyes tight. I want to disappear. When Tony is satisfied, I lay beside him. He cleans his liquid off my stomach. Afterwards, he lays next to me and cuddles me until he falls asleep. I stay awake, watching TV. An old re-run of *Who's the Boss* is on. My favorite character is Alyssa Milano's character. She helps make me laugh after the horrid things Tony made me do.

The next morning, I spend the day with Tony at work in his fancy office job in Greenwich, Connecticut. He works for the credit and collections department for big magazines. During his lunch break, he drives me back home. "Regina?" Tony calls as we enter the apartment. I shut the door behind us. In my bedroom, my side of the room is completely empty. "You are still punished." Tony states. "I told your mother to strip your room of all your belongings so you can learn your lesson," he explains.

"Hey!" Regina appears in the hallway. She is dressed in a shirt and jeans. "You guys made it just in time," Regina smiles.

"For what?" I ask.

"Your doctors appointment," she states. "Thank you so much for watching her, Tony," Regina states with a roll of cash in her hand.

"No, no, Regina," Tony denies the money. "You know that I care about you guys, your company is enough." He smiles. Regina smiles back.

"I will call you soon to update you on what happens," Regina adds.

Regina brings me to a waiting room at a therapy office in Danbury. It is called, 'Aid for Families & Children.' In my session with a doctor by the name of Dr. Jenson, he asks me to remember three things. Socks, crocodile and a meadow. He then begins to question me about my life. I lie to him saying that I am happy and comfortable at home with my family. My biggest fear is spilling the beans and getting taken away, never to see my sisters again.

"Do you like school?" Dr. Jenson questions.

I nod my head, "Math can be hard," I explain. "I like writing, science and art," I tell him.

He writes on his note pad, "So you like to be creative?" he questions. I smile and nod my head.

"Yes, I like to do experiments to see what will happen," I explain. "I like to write movie ideas and draw," I add.

"Maybe you will be a director for a movie one day," he chuckles. "Do you listen to teachers at school?" he asks.

I shrug my shoulders, "Sometimes," I say. "Sometimes I don't care what teachers say because they are bossy," I state.

"Do you think other classmates like you at school?" he asks me.

"I suppose," I state. "Sometimes the kids can be really mean to me," I say softly.

"How are they mean?" he questions.

"Well, everyone thinks that Tony is my dad because he picks me up from school," I state. "One time my Papi picked me up and the teachers were scared to let him take me," I say. "Kids asked me why my dad has dark skin and I don't have dark skin. They said that it was weird to have a dad with dark skin," I explain. I watch Dr. Jenson write on his notepad.

"Who is Tony?" he asks.

"Tony is our babysitter. My mom tells everyone that he is Shannon and I's godfather," I explain. Dr. Jenson nods attentively.

"Do you like spending time with Tony?" he asks.

"Yes, he takes us shopping and to New York to get manicures," I say.

"Well that is nice of him," Dr. Jenson says. "Sometimes he helps me with my homework too," I add.

"Good, I am glad you have someone to help you," he says.

Yeah, like Daddy Warbucks," I state. It felt wrong to say that.

Dr. Jenson tilts his head at me and chuckles. "Alright, so what are the three things I told you to remember when you first sat down?" he asks me. I shake my head trying to remember. However, he asked me so many questions and I need a moment to think.

"Um, cat, alligator and grass," I state.

"Well, that is close enough," Dr. Jenson says.

Later that day, Regina takes me to Walgreens. In the drive through, Regina speaks to the woman behind the microphone. "I am here to pick up a prescription for Maria Colon," she says. Regina hands me the bag with my name on it.

"What is this?" I ask.

"You need to have medication for your behavior. It is going to help you and now you can return to school," she explains as she drives. I look at the bag and see it says 50mg of Ritalin.

CHAPTER 8

Hostage

It is a Sunday afternoon, and everyone around the house is doing their own thing. My thing is writing. I like to write stories about witches, being a spy kid, and the weather. I lean my back against the wall as I hang out on my twin mattress stationed on the floor. I am writing in my compilation journal about a witch who is visiting her witch sisters. I feel very focused and motivated to write because I have just taken my afternoon Ritalin.

"Shit." Shannon rushes through the door. She is wearing basketball shorts and a t-shirt tied in the back. Her hair is in a low pony-tail with two long bangs framing her face. "I need to think," she says sitting on the bed with a worried look.

"What is wrong?" I ask. "Tomorrow is the science fair and I told Mrs. Frost I would create a mashing tool. All I have is 'the masher' printed out and glued to the board," she cries. Shannon points to a cardboard project on the shaggy brown carpet.

I place my journal beside me. "You can use the ice cream jug!" I state. I can feel a light bulb go off in my head. I recall seeing an empty container in the kitchen. "Follow me!" I hop off the bed and lead

Shannon into the kitchen. I dig underneath the sink cabinets. "This would be great for things you are mashing," I explain and pull out a clear plastic container that once held sherbet ice cream.

"Oo, nice!" Shannon smiles. "I can flip it over and cut a hole on the bottom." She grabs a kitchen knife from the dish drying rack. She flips the container upside down and tries to stab the bottom.

"Be careful!" I say.

"Damn, I can only poke one small hole in it." Shannon sighs.

"Mommy!" I holler.

"I am in the bedroom," Regina shouts. We head to Regina's bedroom.

Shannon follows me, whispering, "It is alright, maybe I can figure it out on my own." I hear her but I am persistent for help from Regina.

"Mommy, can you help Sha-" I ask as I become startled by the sight of Regina. "Oh my god, what are you doing?" I gasp.

Regina is kneeling on the shaggy brown carpet in her room. She is twirling around a big, blue, water cooler jug. The jug has no water, just coins and a few dollars inside of it. This jug is Regina's 'savings.' She claims that if we fill it up with money we can go to Disneyland.

"That is Disneyland money, Mommy," I sigh.

"Listen, Miguel used up the rest of this month's food stamps," she explains. I roll my eyes. Miguel has been hiding at our house because there is a warrant out for his arrest. Naturally, Regina thinks it is alright to let him stay here. "I need to buy cigarettes," Regina whines. She shakes the jug with frustration.

"Mommy, help Shannon make a masher," I demand to Regina.

"I put a small hole on the top, do we have a stick or something?" Shannon asks quietly, stepping into the room. She is always hesitant to ask Regina for help. Usually, Shannon likes to do things on her own.

"Her science fair is tomorrow, and she needs her creation to be finished," I explain.

Regina continues shaking the jug, her heavy sighs alert us that she is becoming annoyed. "Oh my god!" Regina shouts, "Just shut up for a second." She rolls her eyes. She pulls out a few coins and a dollar from the jug. "Goddamn it, it's not enough." She tosses the jug to the side. It thumps as it taps the floor.

"We are never gonna get to go to Disneyland," I say watching the jug roll into the wall.

Regina's stands to her feet and yanks the upside-down container from Shannon. "Take this fucking hanger...where is this damn hole?" she says, picking up a plastic, clothing store hanger. She jams the side of the hanger into the bottom of the plastic container. Shannon and I glance at each other. "There, now you have a fucking masher!" Regina says handing Shannon her project.

I giggle and tilt my head at Regina. "Oh look, it can mash things underneath." I lean over and point to the hanger sticking out.

Tears roll down Shannon's face as we walk back to the bedroom. Shannon places, 'The Masher,' on our long wooden dresser. "It's so ugly," she cries.

"At least you have a project?" I question.

"Leave me alone, Maria," Shannon wipes her tears and opens up her blue kitten journal. I sit back on my bed and dig underneath my big pig stuffed animal. Piggy is a gift from Mare, a friend of Regina's. Piggy is big enough for me to hide things like my 'Secret Spy Coding' book, and candy. I exchange my writing journal for a Barbie chapter book. I decide I am going to play teacher. I pull out a red pen and begin skimming through words.

In my mind, I am pretending I am the teacher correcting an essay. I read the words and put a small 'c', for correct, above all the words. "All these words are correct," I say proudly. Crazy how a published Barbie book has no spelling errors. As the night moves forward, I bring my teacher game to life. I play with Karina and Selena in their messy bedroom. They are sitting at the small, yellow play table. I gave them reading books with markers. I guide them as they scribble on the books. I use my red pen to make corrections. I stand over Selena's shoulder as she scribbles.

"Selena, that is not correct." I shake my head and draw an X.

Selena looks at me with her hazel eyes and untamed curls. She hisses at me. Ever since she lost her two front teeth she has been hissing at people. "I want milk," she demands.

I shake my head, "You can't have milk until you do the equation properly," I tell her.

The next morning, Shannon is getting ready for the day while I am in bed, close to having a breakdown. Regina comes into the room. "Maria, what is wrong? Why aren't you up?" she asks.

I sit on my bed, nearly in tears. "I peed the bed." Shannon and Regina shoot a look at each other. Lately, I have been having bed wetting issues. "You peed the bed again," Regina exclaims. "Come on." She helps me up from the mattress. "I don't know why you keep peeing the bed," Regina sighs. I bathe myself and get out of the bathroom. I pick out my outfit for the day. Recently, we rented a movie from Blockbuster. It was a new version of the musical, Annie. The actress in the re-make has dark red hair that is short at her chin. I have been obsessed with the movie because I relate to Annie.

I dig in my dresser and pull out a halter dress that I found in one of our clothing donations. The dress is gray and reminds me of the actress in the re-make of 'Annie.' I begin to layer the outfit with a long sleeve under the dress and my Christmas stockings from last year. The house phone rings.

"Maria!" Regina shouts in the hallway. "Say good morning to Tony," she says. I peek into the hallway and grab the phone from her.

"Hello?" I say holding the phone beneath my chin. "Hi Tony," I say.

"Good morning, sweetheart," Tony says. "Have you been getting ready without any problems?" he asks.

"Yes," I lie, embarrassed to expose that I have wet the bed. "I will take my medicine," I blurt out. Usually that is his first question of the morning.

"Good! I am just checking in," he says. "Have a good day at school. I love you," Tony adds.

"I love you too," I say.

"Remember to behave. I do not need your school calling me about any issues," he states. "

"I promise I will be good," I assure him. I hang up the phone.

"Yo!" A voice shouts from behind the apartment door.

"Mom, someone is at the door!" Shannon shouts.

"YO! REGINA OPEN THE DOOR." I instantly recognize the voice as Miguel. He pounds on the door. Regina lets Miguel inside. "I need money," Miguel says.

"I don't have any for you," Regina laughs.

"You are a fucking liar." Miguel slaps his hand on the wooden wall panels.

"Miguel, stop it," Regina says. "You act like I am not trying to help you." Regina peeks her head into the bedroom. I am putting on sneakers. "Wait, you are not going to school dressed like that." Regina tells me.

I stomp my foot, "Yes I am," I state.

"You look like nobody's child," she says.

"I am dressed like little Orphan Annie," I tell her, stomping my foot. I am an expressive child. The way I feel, I want to show through my appearance.

"People are going to think I don't know how to take care of you!" Regina shouts. "Change your outfit," she demands.

"No, I am wearing this!" I cry.

"Maria, you better shut the fuck up!" Miguel shouts from the hallway. Regina stands in the doorway to the bedroom to be sure I get changed.

Suddenly, Miguel tosses her arm around Regina's neck. "Nobody is going anywhere until I get my money," Miguel threatens. He begins to choke Regina out.

"Hey, stop it!" Shannon runs in from the hallway. Miguel lets go and begins to make demands.

"I unplugged the phone," he says. "Nobody is leaving this house until I get money." He locks the apartment door. Miguel pulls Regina by the back of the head.

"Stay in here," Shannon warns me. She follows Regina.

"What about school?" I question. I race to the bedroom window and see a group of kids at the bus stop. I hear Miguel screaming.

"Show me where you hid the cash!" he yells.

I walk into the kitchen. Shannon is peeking around the corner. Regina's bedroom can be seen across from the kitchen and living room. I stand behind her and try my best to peek.

"Please, Miguel, I don't have any more money," Regina cries. I see my mother kneeling on the floor. Miguel is standing over her with his hand on her shoulder.

"Maria, do not speak," Shannon whispers. Miguel slaps Regina across the face.

My heart breaks, "Don't hit my mommy!" I shout and quickly cover my mouth.

"Maria!" Shannon whines.

"I'm sorry." I look down at my feet.

"Girls, go to your bedroom," Regina shouts.

"Yeah, girls, go into your bedroom and get the money your mother is hiding from me," Miguel cackles.

Miguel grabs Regina's wrist and begins to bend it backward. "I will break your hand," Miguel screams.

Suddenly, we hear Katrina and Selena whimper. We can see the side profile of Selena on the bed in the room.

"OW!" Regina cries in pain. "Stop it, please!" she begs. Miguel pulls back Regina's wrist harder, but suddenly stops. He pushes Regina and kicks her. "You are going to stay in the living room until you give me the money." Miguel drags Regina out of the bedroom. He pushes her onto the couch.

"You little fuckers," he points to us. "Shannon, go cook me breakfast," he demands. "You go and stay in your bedroom." He points at me. "If any of you try to leave, I will beat you up," Miguel threatens.

"Yes, sir." I nod my head. Shannon begins to cook. I walk back to the bedroom. I look out of the window once more. The kids are getting on the bus without us.

As hours pass, Miguel continues to hold us hostage. The phone is disconnected. None of us have cell phones or computers. We are left to our own thoughts as an eerie silence lingers throughout the house. The panic has passed us. Shannon and I are calmly existing around the bedroom. We keep the bedroom door cracked open so we can be on the lookout for an emergency, which is nothing new. We are used to living this way when Miguel is around. Shannon's Gameboy died. Now she and I are playing with a deck of cards. We play Go Fish, WAR, Slap Jack, and Shannon's favorite, 52 pick up. Shannon likes to push on the deck of cards, making them flicker everywhere. Then she counts for 52 seconds as I scramble on the floor to collect them in time. "34...35...36..." Shannon counts. I scramble around the room, collecting the white cards. I reach near a blanket on the floor.

"I am tired of playing this game," I sigh and drop the cards to the floor.

"Maria, you almost picked them all up," Shannon says.

"I need to walk around," I say, walking in circles around the room.

I did not take my morning pill. My ADHD is causing me to feel enclosed in a tight space. I walk down the hallway and into the kitchen. I peek around the corner. Regina is lying on the couch. Miguel is holding Karina and Selena hostage in the bedroom. He moved the living room TV into Regina's bedroom. I can hear a cartoon playing. I begin to tap my feet around. "It's a hard knock life for us," I begin to whisper sing. I take the sink sponge and begin to wipe the fridge. I am acting as if I am in one of the scenes from the musical *Annie* "Its a hard knock life for us." I begin to sing the song 'Hard Knock life.'

"Hey, what are you doing?" Miguel shouts. Regina stands from the couch.

"What are you doing?" she shouts into the kitchen.

"Playing Little Orphan Annie," I state.

"Get your ass back on the couch," Miguel grabs Regina.

"Really, Maria...why don't you ever just listen?" she shouts. "You ruin everything," she adds.

I run into the bedroom. I scrunch my face and begin to cry into my pillow.

My tears make me fall asleep into the next day. I wake up to the smell of eggs and bacon. Shannon is gone from her bed. I peek into the kitchen and see Miguel eating at the table. Shannon shuts the sink off from washing dishes.

"I will be in the bedroom," she tells Miguel.

"Are we going to eat?" I ask her, returning to the room.

"No, he just wanted food for him and his 'real daughters,'" she tells me.

Hours move by, Shannon and my stomachs are rumbling. Suddenly, we hear Miguel shouting. It sounds like he is in Karina and Selena's room. We peek out into the hallway and see him destroying Karina and Selena's room.

"Look what I found!" Miguel yells. Shannon and I follow him to the living room. "300 dollars in cash, Regina!" Miguel yells with rage. Regina screams on the top of her lungs.

"That is my rent money!" Regina cries.

"I found it in the girls' closet," he tells her. "You think you are fucking smart!" he yells.

A hard knock comes from the apartment door. Miguel stomps his way to it. "Who is it?" he asks through the locked door.

"The downstairs neighbor," A man's voice responds.

"What do you need?" Miguel asks.

"Sugar," the voice says.

"We don't got any." Miguel rolls his eyes.

"Open up the door!" the voice shouts back. "This is the police!" they yell. The police begin banging on the door. Miguel rushes into the kitchen, heading for the back deck. Shannon opens the apartment door,

"He is right there!" Shannon points. Suddenly, policemen rush through the door and arrest Miguel on the kitchen floor. Turns out, our downstairs neighbor heard the screams of Regina. They called 911.

After Miguel's arrest, Regina has been cranky. She claims she has had enough with Miguel and is trying to go steady with a man by the name of Eddy. I met Eddy a few times, he isn't too smart of a man. Once he even tried to put Karina's foot in the floor fan. Since Regina is busy with her new boyfriend, she has allowed Tony to come into the apartment to babysit. Some nights after school, Tony will come over, cook, and help clean the house. He will make sure our homework is done. This has been helpful to Shannon. Her grades have improved, and she has time to be a pre-teen. With Tony being around the house so much, he has been advocating for Shannon. When Regina is around, Tony suggests she let Shannon go visit Star. This has led to Shannon beginning to go over to Star's house on the weekends. While Shannon is busy going to Star's house, I have been busy going to Tony's house in New York. Every other Friday I go visit Tony. This set up has been working for Regina. Now, all she has to really focus on is Karina, Selena, and herself.

It is a Saturday morning. I am tired from Tony keeping me awake after we got to his house. His sexual abuse is a part of my life routine. Though no one could guess this because Tony supplies me with discipline. He is the only one checking in on my behavior and my grades at school. In a way, Tony's one-on-one help with homework has helped me understand what is going on in the classroom. On Saturdays, Tony has band practice at church for a few hours. I sit in the back of the sanctuary with a big duffel bag full of toys. Every weekend that I go to Tony's house, he buys me a toy if I come back with good grades. The band and choir practice on the stage. As they sing and the live music is bumping, I use my Barbie dolls as puppets to pretend like they are singing. I dance in the aisle with the barbies. The music comes to a halt.

"Hey, can you turn mix two down?" a gray headed man says over the microphone. The man's name is Patrick. Patrick is the lead pianist in the band. He is retiring and training Tony on how to lead the band into Praise & Worship. Suddenly, I hear Tony's voice on the microphone.

"Little miss thing over there has five minutes before she has to start reading the book for her report," Tony speaks to me.

The choir women giggle. I look at the stage and give everyone a thumbs up.

I clean up my toys and sit on a chair in the way back of the church. I begin to read. The book I chose is called *The Report Card* by Andrew Clements. It is about a girl, Nora, who is a secret genius but gets bad grades on purpose. As I dig deeper in the book, I begin to read and walk around the church. I have become a church kid. I can remember the whole layout of the church. As I read and walk, I also shake my hips. I cannot help myself. The songs they play have live drums, guitar, and vocals. Either I am dancing or mimicking the vocal warmups the choir ladies do. In the hallway, someone steps out of the sanctuary doors. It is Iris, a lady from the choir. She has fair skin, blonde hair, and blue eyes.

"Maria, what book are you reading?" Iris asks. I show her the book. "Oh lovely." She smiles.

"Thank you, Ms. Iris." I smile.

Suddenly, all the choir women exit the door. They are on a water break. "Whew, I don't know about you ladies but I am getting hungry," Angela says. As soon as I hear her voice, I look up from my book.

"Ms. Angela!" I smile and hug her. She has dark skin and beautiful brown sparkly eyes.

"How have you been, sugar?" she says with her southern accent. "I saw you dancing and reading this book," she giggles and takes a peek at the front cover.

"Hey ladies, five more minutes," Mrs. Kathy peeks into the hallway. Mrs. Kathy is the Choir leader. She is Japanese and has a nice figure.

"Alright, whatever you say, Mrs. Kathy." I smile and slap her butt as she walks away. All the ladies around gasp. Mrs. Kathy looks down at me and laughs.

After band practice, Tony picks up a happy meal for me at McDonald's. We arrive back at his house and I sit at the wooden desk in the bedroom, eating my meal while I finish reading my book. Tony barges into the room.

"Are you slapping people's butts at church?" Tony screams in my face. "I just got off the phone with Mrs. Kathy. She says every time she sees you, you slap her butt!" he yells.

I shrug my shoulders, "...it is funny," I say.

Tony shakes his head, "Unbelievable, just when I think you are behaving, I turn around and you are doing something stupid!" he yells. "This is why I need to keep you in my sight at all times," he yells and snatches the book from my hands.

"Hey!" I snap.

"You are only on page 40? There are 174 pages!" Tony screams. "This is due on Monday because you decided not to tell me about it," he adds.

"I am sorry," I say.

Tony shakes his head, "I am going to read and write your report," he scoffs.

"No, I can do it," I say.

"No you can't, look at how slow you read," he states. Tony stomps out of the room with my book in hand.

I won't dare put on the TV, even though I am tempted. I have already made Tony angry today. So, I grab my composition book and write what I remember about the book. I know the main character's name is Nora. She gets good grades but has a plan to do bad on all her tests. As I write, time melts into evening. I have anxiety over how Tony is going to react if my book report isn't finished. So I turn the page in the notebook and begin to write him a sorry letter. He always likes when I write him one.

Dear Tony,

I am sorry I didn't finish reading the book. Please forgive me. I will do better on my next book report.

I love you too much!

I then dig through the desk and begin to make him a creation from popsicle sticks and glue I found. I hear Tony's footsteps approach the bedroom. I lay out my gift for him on the bed.

"Here is a printed copy of your book report," Tony tosses paper on the desk.

"Thank you!" I smile and hug him. "Look what I made you." I point to the bed.

Tony smiles and picks up the letter. "You did this for me?" he asks. "Thank you." He hugs me. Tony sits in the wooden chair. "Listen, just like you said you love me in your letter... I love you," Tony states.

"That is why I spent my Saturday night writing your report," he states. "Now, you have to sit here and read what I wrote," he demands. "In a few hours, I will come back and test you on the report," he says.

By evening, Tony begins quizzing me with questions. I answer them well.

"Good job, Maria," he tells me. Tony moves closer to the bed. He rubs my thighs. "Kiss me." He smiles in my face.

I build the guts up to kiss him when the light is on. Quickly, Tony begins his abusive routine.

"My mom isn't home yet," Tony grins.

He forces my body against his and begins making weird, loud noises. I am horrified to watch him underneath the lamp light. I am very aware of how hairy and ugly his body looks. Tony reaches for my head. I can predict what he expects of me next. Tony begins controlling the movement of my head. I feel his big hands violently shoving my face into his genitals. I can't breathe and begin to gag. "That's right, you want it from me," he shouts and groans. When he is finished, he cuddles by wrapping his arm around me. I stare at the ceiling. He rests next to me as my mind swirls into a never-ending pit of numbness. I feel like no one will ever want to love or hug me. Especially if they find out the things that I do with Tony. This is all my fault. Probably because I am a bad kid. Tony once told me that bad kids get what they deserve for being bad.

As I stare at the ceiling. I see a blue sparkle. I shake my head in disbelief. It looked like a magical blue sparkle. I shrug my shoulders, maybe that is God? Maybe God does hear my prayers. I shut my eyes and my mind drifts to my happy escape. I envision a floating piece of land in the sky with a river, a grassy meadow with a big treehouse in the middle of it. I run through the meadow barefoot as ladybugs and butterflies swirl around me. I can vividly feel like I am at the river bank looking into the water and hopping on big rocks. I can feel the cold river water on my feet. I drift into a deep sleep.

CHAPTER 9

Summer Camp

I have passed the 3rd grade with a C plus. Thanks to the new law of 'no child left behind' and the book report Tony wrote for me. I can now move on to the 4th grade. It is the beginning of Summer in 2003. Regina placed me in a two-week dance camp at the local high school. Today is the last day of Dance Camp. My camp friend, Emily tells me that she is going to be a famous Jewish gymnast one day. She taught me how to do a backbend and point one foot in the air. Since it is the last day of dance camp, each group gets to perform in front of everyone's family. My group is performing 'Most Girls' by the artist P!nk. My camp counselor said she chose the song because she went through a major break up recently. My counselor is an overly emotional and interesting young adult. Once, she even gave us a dance interpretation of the song 'Miss Independent' by Kelly Clarkson.

In the gym, all the campers' families sit on the bleachers of the high school gym. Regina and Tony sit way in the back, high up on the bleachers. I can see Shannon, Lisha, Karina, and Selena. Shannon invited her best friend, Lisha, to watch me dance. Throughout the recital, I can hear Shannon and Lisha shout my name. They even encouraged Karina and Selena to stand on the bleachers and shout my name over people in front of them. Every time I hear my name I wave. My group is up next, we dance to each step like we practiced. As I line up with the other girls. I get ready for Emily's part. She is doing a round-off back handspring. Everyone cheers and claps for her. I wish I could be acrobatic like her.

After my recital, I greet my family at the bleachers. "You did so amazing, Maria!" Shannon hugs me.

"I didn't know you are a little dancer," Lisha says with her bright blue eyes and thick Louisiana accent.

Regina pats me on the back while she carries Selena.

"Well, how about we all head back to the house for some treats?" Tony smiles. "Maria and I will pick them up," he adds. I smile and nod my head.

"Maria!" I hear my name. I look down the bleacher rows and see Emily with a few of our camp friends. "Let me sign your shirt!" she yells coming towards us.

"Who are these girls?" Tony asks with a grin. I look at the way he is looking at them with excitement.

"Just friends," I state and quickly walk away before he asks any more questions. Emily and the others sign my shirt. "Maria, come on, we are leaving," Regina shouts. Everyone in my family begins to move as one. "Well, I like being your friend," Emily smiles at me. She has a cute, round nose and bright brown eyes. I smile at her,

"Maybe I will see you soon!" I tell her. I follow my family down the bleachers. As I leave the gym, I look back to where I just performed. It may not be in a ballet class, however, I feel blessed that God answered one of my prayers. I prayed that I could dance. Once we reach outside, I look up at the big blue sky. The hot sun shines down on us.

"Thank you, God," I whisper to the sky.

In Tony's car, I sit in the front seat of the car and look out of the window. We drive on the road in silence until Tony speaks. "Your friend seems nice," he says.

"She is," I tell him.

"How well do you know her?" he asks.

I shrug my shoulders. "I don't know," I say.

We pull up to the Dunkin Donuts drive-thru to buy coffee and treats for my family. Tony buys me my favorite drink, a coffee coolatta.

"Here you go, to the best dancer I know," Tony smiles handing me my drink. I sip the delicious cold, frozen coffee. "I have good news about the camp in New York," Tony says while he drives to my house.

"Oh yeah?" I look over to him. Tony has been hyping me up with details about a summer camp in New York. It has luxurious details like a pool and field trips. It all sounds so thrilling, I have never been to camp before. I desperately want to go.

"You're mother signed the papers," he states. I smile with glee.

"I get to go swim in a pool!" I take another sip of my drink.

"It is an Olympian size pool," Tony adds. "However, if you want to go to the camp you will need to come stay at my house for the summer," he states. I slowly look up at him.

"Oh, the camp isn't just on the weekends?" I question.

"No, camp is during the week, that is why you would need to stay at my house," he explains.

"Oh…" I say in deep thought. "Would I still get to see my sisters?" I ask.

"We can come visit them from time to time," he states.

"Oh…" I say softly, unsure of how I feel.

"What is wrong?" Tony asks. "You were excited for camp until I said you have to stay with me," Tony rolls his eyes. I stay quiet. "You're ridiculous," he scoffs. "You're ungrateful for the things God has blessed you with in life," he rants. "You know how to love and hug your mother when she gives you a small gift…like a fucking hair tie," he shakes his head. Tony's drives faster as his frustration rises. My stress rises and I stay silent. "If you love me you will come to camp and have a fun summer," he says gently while continuing to drive aggressively. I look down at my drink. I am nervous. I do not want to go because even though there are fun toys at Tony's house. What happened at Tony's house last weekend has haunted my mind all the way back to Connecticut.

A month ago, Tony created plans with a girl from church. Her name is Natalie. Natalie and I share common interests of cheerleading, Lisa Frank, and being Latina. Natalie's mother, Evita, admires Tony for his musical talent. Like everyone else, she is mesmerized by Tony being in the church band on Sundays. Evita realized I was Latina and friends with her daughter, so she invited me over for a playdate. The playdate was so fun. I helped Natalie and her mother cook rice and beans with chicken, then made almond cookies with espressos. Well, this past weekend, Tony invited Natalie to come to his house for a playdate with me. During this time, Tony directed me to watch TV in the extra room with Natalie. She and I hung out on the bed until I heard the golden doorknob jingle multiple times. Tony was standing on the other side with the door slightly opened. He was watching us the whole time. Tony excused me from the room and pulled me into the hallway. He demanded that I pull Natalie close to me and kiss her. His idea made me so uncomfortable. I went back in the room to attempt to do as I was told. However, I failed. I tried to pull on Natalie. I yanked the belt loop on her pink Lisa Frank pants. As soon as I broke it, I knew I could not carry out his requests. I didn't want to engage in the acts Tony was forcing me to do. Since I wouldn't comply, he quickly called the mother to pick Natalie up. The rest of that day he gave me the silent treatment.

I snap out of my flashback of last weekend. I feel like I can never speak to Natalie again. I am too embarrassed. "Well, aren't you gonna say something?" Tony asks. "I will assume you do not love me," Tony says. I snap out of my thoughts.

"I do love you," I tell him. I can't imagine what his house would be like if I live in New York for the whole summer.

"I get it, you don't want to be around me anymore," Tony says softly. "I knew this would happen sooner or later," he begins to cry. I hear him sniffle.

"No, I do," I tell Tony. "Okay…I will go to summer camp in New York!" I tell him.

We pull up to Regina's house. "Make sure you repeat that to your mother," he demands.

Tony and I bring the treats upstairs. "Here is your coffee, Mommy." I hand Regina a white coffee cup. Tony sits at the kitchen table and sorts out the treats.

"Shannon, you have a plain bagel toasted with cream cheese. Lisha, here is the croissant," he states.

Karina and Selena rush over. "Hi, Tony!" Karina smiles. He gives them a hug. "I learned a new song about pudding!" she states.

"Let me hear it!" He smiles. Karina begins to sing while Selena pouts.

"I want donut," Selena whines.

Karina and Selena love when Tony comes by the house. He always has a toy or treat to give them. We enjoy our treats while we chit-chat around the table. "Maria, are you going to go to camp in New York?" Regina questions.

"Yes," I quickly state.

I don't want to be asked this question again. I look over at Tony holding Selena. He helps her eat a donut.

"Summer camp sounds fun." Shannon states.

"Shannon, what do you have planned for the summer?" Tony asks.

She shrugs her shoulders, "Lisha and I want to go to the mall, the beach, and…," she says.

"My family is opening up a pool in their yard," Lisha states.

"That is cool, pools are always refreshing during the summer," Tony smiles and stares directly at me.

"Maria, there is a pool at your camp, did you know that?" he says.

"Really? Cool," I say. I act along with Tony. We just spoke about this in the car.

"Wow, sounds like you will have a nice summer, Shannon." Regina rolls her eyes. "Not even planning on spending time here at the house so I can have someone watch the girls," Regina snaps.

"Please do not start with me," Shannon snaps back.

In a blink of an eye, I am in New York for the summer. It has been a few weeks attending Camp Hummock. Almost every day of the week, Tony surprises me with a brand-new outfit for camp. Every morning, he takes pictures of me in my new outfits. Camp has been a blast. I have made new friends and enjoy learning new camp games. My camp counselor, Danielle, calls me her 'mini me' because we both are Puerto Rican. The only thing I hate about camp is changing for the pool. Everyone gets undressed by the lockers. I get scared having to take my clothes off in front of everyone. Danielle took notice of my fear, so she takes me to the bathroom stalls so I have privacy to change. My behavior at camp for the most part is well behaved. I take my medication every morning. As for my afternoon pill, Tony would need a doctor's note for the camp to give me medication. Though Tony explained to me if I do not behave without my second pill, he will make sure I never see the light of day again. To me, when he threatens in this manner, the only visual I can picture is him hurting me to the point where I won't be able to wake up and see the actual light of day.

Sometimes at camp, I turn on my class clown charm to impress my new friends. They are all from a suburban upbringing. My fearless attitude of cursing and cracking jokes wins popular points. I say the bad words they are afraid to say. Although, I quickly learned that I am being watched at camp. I am careful not to overdo my comedic charm. For, Anna, Tony's mother, works at Camp Hummock. I have realized that she has been spying on me. Anna is a schoolteacher.

During the summertime, Anna and her friend, Corrie, run the arts & crafts program at the camp. I have noticed her walking around the campgrounds. I witnessed her watching me from a distance. Her stare is always cold and bland with her dark eyes. I feel there is this unspoken hatred that she has towards me. Since I noticed her watching me, I understand how Tony finds out about small things that I do at camp. He always claims he 'has eyes everywhere.' My summer life in New York consists of camp, church, and playing alone in the room at Tony's house. If I upset Tony, I am sure to create a drawing along with an apology letter. I have written tons so far. I always start the letters with 'Dear Tony, I am sorry.'

For the 4th of July, Tony drops me off in Connecticut. Regina's brother, David, is throwing a summer cookout.

"I can't wait to see Shannon and the girls!" I say with excitement.

"Oh yeah?" Tony says. "What are you going to tell everyone when they ask you if you like going to camp in New York?" he asks me.

"I will tell them it is fun to go to camp," I state.

"Are you going to say you want to come back home?" he asks.

I panic, "No, no, I am going to say I love camp!" I smile to reassure him.

"That's it?" he asks. "You need to say that you enjoy staying at my house and going to church with me," he states. "Tell them you love meeting my family. Remember, you played with a few of my nieces and nephews at a family event," Tony explains.

"I will say that too!" I state.

"Say what?" he asks. I begin to regurgitate the exact words of what he wants me to say. Tony overly questions me because he thinks this installs a word-for-word reaction from me. He has major anxiety about people questioning his life in New York.

We approach my Uncle David's house deep in a wooded area of Danbury, CT. The house is brown with a huge front yard and deck in the back. "Tell everyone I said hello. I need to rush back to my family's house in New York," Tony states as he pulls up to the driveway. He turns around in his seat. He looks at me with stern eyes. "How you act is a reflection of me, my church, and my family," he warns. "Prove to me that you know how to behave out of my sight," he stares at me with cold eyes.

"Yes, sir," I say.

Tony nods his head and then opens the car door. He lifts his seat up and lets me out. "Behave," he whispers in my ear with a low haunting tone. I feel his hand grip my shoulder. Tony watches me as I walk down the long driveway all the cars are parked in. As I walk, I can hear the crowd of my family on the front lawn. I feel the glare of Tony watching me. I hide behind a car and peer from the side of it. I watch Tony get in his car and drive away.

"Maria!" James shouts from behind me.

"Ah!" I scream out of fright.

"Why are you hiding behind a car?" he laughs.

I shake my head, "Oh, I was making sure my flip flop didn't come off," I lie.

"It is still there," he laughs, looking down at my red, white and blue flip flops.

"Hi James!" I hug my brother.

He is pale with red cheeks and blonde short hair. I haven't seen him in a while, and he looks a bit older. I follow James to the lawn. I see my cousins running from the picnic table to a long blue slip n' slide. Adults are laughing, talking, and eating. Uncle David's pit-bull dog, Madea, rushes up to me. I step backward with slight fear, she always jumps on me.

"Down, girl." Uncle David smiles, pulling Madea back. I pet her head gently.

"How are you, Maria?" Uncle David smiles with his dark red beard.

"I am good." I smile.

"There you are, Maria!" Grandma Leona greets me with a hug. "How is summer camp going?" Regina asks while reaching down to hug me.

"Good, I go in the pool at camp." I smile. "They give me a red special bracelet because I am short, the counselors are scared I will drown," I explain.

Regina chuckles. "Oh, and I go to church on Sundays with Tony and I love his family," I add, trying to remember Tony's rant of what he wanted me to say.

"Well, that is great!" Leona smiles.

I look around at the crowd of the party. I notice that Uncle David's wife, Diana, invited her Mormon family members. I try my best to greet them. However, they scare me because they don't really speak to anyone besides each other. When I say hello, they smile and awkwardly stare at me with their bright blue eyes. I head over to the slip n' slide. I play with my siblings and cousins.

For Dinner, we all gather on the back deck and eat tons of food, like hamburgers and hotdogs. Regina made our favorite Spanish rice and beans with chicken. Afterwards, Uncle David hangs a string along the side of the house, we play a family game that we always play when we gather for events: the donut eating contest. Each child gets a donut that hangs down. In competition, we put our hands behind our backs. Whoever finishes the donut first, without using their hands, wins. This year Shannon beat everyone. The day turns into night. Fireflies zoom around the front yard as we shoot off store-bought fireworks. I hold a sparkler in my hand, running up and down the yard. I feel happy. I feel like there isn't any pressure on how I must act. Towards the end of the night, my family says goodbye to everyone. We hop in Regina's car back to Naugatuck. I watch a movie with my siblings.

"Girls, I am going to sleep, don't stay up too late," Regina states. She steps off the couch and walks into her bedroom.

Shortly after, Shannon puts Karina and Selena in their beds. In my bed, I look around the room. It feels weird to be back home. I cuddle my stuffed animal, Piggy.

"Did you have fun today?" Shannon asks as she gets cozy in bed.

"Yeah! I can't believe you beat James in the donut contest." I laugh.

"He was too slow this year." She giggles. "Goodnight, Maria. I love you," she says through the dark.

"I love you too, sissy." I smile. I stare at the darkness. Suddenly, I see a blue magical sparkle. "There you are," I whisper. Slowly, my eyes drift to sleep. I think about my treehouse in the meadow by the river.

"Maria!" I hear my name being called. I wake up startled to see Tony standing at the foot of my bed. "Good morning." He smiles. "Why are you still in bed?" he whispers with anger. "This makes you look lazy," he adds. I look over to Shannon's bed. It is made and empty. I stand to my feet. "I bought Dunkin' Donuts," he says, loudly changing the tone of his voice. I follow him into the kitchen. My family sits at the table enjoying their morning treats from Tony. "We have to get going soon," Tony states as I sit at the table. I grab a bagel with cream cheese.

"Today is Tuesday, do I have camp?" I ask Regina.

"Oh, I don't know." She looks at Tony.

"Actually, you are missing camp today," he states. "I would rather you see your family," Tony says.

Regina smiles. "I have to get ready for work, I love you." Regina stands to her feet. She gives me a kiss on the cheek. I look up into her blue bright eyes and smile at her. I guess when I am away for a while, Regina misses me so much she likes to hold me and give me kisses. I eat my breakfast and quickly get ready to head back to New York.

In New York, the house is silent. Anna is working at camp for the day. Tony lets me go into the bathtub with my bathing suit, I pretend I am a mermaid in the sea. After, I step out of the bathroom with my wet bathing suit and towel.

"Alright, you can watch TV," Tony says.

"Actually, can I play on the computer?" I ask as I place my towel in the dirty laundry pile.

Tony looks me up and down. "Sure," he says. "You can stay in your bathing suit, if you want," he tells me with a wide smile. The look in his eyes makes me feel like that was a command. He walks over to the desk and turns on the thick, white computer. "Stay in your bathing suit, play a few games and relax," he smiles. "Have a seat." He pulls out the wooden desk chair. I sit down at the desk. I place a CD-ROM game called, 'Freddie the Fish.' "Put these on," Tony says, handing me the black headphones. He walks away and shuts the door behind him.

Time begins to pass by while I enjoy playing the computer game. Suddenly, I get a sense that something is behind me. I can't hear anything, so I move one headphone to the side of my head. I look behind me and notice the jackets hanging on the back of the bedroom door sway. Was the door just moving? I remove the headphones. I notice the door is slightly cracked open. I stand up and walk over to the door to open it. I see Tony standing there, I notice him pull one hand out of his black sweatpants and adjust himself. He stares and smiles at me. My intuition alerts my mind with the question, 'Was he just touching himself behind the door?' Peeking behind doors seems like a reoccurring habit Tony has.

"Oh, hey." He smiles. "I was just coming to check on you." He opens the door all the way. "How is your game?" he asks.

"It is fun," I say plainly. Fear fills my chest. I am unsure what Tony has planned for me. The look in his eyes is dark and focused. Tony opens a drawer in his tall dresser. I sit back at the desk and place the headphones back on. "Smile," he says holding up a disposable camera. I look up at him and smile as I sit on the wooden chair. He takes the photo and places the camera down. I feel him rub my shoulders and move down my back.

Suddenly, I am laying on the edge of the bed. Let's pretend I am a friend from school," he whispers while he touches himself. "Give me a name of a friend," he demands. I stay silent. I hate when he plays this game. "Come on, give me a name," he persists. I try to think under pressure. I can't think of anyone because I do not want to name anybody. Tony whines. He gets frustrated when I am stay quiet. I feel frozen. Out of nowhere, a voice calls from the hallway.

"Tony?" Anna calls. Tony's eyes widen with fear. Relief fills my chest. Anna is here. This means he has to stop this sexual act.

"Shut up and get dressed in pajamas," he whispers to me. He fixes himself and steps into the hallway.

"Hey, Ma." He shuts the door slightly behind him. In the heat of the moment, I rush over to the long dresser and pull out a change of clothing. "It is 3 o'clock, already?" He laughs.

"Yeah, I was thinking we can make ravioli, tonight?" Anna suggests. I rush back to the desk to play my video game. I stare at the screen relieved that I am clothed. Tony opens the door, "Hey, I will be in the kitchen," he tells me. The bedroom door is left wide open as I play my game until dinner time.

After dinner, I lay down, watching TV until I fall asleep. Tony wakes me up. "Let's finish what we started," he whispers into my ear. It is 2 a.m. I can tell it is early in the morning because that is when the re-runs of 'George Lopez Show' comes on. As he engages in his sexual acts with me, I feel Tony's hand aggressively tap my shoulder. "Wake up," he demands in my ear. I open my eyes. I am looking at the white and pink striped bed sheets. I lift my head from his shoulder while I lay on top of him, naked. I fell asleep while he was in the middle of directing me. Oddly, I dozed off, dreaming about a large tree on a dirt ground with worms. Then, I saw a big purple snail inching its way along the dirt ground. I could see the roots below the tree. When suddenly, a giant metal drill digs up from beneath the ground, destroying the roots. The dream was odd but seems like a reflection of my life.

I snap my head up and look at him. My body feels uncomfortable as I feel his genitals within mine.

"I am sorry." I tell him.

He places me beside him and stands up with an attitude. "You really couldn't stay awake?" he barks.

"I am sorry."

I reach out and grab his hand. He snatches it away, "It's too late, just go to sleep." He rolls his eyes. I watch him leave the room and shut the door behind him. Now, I feel wide awake with my fear that I upset Tony. I quickly stand to my feet. I use the TV light to guide me on finding a piece of paper and pen. I sit at the desk and begin to write him an apology letter. I am hoping Tony will not stay mad at me for too long. Suddenly, I hear the golden doorknob open.

Tony steps back into the bedroom, "Are you drawing?" he scoffs. "I thought you were tired?" He shakes his head.

"I am writing you a letter," I state.

Tony crinkles the paper and tosses it to the side. He jabs his finger on the power button of the TV. The room goes dark. "Get to sleep, you better not make me late in the morning," he states. I take a deep breath as I feel my way back to the bed. I build up the courage to speak up about how I feel.

"I want to go home," I bravely say within the dark.

"Did you really just say that to me?" he says in an aggressive whisper. I gasp as I hear his feet move towards me through the dark. I feel his large hands squeeze my arms. "After everything I have done for you, you are not going anywhere," he states. My eyes adjust to the darkness. I see a small outline of his face hovering over mine. I am frightened.

"I am sorry," I say.

"Fuck you, Maria," Tony says. I hear him walk out of the room and shut the door behind him. It took a lot for me to speak up to him, although I know my true feelings will never win. Tony is an emotional and sensitive man. I always have to lie to him, so he won't get upset. Alone in the bed, I being to cry. I miss my mom and sisters. I don't want to be in New York. I am angry at myself. I was just home yesterday. Why didn't I just tell Regina I wanted to stay home and never go back to New York. This is all my fault.

A few hours later, it is daylight. I hear movement around the bedroom. "Get up!" Tony shouts over me. "Take this?" He shoves my ADHD pill in my face with a glass of water. I sit up and take my pill. "You're not going to camp today," he informs me.

"It is Wednesday," I state.

"Who cares, you want to go home," he says, avoiding eye contact with me. "Pack your bags," he tells me. "Maybe I'll drive you or just pay for your bus ticket back to Connecticut," he explains.

"Bus ticket?" I question.

He begins to sniffle and wipe his eye with his hand. "I give you everything and this is how you treat me," he exclaims. I lean against the wall and listen to him speak. "After all of the money I spent on sending you to camp. You want to go home and leave me." He begins to cry. "Like I am nothing to you," he adds. He leans his elbow on top of the tall dresser. Tony dramatically slams his hand on the dresser. "They have photos of us, Maria," he mumbles.

"They have photos of us kissing," he states. My eyes widen, I begin to panic inside. Who has those photos? How did they get them? When did someone take photos of us kissing? I question to myself. "You won't ever see me again, say goodbye to me now," he states.

"No," I say.

"Oh, now you don't want to say goodbye to me?" He turns to me with red, watery eyes. "You wanted say goodbye last night," he states. "What are you going to do when they show everyone the photos?" he questions me. "Are you going to tell them I made you do it?" he asks.

"I-I-I..." I stumble over my words.

"You kissed me, it is your fault," he states.

"I know, I am sorry!" I cry with shame. "I want to stay here," I lie to him.

Tony sniffles, "They are gonna come and take me away," he says.

I panic. I believe everything he is telling me. "I won't say anything about the pictures," I declare. "I will say they are lying," I add. "I love you and I will tell them they can't take you," I state. Tony shakes his head.

"The police are already on their way to come get me," he cries. I panic and look at the door. "They are going to tell your mom and show her the pictures," he explains.

"No!" I panic. I jump off the bed and walk over to Tony. I hug his side. "I love you, so they can't take you," I state.

"Are you going to miss me if I am gone?" he asks.

"Yes! I will miss you so much," I state. "Tell the police not to come!" I beg. Tony's face switches up.

"Look at you," he laughs. "There are no pictures, Maria." He wipes his tears from his performance.

"Huh?" I ask, backing away from him.

"Well, now at least I know that you truly love me," he smiles. "No one knows our secret. But, I am going to give you a moment to decide what you want to do," Tony tells me. "Stay in this room, decide if you really want to stay here," he demands. "God is watching you and waiting for you to make the smart decision," Tony adds.

Alone in the room, I am confused. I want to go home but I am scared to tell him that again. I need to think of a way to fix Tony being mad at me. I rush over to the desk. I pull out a piece of paper and pen. I begin to write him a letter.

Dear Tony,

I am very, very sorry I hurt your feelings. I want to stay in New York and go to camp. I do not want to leave. I will do whatever you want me to do. I love you so much! I forgive and forget.

Love, Maria.

I fold the letter up and walk out of the bedroom. Tony is watching TV in the living room. I walk over to him and hand him the letter. "You think this is going to solve everything?" he questions. "Now, this is the Maria I know and love." He dramatically cries into the letter. Now I can tell he is faking. "This is the Maria I want staying with me in New York," he adds.

At the end of summer, Tony sits in the wooden chair, while I sit on the bed. My belongings are packed to head back home to Connecticut. "I am going to miss seeing you every day." Tony slowly reveals a smile. "I have some bad news," he tells me. I sit up, ready to hear his news. "I have feared this was going to happen," he says. My heart races. "Over the summer, your family moved into a shelter," he says. "A homeless shelter is where you will live with other families until Regina can find a new home," he explains. "Your family is homeless right now." He shakes his head. "Don't worry, I have people at the church praying for you and your family," he states. "I will help your family in any way because I love you so much," he says.

"Thank you, Tony." I give him a hug. "I love you." I add. As I lean on his shoulder, I blankly stare into the air. I feel numb inside. Tony's bad news wasn't exactly shocking to me. Though, I have no idea what I am walking into when I go back with Regina.

While playing with a disposable camera, Maria snaps photos of the room at Tony's house.

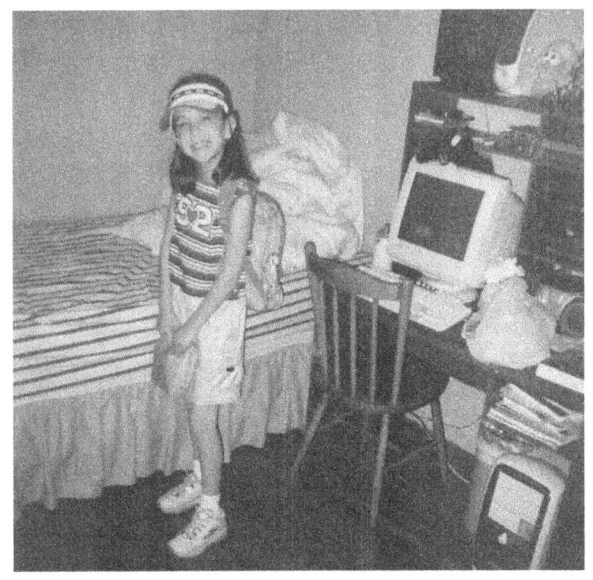

Maria's first day of camp in New York

Karina and Selena

Maria and Selena

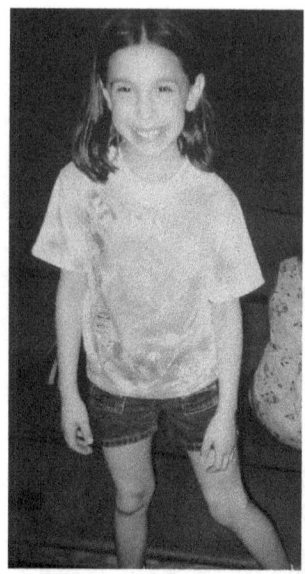

Maria at her dance camp performance

Karina and Maria

Shannon, Maria, Lisha, and little Brianna at the dance camp performance

Maria in 3rd grade

Maria dressed up as a Spy Kid for Halloween, 2003

CHAPTER 10

Green Cup

My family and I live in a homeless shelter called Hope House in Danbury, Connecticut. We are here for a short while, sharing a room with three beds and our belongings stuffed into garbage bags. It is a pain to dig through the bags every morning for an outfit, then having to wait for other families to get ready in our shared bathroom. At least we aren't sleeping in a car or park. For that, I am grateful to dig clothing out of bags and wait in line for the bathroom. Regina has made some friends with the other mothers here. However, as the school year began, Regina ignores signing us up for school. She is undecided where we will live after our shelter contract is expired. Since Regina can't leave us unattended at the shelter, she found a babysitter named Pam. Pam is mainly a stay-at-home mother while her husband works construction. Regina drops us off at Pam's house so she can go to work as a nursing aid. When she works overnight, we sleep over. Pam has long, curly, dirty blonde hair and green eyes. Her house is different than other homes Regina has left us at. Pam has a certain type of parenting style she abides by.

Pam has four children between the ages of three and ten. Her parenting style goes by the idea to let children engage in slightly dangerous activities on their own. For example, in her backyard she has very tall metal monkey bars and a fire pit. She lets her kids swing and dangle from the monkey bars. They taught me how to go upside down. She also has a big fire pit in her backyard. Pam taught them how to be safe with the fire. It was fun tossing things into the pit and watching them turn to ash. Lastly, there is a graveyard directly next to the backyard. I have gone on walks with her daughter, Ella, in the graveyard. It was peaceful and a fun type of fear to walk through the haunted looking place. Pam lets us jump on the beds and dig in the mud. Shannon and I play all day while Pam takes care of Karina, Selena and her three-year-old son. Tony checks in with me, by phone, in the morning and afternoon. He calls to ask his 20 questions of what I am doing and who I am with.

It is early October, and it is starting to get cold. Regina isn't able to stay in the shelter much longer, so she found a cheap apartment in Waterbury, Connecticut. The apartment is not finished, and the floors are wooden corked panels. We can see the pipes in the unfinished wall in the kitchen. There isn't any heat. For the first few nights, we all slept in the living room on a big mattress. Shannon, Karina, Selena and I cuddle with Regina while she sings our favorite lullaby, 'Hush Little Baby.' I always visualize my mother doing what the lyrics say. Though, her motherly affection doesn't last very long. This apartment and our struggle for survival affects Regina mentally. Every morning, she complains throughout the hallways, cursing us out and smacking us if we get in her way. I stay in the small bedroom designated to me. I just hopped out of the shower. I dig through a black garbage bag for clothing as I balance to keep my towel wrapped around me. "I am so fucking over this shit!" Regina shouts in the hallway. "Let's go Maria, get ready!" Regina shouts. "You too, Shannon!!" Regina screams.

"I am mom! I just got out of the shower!" I yell at the top of my lungs. Her consistent complaining is stressing me out.

"Tony will be here to pick you guys up!" she screams back. Since we still aren't enrolled in school, Tony offers to watch us.

"Look at you, you aren't even dressed!" Regina yells and storms around the room.

"I am looking through all of the bags, none of them are my clothes," I sigh.

Regina picks up a white metal curtain rod in a pile of items. She whacks my bare back. I begin to cry. "Get dressed, little bitch!" she yells and walks out of the room.

"Hello?" Tony's voice speaks as he enters the apartment.

"Tony, go and get that girl," Regina snaps.

"What happened?" he asks. "She always makes me fucking late for shit," she whines.

Tony steps into my bedroom. "You alright?" he whispers. I sit on the edge of the bed crying.

"No," I cry.

"She hit you?" he asks.

I nod my head, "On my back, with that." I point to the rod on the floor. He looks at my back and then leans down. I feel him hold his kiss on the side of my head while he hugs me. For a glimpse, I feel seen and loved.

"Get ready so we can leave." He stands up and walks out of the room. I take a deep breath and continue to search for clothing.

It is late November, Regina's section 8 got reinstated. We quickly left the unfurnished apartment, moving back to Danbury. We move to one of the dirtiest houses on Franklin Street. Though people see it as dirty, my family sees it as heaven sent. We have mice and roaches that live in the apartment, although, my family and I are used to living around pests. In the kitchen, the washer and dryer are plugged in along the wall, taking up most of the space in the kitchen area. There is no table. Just the washers, a refrigerator, a small countertop with a sink and cabinet above. The apartment has four bedrooms:

two upstairs in the attic and two downstairs. Each of us have our own bedroom. However, Regina is scared to sleep in the attic, so she uses the living room as Karina's, Selena's, and her bedroom. I place my bowl in the sink after eating my morning cereal.

"Hi Ria!" Karina smiles. Her curls bounce as she runs to give me a hug.

"Hey, Karina." I hug her back.

"Today, I go to kindergarten!" Karina shouts with glee. She is happy to be starting school. Shannon and I have started school, too. Shannon is in 6th grade, and she is attending middle school. I am in 4th grade, and I attend Prince Street Intermediate. Karina is in kindergarten while Selena is in Pre-K. They both attend Prince Street Primary.

Being at Prince Street Intermediate has been great for my learning. The school is mainly a district for upper and middle-class children in the area. They have a fund dedicated for learning development. They help kids with learning disabilities. I battle with my ADHD and dyslexia. The school also has extracurricular activities that happen during the school day, so I signed up for the band to play the clarinet. My 4th grade teacher is Mrs. Carboni. She has short blonde pixie hair, green eyes, and patience that can last forever. Her grace and complexion remind me of Princess Diana. She runs her classroom using a method of understanding that each child learns differently. She can handle my phases of being the class clown, having a slick mouth, and distracting others, all while having my moments of showing her that I am actually paying attention and have skills.

My first few weeks of school, I became friends with Dylan and Roy. The three of us are a force to be reckoned with. We all play off each other's energy during lessons, cracking jokes and comments across the room. So much so that Mrs. Carboni groups our desks together next to her teacher desk. Surprisingly, this works out because we aren't shouting across the room to each other. During group activities, we work together. Somehow, I agreed to 'date' Roy. In the morning, when we get off the bus. We meet by the bushes and give each other a kiss on the lips. Roy's kisses feel different from Tony's. Roy's are less slobbery and more kind towards me. This year, I have managed to gain many friends. Alex, Arianna, Skylar, and Myra. I motivate them to play a game we call, 'Cheetah Girls.' It is based off my latest favorite movie on Disney Channel, 'The Cheetah Girls' with Raven-Symoné. Just like Alexa Vega, I am obsessed with Raven-Symoné. She is pretty and funny.

It is dismissal, and I walk with two girls from my class who take the same bus as me: Skylar and Vanessa. I am updating them on my fake life I have been lying to them about. Since I am used to always being a new girl, I figured why not fabricate my life a little bit? Skylar and Vanessa think that I am a spy kid who is cousins with Britney Spears. I also told them I have a secret house in Puerto Rico where my twin lives. Yeah, the lies seem unbelievable but, to children my age, it could possibly be true.

"Yeah, I might have to go on a mission this weekend," I say as we walk to the bus.

"Where?" Skylar asks.

"She can't tell you, it is top secret," Vanessa tells Skylar.

I look at Vanessa. She has fair skin, short and has long dark hair. Personally, I find Vanessa annoying because she likes to copy things I say and do. However, it is interesting to see the serious look in Vanessa's eyes as she believes me. I look at Skylar. She has dark skin, bright eyes, and her hair in long braids.

"Can't you tell me, Maria?" Skylar asks.

I shrug my shoulders and then whisper in her ear. "I have to go to San Diego," I tell her.

Skylar gasps with a smile. I think Skylar is cool because at recess we go on secret missions. She knows how to play pretend just like me.

"I want to know!" Vanessa whines.

"She can't tell you," Skylar states.

On the bus, I am silent. I had a busy day of my storytelling, making students laugh and trying to learn. I hop off the bus and see Shannon outside of our apartment talking to somebody. As I approach her, I realize it is our older brother, James.

"Ugh, what happened to your face?"

I shriek at the sight of his bloody face. He is wearing shorts and sneakers with crew socks. His sleeveless shirt has specks of blood. James's pale skin is red and sweaty.

"I was a few streets over hanging out with some guys. I know them from the dojo I fight at," he says. "They randomly caught me off guard and fought me," he explains.

"Did you at least beat some of their asses?" Shannon asks. I watch Shannon flip her hair, revealing her big hoop earrings.

"Yeah, I beat some," he states rubbing his eye.

"Shannon fought someone last week," I state.

"Really?" James laughs.

Shannon rolls her eyes, "Yeah, some dumb bitch kept starting problems with me." She laughs.

"It is hard growing up on the streets of D-Block," James says.

Shannon and I look at each other. "Don't say that, James." Shannon shakes her head. "

What? Danbury is ghetto," he states.

"There are worse places than Danbury." I giggle.

James rolls his eyes. He hasn't experienced the truth about 'living in the ghetto' or being from the 'projects.' He has been sheltered in the bubble of stability and comfort with Grandma Leona.

"Wow James. Your eye looks disgusting," I tell him.

"Let's go get him some ice," Shannon suggests.

"Don't let mommy know I am here," James states before we head inside. "I don't want Grandma to find out I am walking around alone," he explains. "She might ground me from dojo class," he adds.

In the apartment, I head to my very own bedroom. In a glass fish tank lives Mooky, our guinea pig. We received Mooky from one of Regina's friends. They didn't want the pet anymore.

"Hi, Mooky," I say, tapping on the glass. Mooky is multi-color of white, brown, and black spots. I feed Mooky and sigh. I have nothing to do. That is until my eyes look upon the door that leads to the attic. Regina claims it is haunted upstairs. One night she was drunk, and she claimed she saw an evil spirit. Ever since then she tries to stay away. I have an urge to go upstairs, however, I ignore it. I sit on the carpeted floor and turn on the thick, gray TV. Tony gifted Shannon and I with our own TV's since we now have our own rooms. I watch TV, though it does not entertain me. So, I stand up and rush over to the attic door. My curiosity leads me up the dirty carpeted steps.

The walls are painted turquoise. The paint is chipped, and the top of the walls have a strange, dirty smog on them. I see nothing so far. Why are attics always scary looking though? I begin to dig through random bags and boxes of Regina's belongings. It's all random junk; Christmas decor, unwanted donations, and memoirs my mother holds on too. I find a box of VHS tapes. Excited, I pull out a few and read the titles. I come across a fun looking VHS cover. It is a yellow box with colorful font. Printed on the box is a picture of two young women, a dark skin woman and a fair skin woman. The title reads 'The Incredibly True Adventures of Two Girls in Love.' Not fully comprehending the title, I assume the movie is about two best friends that go on an adventure. I choose this VHS. Holding the VHS tape in my hand, I enter the doorway for the second room. The floor is unfinished, just planks of wood. This room is dirtier than the first. This room was going to be for Karina and Selena. I can see why Regina thinks it is creepy in here. "Oh jackpot!" I smile at a huge pile of clear bags.

I climb over some of the bags and see that it is full of clothes. I place the VHS under my arm as I rip open a bag and start searching.

"Whoa!" I gasp. I snap my head to the right. It felt like someone was behind me. I chuckle at myself and shake my head. Continuing to dig, I come across a shirt in my favorite color, Barbie Pink. Suddenly, I get a weird feeling in the pit of my stomach. "Ah!" I yelp and jump back. I hold onto my newly found treasures and turn towards the door. "No way, man." I shake my head. I can no longer take how spooky it is beginning to feel. I race over to the doorway. I feel my foot slip between two bags. "Let go!" I shout. Startled, I feel as if I am not able to fully walk. I feel like something is dragging me down. I grip tightly to my treasures and yank myself forward against this strange force. A breath of relief comes when I feel my feet land freely.

I run down the steps, back into my bedroom. I slam the door shut. I catch my breath. Although I felt scared, I feel as if there was an adrenaline rush about the whole thing. It is interesting to think that a spooky spirit can linger around the house. I place the VHS tape underneath my bed. As I place it there, a random memory floats across my mind. I remember at my Abuela's house, she used to talk about how energy can be evil. She would remind us that evil energy can be in people and spooky spirits. I remember exactly how she would cleanse us with an egg. I shake my head and tilt it with curiosity. That ghost's energy felt scary. I must do an egg cleansing, immediately. I rush into the kitchen. "AH!" I scream, bumping into Karina.

"Hi." Karina smiles. "What are you doing?" she asks while her moisturized curls bounce around her rosy, chunky cheeks.

I pull an egg from the fridge. "An experiment," I tell her. "Wanna watch?" I ask.

"Alright." She smiles.

Karina is used to watching me do experiments in the kitchen. Karina leans against the washing machine to watch. I fill a glass cup with cold water and place it on the kitchen counter. I run the egg along my arms, legs, back, and face. I think about taking away the evil energy from me.

"Hahahaha!" Karina cracks up laughing. I must look silly to her as I place an egg all around me. I giggle and crack the egg open into the glass. Karina and I look up at the side of the glass. The yellow yolk sits at the bottom of the glass as pieces of the egg whites are spiked up.

"WOW!" I say observing the egg cleansing. "What are you girls doing?" Regina comes into the kitchen. "What is that?" she asks, pointing to the glass.

"My experiment" I state. Regina shakes her head and pours the yolk down the sink.

"No more experiments, you always make a mess," she states.

I gasp. "Mom, that was mine," I fold my arms. "Take that look off your face and go do something else," she demands. I roll my eyes, there is no use in arguing with her.

For the rest of the night, I hide in my room. I sit with Mooky on the floor. I am watching the VHS I found earlier today, 'The Incredibly True Adventures of Two Girls in Love.' As the movie unfolds, I begin to understand that the two best friends are in love with each other. I find it fascinating to think two girls can kiss. As I continue to watch the movie, a sexual scene appears. Which doesn't really phase me. I am used to seeing sexual things on TV. Suddenly, my mind begins to fight the urge to think about how gentle the girls look as they kiss and touch each other. It is less rough than how Tony touches me. I am fascinated as I learn through the scenes that other people become angry with the girls for being 'Lesbians.' I feel a tear roll down my cheek as they are made fun of. All they want to do is love and hug each other. The credits roll. I quickly pull the VHS tape out of the TV. I hide it underneath my bed, this tape must never be found in my room. However, I want to watch it again later. "Goodnight, Mooky." I smile and place her back into her cage.

The next morning, I wake up to Karina and Selena going through the items in my room. I toss my hands up in the air and do a big stretch. The egg cleansing really made me have a good night's sleep.

I gasp as I look at the girls in the corner of my room. "Don't touch!" I demand as I hop out of bed and grab my clarinet case away from Karina.

"Where is Mommy?" I ask.

"Laying down," Karina answers

"Just get out of my room," I yell at Karina and Selena as I shoo them into the kitchen.

Regina runs to the front door. I watch her scream and swing the door wide open. "No, no, no," she cries over and over again.

"Mom, what is wrong?" Shannon comes into the kitchen.

"My father is dead!" Regina cries with her hands in her face. The phone falls from her grip. She sits in the middle of the doorway.

"I am sorry, Mommy." Shannon pats Regina on the back. A tear rolls down Shannon's cheek. I feel sorrow for my mother. Regina and her father's relationship wasn't the greatest. She rarely saw him. For me, it was hard to mourn somebody I never got a chance to know. From what I can recall his name was Ray, he was a veteran and a functioning alcoholic. I remember waving to him from my grandmother's living room once. He was visiting her and everyone told me that he was my grandfather. I wish I got to know who Grandpa Ray was.

Later that day, Regina spends the rest of her hours mourning in the living room.

"Have you seen, Karina?" Shannon peeks into my bedroom.

"No," I say.

"The door has been left open and I can't find her," Shannon explains.

Quickly, we search the house.

"First my father and now my baby is missing!" Regina cries in the kitchen.

"We need to check outside." Shannon pulls on my arm. I follow her down the deck stairs and search the back parking lot. Suddenly, we see Karina walking up the sidewalk from the corner store.

"Karina!" Shannon shouts. "Where have you been?" she asks, picking her up.

Karina is in her pajamas, her curls bounce as Shannon hugs her with relief.

"I wanted candy from the store. The man said to come back with money," Karina explains.

We get Karina back upstairs. Regina hugs her. "He should have called the police or asked her where her parents were," Regina explains. "I am going to go talk to that motherfucker!" Regina rages.

Boy, I hate to be the man that pisses Regina off when she is in mourning. Shannon rushes after Regina to be sure she does not do anything that will get her put in jail.

Regina, James, and Shannon attend Grandpa Ray's funeral. I was supposed to go, however, Tony made me scared to go. He said it wasn't healthy for me to be at a funeral. He said I am too young to see a dead man in his casket. So, with fear, I listened to Tony and told Regina I did not want to go. A few weeks after the funeral, Regina has turned mourning her father into a non-stop party rage. Almost every weekend she goes out. I see Tony sitting on the living room couch with Karina and Selena.

"Hi, how are you?" He smiles. "How was school?" he asks.

"School was good," I tell him.

"Why don't you go get comfortable and start your homework?" Tony suggests.

I nod my head, "Alright."

I walk into my bedroom. I kick my shoes off and lay on the bed. I like to relax before having to do a big task.

"Knock knock," Tony says while entering my bedroom. "Your mother will be home soon," he states. "She is going to shower and get ready to go out," he explains.

"Where is she going?" I ask.

"Well, she said that she needs to have fun," he explains. I nod my head. "Wait, where is your homework?" Tony asks.

"I am gonna do it in a little bit," I answer.

Tony scoffs at me. "This is why you can't do anything right when you are out of my sight," he says, annoyed. "Sit up," he snaps. With fear I sit up in bed and grab my backpack on the floor. "Listen, I am sleeping over tonight. I dare you to test me," he warns.

Later that night, I stand in the bathroom and watch Regina get all dolled up to go out for a casino night with her friends. She uses her fingertips to apply her CoverGirl liquid foundation. After she is ready, Regina does a twirl for everyone in the kitchen.

"You look pretty, mommy!" Karina shouts.

Regina is wearing a long-sleeved light blue blouse with jeans and short black heels.

"Bye, Regina, have fun and be careful," Tony says shutting the apartment door behind her.

"Can I have some of the ice cream now?" Shannon asks while she places her dinner dish into the sink.

"Yeah, let me get that ready for you girls." Tony smiles.

I watch him open the freezer. He pulls out an ice cream tub.

"Maria!" Shannon calls.

I step into the living room. The couch has a mixture of blankets and pillows. "Sit with us," Shannon says. She tosses a pillow aside. "We are watching *The Brave Little Toaster*." She smiles.

I lean on Shannon as we watch the movie.

"Here girls," Tony passes out our treat for the night. "I am going to change into my pajamas," Tony tells us.

Shannon, Karina, Selena, and I finish the movie with our bowls of ice cream.

Suddenly, we hear Tony shout in terror from the bathroom. "What the fuck!" he yells.

What happened?!" Shannon shouts from the living room.

Tony steps into the room chuckling. He is dressed in his black sweatpants and white t-shirt. "A damn rat just ran across my foot," he says.

Shannon and I laugh. He isn't used to seeing a rat randomly run by.

"That is funny," I giggle.

"I am glad I can make you guys laugh," he chuckles. "Alright, time for bed, you girls have school tomorrow," Tony tells us as the movie credits roll.

"Shannon, can you help get the girls to sleep?" he asks.

"Sure," Shannon answers. I hug my sisters and get ready for bed. I place my headphones on my head and turn on my pink CD player. Julian got me this CD player. It says 'Princess' on it. Every time I use the CD player, I think of my father. Julian is the type of man to always have his Walkman cassette player on him. He gave me this CD player and told me to always remember that music helps fill in life's little moments. I press play and 'Beauty for Ashes' by Crystal Lewis begins to play. Crystal Lewis is a gospel singer. Tony strictly only lets me listen to Christian music or Disney music. However, when I am at Regina's house, I listen to reggaeton, rap, and hip hop, which I enjoy. Linda gifted me with a Crystal Lewis CD. I find this singer's voice relaxing as well as appropriate just in case Tony comes and checks on what I am listening to.

I lay in bed with my side table lamp on. I rest while I listen to my music. I see Tony walk into my room. He is holding a tall, plastic, green cup. I take off my headphones.

"Where did you get that?" he questions my CD player.

"My Papi gave it to me." I smile.

He rolls his eyes. "My Papi gave it to me." He mimics my voice. I hate when he mimics me. I don't sound like that. "Isn't that just lovely, everyone else does his job while he leaves small gifts?" he chuckles.

"What are you listening to?" he asks and yanks the player from my hand.

"Crystal Lewis," I answer.

Tony scoffs and shakes his head, "I told you to leave this CD at my house," he barks.

"I am sorry. I wanted to listen to it here," I tell him.

Tony holds out the green cup in front of my face. "You need to drink this," he says.

"I am not thirsty," I state.

"Your mother says you need to drink this before bed," he says.

"She did? Why?" I ask.

"She told me your digestive system needs a boost. It will make you poop." He chuckles placing the cup in my face. I look up at him and take hold of the cup. "I put some lime juice in so you can't taste the medicine," he states. I look at him and take a sip of the cloudy water.

"Ahh." I stick my tongue out as I swallow. "I don't want this," I say.

"Well, you need to drink it. I will be back soon to check on you." He steps out of the room. I sit up in bed and I stare at the drink in my hands. I try my best to gulp it down.

I place the green cup on my side table. Resting on the pillow, I stare at the dim orange glow of my lamp. I begin to feel sleepy.

"Did you finish the drink?" Tony asks, appearing in the bedroom. He picks the green cup up and looks in it.

"Yes, and I am very tired," I whisper. I shut my eyes and fade into a deep, dark slumber.

As I sleep, I hear my name being called. "Maria," I hear a whisper. Slowly, I open my eye lids. My lamp is still on. I see a blurry version of Tony's face and his arm extended towards me. Everything feels like I am in a tunnel. Tony's voice turns into a mumble. I keep my eyes open. I see Tony's feet and sweatpants standing by my bed. I watch my feet slide across the floor. He is moving my body with him. Tony guides me to the center of the room. Everything is moving so fast, yet slow. I begin to feel a cool breeze on my body. I become aware that my bare skin is exposed. I can feel a carpet fabric on my bare back. My back is sliding as Tony hovers over me. He is moving around on top of me. I watch his hand grip the top of my bent knee. I am trying to gain control of my vision. I turn my head to the side. I am on eye level with the view underneath my bed. I can see the yellow VCR box that I hid under there. My vision fades, I close my eyes.

The next morning, I wake up in my bed, feeling hazy. My lower back feels like it got a rug burn. I stare at the daylight within my room. Something feels strange, I look over and see the green cup is still on my nightstand. I hope that I don't end up using the bathroom at school today because of the medicine. As I wiggle in bed, my body and lower stomach feels sore. I stare to the ceiling. My mind is racing, I am trying to figure out why I feel different. Last night, I remember seeing Tony's feet and hands. The room was low lit.

"Hey, sleepy head." Tony walks into my room smiling. He walks over to my bed. "Breakfast is ready." He smiles. I watch him reach over and pick up the green cup.

"Okay," I say softly. I sit up in bed. I place my feet on the floor and look down. I look down at my feet, I get a flash in my mind again of his hands and feet. I shake my head, too much to think about right now. I just want to wake up and eat. I am starving. It feels like I haven't eaten in a while.

Tony drives me to school. I build up the confidence to ask him when the digestive medication will affect me. "Am I going to poop at school?" I ask him.

Tony snaps his head to me. "What kind of question is that?" he chuckles.

"Cause the medicine for my stomach," I state. "Oh." Tony eyes widen. "Yeah, it should work," he says. "Remember to behave at school," Tony warns me, changing the subject. I smile and nod my head as I stare at him. Tony gives me his whole rant about how my behavior is a reflection of him. "Love you!" Tony shouts through the open window. I walk down the hallway, I realize, I did not take my ADHD medication this morning, which is strange because Tony is always sure I take my medication. He is like the pill police when it comes to my behavior. Stepping into the classroom, I feel low energy and annoyed. I do not want to talk to anyone.

"Hi, Maria!" Mrs. Carboni smiles.

"Hey," I say plainly and sit in my desk. The class chatters. I sit in my desk and drift off into my thoughts.

Mrs. Carboni begins her morning lesson by writing a lower case 'a' in cursive. "Imagine it being an upside-down roller coaster," she chuckles while writing on the chalkboard. My mind recalls standing up last night, looking at my feet. I remember the green cup. I gasp as my mind flashes to a blurry imagine of Tony hovering over me. I remember viewing underneath my bed. I saw the yellow VHS box. My mind can't bear the thought of what happened last night. I push my chair out and stand to my feet.

"Where are you going?" Mrs. Carboni asks.

"The bathroom," I state. I walk across the classroom. This school is so fancy, it has a bathroom built in each classroom. I shut the door behind me. Finally, I feel like I can think in peace. I stare in the mirror and let my mind drift into the thought I kept ignoring. I was naked with Tony last night. I was on the floor. Tears roll down my eyes from frustration. Usually when he touches me, I am aware and he directs me to do things. I am aware of what sex is. Tony always tries to stick himself inside me, though he always stops mid-way. I believe that Tony fully penetrated me last night. I roll my hand into a fist. I want to scream and run away. Suddenly, I lift my fist in the air and punch the tiled bathroom wall. "OWW" I shout as my right hand begins to throb.

Mrs. Carboni knocks on the door. I open it, "I hurt my hand," I tell her.

"How?" she asks.

"I punched the wall," I answer.

"Well, if you need to express any anger, you can try and use your words," she says bending down, looking directly into my eyes. Her kind eyes make me want to hug her and never let go. I stay quiet. "You don't have to tell me," she sighs.

"Hey, Alex," Mrs. Carboni calls. "Can you escort Maria to the nurse's office please?" she says. Alex smiles as her big blonde curls bounce.

"Is she alright?" Alex asks, looking at me with concern. Once I told Alex that my mother and sister fist fight, since then she has been very caring over me. Alex wraps her hand around my back as she escorts me to the nurse's office. "Well, I hope you feel better." Alex smiles. She reaches over and gives me a hug. Her big blue eyes sparkle.

"Thank you, Alex," I say. I go and speak to the nurse to tell her what happened. The nurse calls my mother to come and pick me up. Regina isn't too thrilled to come and get me after being hungover. She drives me to the hospital. The ER doctors gives me a splinter to put on my fractured pinky.

CHAPTER 11

The Things He Said to Me

I attend Camp Hummocks for another summer. Tony continues his abusive nightly routine as if we are an adult couple. I like going to camp, however, I am glad that it is the last day. Camp Hummocks does an annual talent show on the last day of camp. We perform a dance created by our camp counselors. After the show, Tony takes me to McDonald's. I sit in a booth with Tony across from me. I am eating chicken nuggets, however, I eat them in a peculiar way. I rip off the crispy skin of my nuggets, leaving the chicken exposed. I place the crisp skin on the side, open the sweet and sour sauce. In fragments, I eat the crispy skin first then move onto the chicken itself. Tony shakes his head at me, "You do such strange things." He laughs. I giggle and look up at him.

"I like to eat the crispy parts first." I laugh.

"Hey, now that you are off from camp, Linda will watch you for a few hours somedays," he says.

"I love Linda," I say.

"In the mornings, you might be home alone until she can come pick you up," he adds.

"Why?" I ask.

"Well, I need to go to work and my mother is going to stay a few weeks at Marcella's house," he explains. I begin to individually touch each fingertip on my thumb. I have gained this skill from a therapist I went to once. I get nervous about being home alone.

"Stop that!" Tony scoffs. "You know I hate when you do that." He looks at me with disgust. I move my hand and continue my anxiety exercise underneath the table. "Your mother thinks camp ends at the very end of August." He chuckles.

"Wait, but today was the last day of camp." I say.

"Yeah, but it is only the 8th," Tony says. "She is expecting you back on the 25th of August," he adds.

"Why am I staying longer?" I ask. Tony's face becomes serious. I watch him aggressively begin to collect the trash on our table. In the car, he is silent. I sit in the back seat, "Tony, what is wrong?" I ask.

"Fuck you, Maria." Tony points his rearview mirror down at me. "You want to leave so bad, I will pack you up tonight," he adds while his driving speed picks up. I hate when he curses at me. I slip my hands underneath my thighs. As I sit on my hands, I stick up my middle fingers in a secret protest, saying 'fuck you' back to him. I do this when someone is rude to me, but I am not allowed to be rude back.

"Tony, I am sorry, I want to stay. I don't want to go home," I tell him.

At Tony's house, he paces around the small room while I sit on the bed. "Did you know that I was once engaged to be married." Tony states.

I shake my head. "No," I say.

"I was going to get married," he says.

"Why didn't you?" I ask.

Tony scoffs. "My fiancé turned out to be a cold bitch," he says while his eyes begin to water. "She found out she was pregnant with my child and she aborted it," he cries loudly and dramatically. "You know what that means?" he asks.

"When a woman kills the baby inside her," I explain. I feel the sadness from Tony's story.

"I didn't even get to know if it was a boy or girl," he sobs. "Then she left me," he cries. "Now, years later, I meet you." He smiles. "You were at Star's house and I saw you were not loved by your parents," he states. Suddenly, I feel a deep emotion arise in my heart. Hearing Tony's words of how I am not loved by my parents stabs my heart.

"Don't cry." He wipes my tear.

"When I met you, you made me smile. I felt like I wanted to give you everything in the world," he adds. His watery eyes look deep into mine. His sad eyes quickly turn angry, "Now, here we are today… All you are worried about is when you get to go home?" he snaps. He stands tall to his feet. "You don't appreciate all that I give you." He storms out of the bedroom.

I flip over on the bed and dig my head into the pillow. My chest hurts. I let out tiny screams so Tony can't hear me. It feels like a neverending battle with Tony. My crying fit comes to an end. I sit up in the bed to take a deep breath. I look around the room and wipe my tears. No matter how much I cry, it is not going to fix the fact that Tony is angry with me.

If I am going to be staying in New York longer, I know I have to figure out a way to make things right with him. I look in the mirror and fix my hair. I pat under my eyes, hopefully the puffiness will go down. I must write Tony an apology letter. However, I feel this one needs to be more impressive than any other letter. I begin to search the room for inspiration. I sit at the desk and move the computer keyboard aside. I open to a clean page in my journal and begin to write, 'Dear Tony,' I use a fancy 'Y' with a loop. I flip the page because my 'Y' didn't come out neat enough. I write it again, yet I feel stuck on my apology to him. Why am I sorry? What have I done to him that is so wrong? I glance beside me. The children's bible that Linda gifted me is on the shelf of the wooden desk. I pray to God for guidance. "God, if you love me and hear me... please help me write this letter to Tony," I say softly.

Tony loves church. If I can find a way to write in my letter about the Bible, maybe he will forgive me for upsetting him? I flip through the pages of the Bible and come across a man named Job. Job is a man that argues with God and then is tested. In the end God forgives him. I sit at the desk and write. Suddenly, I hear a noise from behind me. I turn around and notice a note is slipped underneath the door. I walk over and read the writing on the lined paper.

You broke my heart, this time it hurts me so much.

The note reads. I turn the golden doorknob and open the door. "Stop it!" Tony cries. He is sitting on the floor in the hallway. "Don't look at me!" he shouts and pulls the door shut. I rush back to the desk to finish the letter.

Dear Tony,

Please forgive me for my attitude I had. I know that I am not a great listener. I will do better, I promise. I am excited that I get to stay longer at your house. I love you so so so very much. Please forgive me like God forgave Job in the Bible.

I take a deep breath as I fold the letter in half. I open the door. Tony isn't there. I find him in the kitchen. He is at the table eating a sandwich.

"This is for you." I place the letter on the small kitchen table. Tony stares at me as he finishes chewing. His silence is enough to make me turn around and head back into the bedroom. I sit on the bed, hanging my head low. Suddenly, the golden doorknob jingles. Tony walks into the room.

"This, this makes me feel like you have been listening and actually learning when you read the Bible." He smiles. "You are forgiven," he says gently while he wipes his tears. I am relieved to have fixed his mood, yet I have a big headache from crying. He sits down on the wooden chair and begins to tell me the story about Job. "You know, Job was a man who had everything," he says. "Then God took it all away from him to see if Job would still believe and worship him," he explains. "What do you think Job did?" he asks.

"I think that he continued to praise Jesus," I state.

"Eh, kind of. Jesus wasn't alive yet," he says.

I nod my head. I still have a hard time knowing the different between God and Jesus. I always thought that Jesus is a small fairy man in a robe that tries to jump inside my heart so I can accept him.

"Now that I forgive you, let's go watch TV in the living room." He smiles.

I nod my head and follow Tony. He sits in the reclining chair as I get cozy on the couch. He begins to flip through the channels. "Ut oh," Tony gasps with concern. He turns the channel to the news. "Is your child safe?" a news woman's voice speaks. "Today we are responding to Kidnapping, Is Your Child Safe?" the newscaster explains. The news begins its segment. I watch as a lady speaks facts about kidnapping rates. They show a clip of a child playing on the swing. Then, a moment later, the child vanishes, leaving the swing empty. "Kidnapping, a major issue for children between the ages of infant to 16 years old," a newscaster speaks. I gasp, I fit in that age gap. I turn to look at Tony. "This is why I always need to know where you are," Tony states. "You could get kidnapped in the blink of an eye," he states.

Just like that, a new fear of being kidnapped rises within me. Trying not to expose my fear, I sit up. "Can we watch something else now?" I ask.

Tony flips through the channels again. "Oh, this is my favorite show," he says. I recognize the show. Tony and Anna spend hours together watching this show. Law and Order: Special Victims Unit on the 'USA Network.' I watch the screen. There are a bunch of adults talking. I tune in, gaining the show's perspective. I see a bald man in nice clothing next to a woman. She has light brown pixie hair, kind brown eyes, and nice clothing. They are standing next to a morgue table with a dead body covered in a blue blanket. "Oh, I have seen this episode before," Tony comments from behind.

"Oh yeah?" I say staring at the TV.

"Under the blanket is a dead girl," he states.

I gasp. "Why is she dead?" I ask.

"She was kidnapped and killed," he explains.

"Why?" I ask with concern.

"Maybe she wasn't a good listener and got herself into trouble," Tony states plainly.

The woman on TV, with the short pixie hair, speaks. "Melinda, what is the cause of death?" she asks another lady.

A woman with dark skin and tight curly hair turns to the other woman. She says, "Olivia, it was a struggle... Strangulation and stabbing wounds. But the girl fought back, she might have DNA under her fingernails," the woman explains.

I sit and watch the show. "You are continuing to watch the Law and Order: Special Victims Unit marathon. We will be right back," the TV announcer states. I sit there and watch the rest of the episode. Tony falls asleep in the chair as the next episode of Law and Order comes on. The show is scary, yet I stay to watch because of the woman character, Olivia, played by Mariska Hargitay. I have always wanted to be a secret agent like the movie Spy Kids. Olivia is a detective who goes on missions. I have never seen a show with a female agent besides the movie Spy Kids or Nancy Drew books. I try to watch the next episode, but I become frightened at a bloody scene. I stand up and rush down the hallway. I do not want to watch that show anymore. I throw myself in bed and wrap the blanket around my feet and shoulders. I may be frightened, but at least tonight I have the bed to myself.

Over the summer, Regina moved us into a new apartment on Foster Street in a two-family house. Before Tony dropped me back home, one important thing happened before leaving his house. Tony explained that Regina has relocated us once more. Now we attend a new school, once again. It is no surprise to be starting a new school. Every year it seems like we begin a new one. I am excited to be in the 5th grade. Since living in Foster Street, we now attend school at Parkland Ave. Fun fact, my dance camp friend, Emily, is in my new class. Karina and I ride the same bus.

"My teacher said dinosaurs existed a long time ago," Karina speaks while sitting next to me on the bus.

I smile and nod my head. I am not listening to a word Karina is saying. My mind is too anxious at the idea of getting dropped off down the road from our house. I am so scared we both could get kidnapped as we walk home. The bus comes to a stop.

"Karina, come on, it is our stop." I panic. The bus stops about 9 houses down from ours. I quickly rush down the bus stairs. I run down the sidewalk and hop up onto our neighbor's front yard. They have a hill that is aligned with the stone wall leading to our side yard. I reach the top. "Come on, woo woo!" I call Karina by her nickname.

Karina tries to follow me up the grassy hill. "I can't climb the hill!" she shouts at me. "I am too chubby and cute for this!" Karina hops her feet back on the concrete.

"Someone is going to take you!" I shout at her. Karina rolls her eyes and walks away. I shake my head and walk towards the front porch.

"Hey," Regina says as she smokes a cigarette outside. "Where is Karina?" she questions. I shrug my shoulders.

Karina comes stomping up the concrete steps. "Mommy, she tried to make me go up the hill, again," Karina whimpers.

"Maria, goddamn it," Regina snaps, "Didn't I tell you to stop making her climb that hill?" Regina yells and hits me on the back of my head.

"Ow, stop!" I yell at her. "She just doesn't listen! Someone can take her if she isn't careful!" I yell.

"Maria, no one is going to kidnap you! I don't know why you keep acting like this," Regina says puffing on her cigarette. I shake my head and walk around to the front door. She wouldn't understand my fear.

Around the apartment there are small plots of land, and a backyard with a tall stone wall. Below the stone wall there is depth within the grounding, which is where the side yard land begins. A tall, climbable tree lives beside it. This tree is my favorite place to be after school. I talk on my new cell phone that Tony got me. It is a Cingular gray flip phone. Tony convinced Regina that getting me a phone will help with my kidnapping anxiety. I talk to Tony and update him on my day. "I promise I will do my homework," I assure Tony. I hang up the phone and toss it on my bed. I head outside to the side yard. When I am in the side yard, I feel slightly safer from kidnappers. I climb the tree nearby. In my tree, I can see over the house and street. I feel like a secret agent hidden away because she is on a mission. Also, playing up here, I feel there is less chance of being seen playing, which lessens my chance of being kidnapped in the yard. I have real bad anxiety about that.

However, it is relaxing to watch the active neighborhood. Across the street there are apartments with the same white, dingy siding as our apartment. A Mexican family lives over there. They always make me smile. On nice days, the family of four sit on their stoop. The parents set out child play tables and chairs for their son and daughter. Then the parents sit on their chairs while they enjoy a home cooked meal outside. They always look happy and content. I can smell the yummy spices in their food from across the street. As I move my eyes along the road, I see a teen boy begin to head in our direction. He climbs up from the sidewalk, up a small grassy hill onto our side yard. He knocks on our bedroom window that looks out to the yard. I shake my head as I remember that is where Tony stands to knock on our window. Why could this boy be knocking?

Shannon opens the blinds with a smile on her face. She spends her time between our apartment and Star's condo. I hadn't realized she was home. Shannon points her finger. The teen boy walks around the back of the apartment to our bedroom's second window. He steps into the bedroom. I gasp and climb out of the tree. Shannon is sneaking a boy into the house. I must investigate. I enter the apartment and check on Regina. She is sleeping in her bedroom. Karina and Selena are watching TV on the couch. I step into our bedroom and shut the door behind me.

"Hey Shannon, you are home," I say. "Oh, who are you?" I ask the teen boy.

"Hey, I am Angel." The boy smiles.

He is a Puerto Rican boy with a kind smile. He is fashionable with a red shirt, baggy jeans and lots of gold jewelry.

"Maria, take this and take pictures of us," Shannon demands as she places a disposable camera in my hand. She looks into his eyes and smiles at him. He smiles back and they hold hands. "Take the picture from the side," Shannon demands through her smile. I snap a photo. "Keep taking pictures," she states. To me this is a fun game, I stand on the bed and capture moments of their young love.

Quickly after, Shannon shoos me out of the room. So, I go into the bathroom. There is clutter everywhere within the house. However, the best clutter is in the bathroom. Regina's make up clutter. She has CoverGirl cover up, eyeliner, and mascara. I see that Regina has a brand-new bottle of Barbie pink nail polish. I sit on the side of the sink with my cell phone beside me. I begin to polish my toes. My cell phone vibrates.

It is Tony calling to check in. "Hello, what are you doing?" he asks.

"Nothing, just finished my homework," I lie.

"You better have, your grades always show when you don't do the homework," he reminds me. "Where is your mother?" he asks.

"Sleeping," I say.

"Alright, don't leave the house," he says.

"I won't, it is dark out," I say.

"Even if it was daytime, you shouldn't step foot outside that house," Tony says.

"Why?" I ask. Tony begins ranting. As I listen, I begin to over paint my toes to the point where I am painting my whole foot to make it look like I have a pink sock on. "Have you been leaving the house? Where have you been going?" he asks frantically. I look at myself in the bathroom mirror. I feel like I should just keep lying to him.

"No, I always stay in my room," I tell him.

"You better. I will call you in an hour. Get ready for bed soon," he says and hangs up.

The next morning, I wake up hungry. Tony guides my morning over the phone. Regina likes that Tony calls to wake me up. That way she only has to focus on getting Karina, Selena, and herself ready for the day.

I sit in the classroom at Parkland Ave. My teacher, Mr. Karft is a short man with fair skin, green eyes and glasses. He is a funny teacher and nerdy. I like all the facts he teaches on Math and English. My friend, Emily from dance camp, is in the same class as me. We both signed up for instrument extracurricular activities and the 5th grade play. We both decided on playing the viola instead of the violin. We thought it would make us 'different.' At recess, there are many games going on. The jungle gym, swings, wall ball, and four square. I play four square, my favorite playground game I learned here. There are four painted squares on the ground. Each middle corner of the square has different suits. King, Queen Knight and joker. The players let the ball bounce once in their square before passing it. The objective of the game is to become the king by staying in the game long enough without a fault of the ball bouncing out of the box. It gets intense. It is my turn in line, I step into the Joker box.

"Ut oh, Maria in stepping in the box," Jorge states. "I am going to overthrow you," I threaten. Jorge smirks. Jorge has glasses, and curly black hair. He and I like to play spy kids. He is good at coming up with fake missions. He and I like each other. Sometimes I kiss him in the back of the bus.

"No you won't, I am next to the throne," Douglas laughs. "So you will have to overthrow me," he says.

I laugh. "Well, get to it, let's see what happens," I demand. Douglas winks at me. We ride the bus together too. I have kissed him as well.

"Beat them, Maria!" Chris shouts from the game's line of students. I look to the side and smile. Chris is another boy that I kiss, his hair is white and he is half-Japanese. The game begins until Douglas overthrows Jorge and I am in the queen box. Suddenly, the bell rings.

"Wait. Tomorrow, Chris is the Joker, Maria is the queen, and I am King." Douglas says.

"Deal." Chris and I say, waiting to meet up.

Coming home from school. I quickly run up the side yard's hill into the house to avoid being kidnapped. Entering the kitchen I see a man by the name of Presley sitting at the kitchen table. "Who is this?" I ask Regina as she stands over the stove.

"I am Presley." He smiles. I see a gas station teddy bear with a fake rose and heart on the table. I begin to understand this is one of Regina's new boyfriends. Presley has tan skin, a thick Dominican accent, brown almond eyes and he is decked out in gold jewelry. My phone vibrates. It is Tony.

"Hey, one second," I say.

"Nice meeting you, I am going to go put my bag away," I say respectfully.

"Wait, Maria, your birthday is coming up," Regina says. "What do you want?" she asks.

"A birthday party," I say. Regina laughs.

"What do you want me to buy you?" she questions.

"A karaoke machine so I can sing on a microphone," I state.

I look at Regina. She has an odd, motherly smile on her face. It feels off-putting. "Alright, I am going in my room," I tell her.

"If she throws you a birthday party you better tell her you want me there," Tony demands, as he has listened to the whole conversation.

I enter the room. "Who is that man in the house?" he asks.

"Her new boyfriend," I say. I place my bag down and pull out my sketch pad. Drawing helps keep my mind occupied. I have a book on how to draw Nickelodeon cartoon characters.

"I forgot my birthday is soon," I tell Tony.

"If you behave, I might get you something you really want," he says.

"I want to do cheerleading," I tell him.

"Hmm, maybe. I would drive down to bring you and watch you at cheer practice," he says. "Would you like that?" he asks. "If I watched you do cheerleading?" he asks.

"I guess." I shrug my shoulders.

"Anyway..." Tony says, disappointed. "Do your homework, I will call you soon," he says and hangs up.

Shannon barges into the bedroom. "Maria, get your shoes on." Shannon smiles as she rushes into the bedroom.

"Why?" I ask.

"Papi is outside we are going to his house," she says. I quickly put my sneakers on and tag along with my sketch book. I look at Shannon, her eyes are a bit low.

"You alright?" I ask.

"Yeah, I am feeling chill," she chuckles. She seems a bit different.

Julian moved into a studio apartment around the corner from our street. Outside on the sidewalk, I see my father.

"Papi!" I smile. He lifts me up high. He smells like marijuana. "Oh, your arm pits smell," I state. Shannon and Julian look at each other and laugh. We walk to Julian's apartment. "I haven't been here since we watched all of the Lord of the Rings movies," I say. Julian sits on his futon couch. "And you made fried ice cream for us." I smile.

Julian smiles and reacts slowly. His eyes are low like Shannon's. "I wanted to give you a gift for your birthday in case your mother won't let me see you," he states. I sit up straight, and he hands me a wrapped square. I unwrap the gift. It is an Apple product.

"An iPod Nano!" I squeal. "The girls at summer camp in New York have these!" I smile.

"Music is important to have in life," he tells me.

"That's what you said when you gave me a CD player." I smile and hug him.

For an hour, Shannon and I spend time talking with Julian. He begins to explain how he has a comic book idea. He is a superhero like Wolverine. Shannon and I are his superhero daughters. "Shannon, you have the power of fire and strength," he says. "Maria, you are air." "You have the power to hover in the air and control other people's emotions," he explains.

Suddenly from his dresser he pulls out small, white artist cardboards. It has drawings of superheroes in armor. Julian drew us as the superheroes he spoke about.

"Look, I draw too." I smile and hand him my sketch pad. Shannon and her boyfriend hang out by Julian's front door. Julian sits with me. He turns my sketch book to a fresh page. "This is how you draw and shade in a snow man," he explains. He draws in my sketch book.

"Papi, it is dark out now!" Shannon shouts through the screen door. Julian walks us home. I hug my father to remember these last moments with him. I am not sure when I will be seeing him again. He only really likes to hang out with Shannon.

"Can you take me boxing with you and Shannon?" I ask him. "Just like you used to do when you first moved close to us." I smile. I am trying to guarantee a time and place so I can see him again. Shannon walks inside the house. A car pulls up to the sidewalk. All the windows are rolled down.

"Yeah, maybe," he says. "My ride is here." He opens the door and sits in the passenger's seat. I see a man driving the car.

"Wait," I say. Placing my hand through the window, I touch Julian's arm.

"What?" he says, annoyed.

"Thank you again, I love you," I say. "I am going to miss you," I add.

Julian looks me up and down. "Let go of me." He moves my hand off of him. "Look I gave you the gift, now your mother can't tell the court I didn't do anything," he says.

"Huh?" I lower my eyebrows and back away from the car.

"If you are my real daughter, then you were a mistake," he states, looking into my eyes. My heart breaks. Julian lifts his fingers up to the man driving. The car begins to roll away.

I run up the concrete steps and into the apartment. I am confused. I just had a fun time with my father. I cannot comprehend why all of a sudden he looked at me with disgust. I bolt into the bedroom and toss myself on the bed. I lay there silently crying into my pillow until I fall asleep. I will never know why Julian said the things he said to me.

CHAPTER 12

Outside

I wake up and start my day listening to a CD I stole from Tony. It was so worth the worry if he wouldn't notice me stealing. I guess all his claims of always watching me aren't all too true. I stole the 'Butterfly' album by Mariah Carey. I just love her gentle, angelic voice. She soothes my ears, makes me feel calm. On repeat is track 12, 'Outside.' I have lots of knowledge on how Mariah Carey grew up poor and biracial, always living on the outside of life. Suddenly, my morning is interrupted by Shannon.

"Sissy!" I smile and run up to give her a hug.

"Hi, Maria." She smiles. "I am here to pick up a few things," she states. "I have to hurry, Star is in the car," she adds.

"Shannon, you are home!" Regina stops by the bedroom. "Can you watch the girls?" Regina asks.

"No, I have plans," Shannon scoffs.

"Miguel said he can't watch them." Regina whines.

"Why is Miguel even here?" Shannon questions.

"I am helping him out, he is the father of my two girls," Regina snaps.

Shannon rolls her eyes. She has a mean mug on her face. "Well, you are a fool for letting him back in your house," Shannon states. She searches her side of the room for an item.

"Well fuck you, Shannon," Regina yells. "Get the hell out of my house and never come back!" Regina demands.

I grab Mooky, my guinea pig. I sit at the top of my bed and watch them yell in each other's faces.

"Consider me moving out, I wish you were dead, bitch!" Shannon flicks Regina's glasses. "When you die I am going to spit on your fucking grave!" she adds.

"Miguel!" Regina screams. "You need to watch the girls, I have plans tonight," Regina states.

Continuing to hold Mooky, I walk into the hallway.

"Hi, Miguel," I greet him. He is holding Selena while Karina runs around him. They are happy to see their father. I smile at their innocent love for him. It reminds me of when Shannon and I were little. So happy to see our Papi, yet waiting for the shoe of disappointment stomping on our hearts. It's just a matter of time for Karina and Selena to understand. Regina changes into causal wear.

"Where are you going?" I ask her.

"None of your business," she says, perky.

"Going to see Presley?" I giggle.

"Can you shut up? I do not need him hearing about my dating life," Regina whispers and points to Miguel.

"Can you hurry the fuck back so I can do what I need done?" Miguel states while Karina and Selena try to climb him.

"I think they want to play with you," I tell Miguel.

"They have toys in their bedroom," I suggest, pointing to their bedroom door. I look him up and down as he guides the girls to the bedroom. I always wondered what went wrong in Miguel's life for him to end up so angry.

I linger over to my bed and continue to play track 12. This song by Mariah Carey has been opening my mind to deeper thinking. In the song, she uses words like 'ambiguous,' meaning uncertain of being understood. I feel ambiguous when it comes to relating to family members. They are all in a rush to get things done. They never want to spend a moment to look around and observe life with me. At school, I move so many times I have no idea what type of friend I am or how to keep a stable friendship. At camp, I feel more like an alien because all those kids are wealthy and have parents that look after them. At Tony's house, that is where I feel extremely alone and misunderstood. I feel like I live so many lives. Which Maria is the correct Maria? I lean my back against the wall and begin to sketch cartoon characters out as I listen to music on my pink princess CD player.

Time passes, and I realize Regina is still not home. I venture out of the bedroom and down the hallway.

"Mom?" I shout. No answer. I see that Karina and Selena sleeping on the couch.

"Miguel?" I call out. No answer. I notice the bathroom light is on. I investigate. "Miguel, are you in there?" I knock on the door. I turn the doorknob. It is locked. I begin to slightly panic because the sun is going down. What if a kidnapper comes in the house.

"Miguel!" I bang on the door. Silence. I hop down to the floor and peek underneath the bathroom door. It looks like someone is in the bathroom. I begin to panic and think of a plan. The only solution I can find is taking off the doorknob. I grab a screwdriver from the kitchen junk drawer. The other knob falls off on the other side of the door as I unscrew it. Before opening the door, I peek through the knob hole and see Miguel laying on the floor.

I gasp and open the door. I spy a small orange rubber tip next to a syringe needle on the bathroom sink. I am too stunned to speak. I stand there and observe the scene. So this is what drug use looks like? Using a needle and falling to the floor.

"Miguel!" I tap Miguel on the shoulder. I begin to panic. I am not sure if he is breathing. Unconsciously, I do what I have seen Olivia Benson do on *Law and Order: SVU*. I kneel on the floor. I check for breathing and a pulse. "He is alive!" I shout and look up in the air. "Miguel, you are laying in a pile of dirty clothes." I shake Miguel aggressively.

"Hmmhmm," he groans. I notice the other doorknob is on the floor.

"Shit." I stand to my feet. Regina can be home any second. She will flip out if she sees this. Miguel begins to move around a bit while he lays on the bathroom floor. I begin to reinstall the doorknobs as best I can.

I turn around and I scream. Suddenly, Miguel is standing to his feet, swaying. He looks like a zombie. "Miguel, are you alright?" I ask him. He begins to walk slowly to the front door.

"Wait, don't leave!" I tell him. He groans and proceeds to find the strength to open the apartment door. "Wait, don't leave!" I beg. "We need an adult to watch us," I cry and begin to push his hands away from the door. Miguel turns around and heads down the hallway. I follow him and watch how he plants himself on Regina's bed. I take a deep breath. "Great, if someone breaks in the house, the adult is on drugs and sleeping," I mumble with urgency. I race around the house to be sure all the windows and doors are locked.

Late in the night, Regina arrives home. She is searching the house. "Maria, where is Miguel?" She steps into the bedroom. I am watching TV in the dark.

"In your room. He is on drugs," I tell her.

"What?" she asks. I stand to me feet.

"Look in the bathroom." I open the door and show her the needle on the sink.

"Alright, stay in your room," Regina demands. "Where are the girls?" she asks.

"I put Karina and Selena to sleep on Shannon's bed so they wouldn't get kidnapped," I explain.

Regina walks into her bedroom. I lay back on my bed, shutting the TV off. I stare into the dark while my headphones play track 12, 'Outside.'

The lyrics to 'Outside' by Mariah Carey:

"It's hard to explain
Inherently it's just always been strange
Neither here nor there
Always somewhat out of place everywhere
Ambiguous
Without a sense of belonging to touch
Somewhere halfway
Feeling there's no one completely the same"

"Standing alone
Eager to just
Believe it's good enough to be what
You really are
But in your heart
Uncertainty forever lies
And you'll always be
Somewhere on the
Outside"

'Always somewhat out of place everywhere' is the definition of my life. I do not feel like I belong to anybody or anywhere. *'Without a sense of belonging to touch.'* This line stabs my heart the most. The word 'touch' is triggering to me. I don't know what it is like to be touched correctly. If someone is touching me it is because they are using me for their own gain. Tony uses me for his satisfaction. When

I look to my mother for affection, she either uses me because she needs a hug or pushes me away. Lastly, *'Eager enough to just believe it is good enough to be what you really are.'* I am so eager to make connections with the people around me. Yet, I feel so far from them. I do not even feel good enough for my own father. I want to be someone to somebody. Somebody who truly loves me for me. I bet if someone gave me a chance, they would see how smart, funny and creative I can be. At 10 years old, this song has taught me the words to describe my inner sorrow and fears.

CHAPTER 13

Cluster C

Regina has kept us in the same apartment for a year. However, the new school switch is because I am starting middle school. I sit in the gymnasium with a mixture of grades. We all sit on the bleachers waiting for our names to be called to a cluster. It has been explained that after we are assigned, we will take a group school photo. As we wait, I look around to observe my fellow classmates. I realize that I sat next to a group of 8th graders. 8th grade girls cuddling all over their boyfriends. The 8th grade boys are clowning each other with fun jokes as they let the girls hang on them. The girls seem older and cooler than me. To impress them, I sit up straight. I am proud because Regina put thick 'blonde' highlights in my hair. The highlights turned a bit orange, however I have pride that I was allowed to dye my hair.

I am wearing velvet orange pants, a pink fuzzy vest, and a long-sleeve white shirt. I am hoping that the cool girls recognize my pants from the 'That's So Raven' clothing line.

"You look like you really like pink and orange." One of the older boys point to me. They laugh.

"Yeah, so does your hair." They chuckle at my horribly done highlights. I side eye the group, there goes my chance to come across as cool.

"Shut up," I say.

"What is your name?" another boy asks.

"She looks too young to be in middle school bro," another boy comments.

"Maria," I say. "I am starting 6th grade," I state.

"Oh, you should be on the other set of bleachers," the first boy tells me.

"Yeah, you are going to miss your assigned cluster," he says.

"She is going to get assigned to cluster B," one of them shouts.

"Nah, man, you think?"

They discuss. "Are you fully white?" A boy asks.

I tilt my head, confused. "What do you mean?" I question.

"She looks Spanish," I hear.

"I am half Puerto Rican," I say.

"Oh yup, cluster C," another comments. I am heavily confused.

"All Puerto Ricans are put in cluster C," a kid laughs.

"Bitch, I mean look at me, I am in cluster C," a Spanish kids laughs.

"Even if you are white, if you are on food stamps..." a boy says.

"CLUSTER C!" three other boys say simultaneously.

I am taken aback at how they are speaking. I am aware of racism. I know not to say the N-word or judge someone on their skin color. I am confused as to why these 8th graders are so prominent on which race goes in which cluster.

"Guys, stop fooling around with her," a pretty girl next to us shouts. She has tan skin, curly gelled hair and has a belly shirt on. She looks so cool.

"Babe, you need to go to the first bleacher, over there," the girl directs with her finger. I stand to my feet and hold my fabric binder in my hand.

"Thank you," I smile.

"And don't listen to them, your highlights look good," the girl adds. I blush, hold my big binder to my chest and walk away.

Ironically, I am assigned to the 6th grade cluster C. All those boys were right. Now that they pointed out race, I can't unsee how each cluster is grouped together. At lunch, I run into Chris from Parkland Ave. We used to 'date' and kiss in the school library.

"Hi, Chris." I smile.

"I like your hair," he says.

I smile and smack my gum. "What cluster are you in?" he asks.

"Cluster C," I say. I then remember Chris is mixed with white and Japanese. "Are you in cluster C?" I say with hope.

"No, cluster A." He smiles and points to cluster A's lunch tables.

"Oh..." I say.

"Do you want my Doritos?" he asks. I smirk. He remembers from 5th grade that I would always take his bag of Doritos. I follow him to a lunch table.

"Chris, who is that?" A girl with long dark blonde hair asks.

"Julie, this is Maria, I know her from last year," he says.

"Hi." I smile.

Chris hands me his bag of chips that has been sitting in a lunch box. He sits next to Julie.

"Looks like you are a copycat," Julie laughs.

"What do you mean?" I smile, smacking my gum.

"My friend Mykayla just got her hair highlighted too." Julie points to a girl next to her. She has the same color highlights.

"I don't know her, how could I copy her?" I question.

The girls giggle. Julie rolls her eyes. "Let's hope she doesn't try out for the cheer squad this afternoon," she comments.

"You are a rude bitch," I state.

"Really? Have some class," Julie replies.

I walk over to her. Julie scoffs and waves her hand to shoo me away. I spit my gum into her long hair.

"Ah!" she screams.

I laugh and start to walk away. "Chris if you are going to be my boyfriend, you are not allowed to talk to that girl anymore." I hear Julie cry. "It's stuck in my hair!" she yelps.

I roll my eyes. I guess I see what the 8th graders mean when one of them said cluster A students are stuck up and rich.

Towards the end of the day, I am excited to leave school. Tony texted my cell phone explaining that Shannon is picking me up after school. Apparently, we are going to meet Star at a diner called JK's. I head to the main entrance of the school. Shannon called to tell me she is outside.

"Hey, pumpkin hair." Julie says, from behind me. I turn and see Julie dressed in a blue and white cheerleading uniform. She has 5 other cheerleaders with her. I step back until my backpack touches the wall. The girls form a semi-circle around me. I am trapped between them and the wall.

"What do you all want?" I ask, looking each of them in the eye.

"Apologize for putting gum in my hair," Julie demands. "I had to cut pieces of my hair off," Julie whines.

I laugh at her and look around at the girls. In my mind, I do not feel threatened. I actually feel like I am in a secret spy agent movie. I know that I can't fight all these girls myself. However, I can escape. Those are two different things. I think of what a smart spy would do to remove herself from this situation. I see a gap between Julie and another girl standing next to her. I feel as though I have the ability to run through them.

"I don't care how you feel, Julie," I state plainly. I throw my binder between Julie and her friend,

"She is untamed," Julie says. I run between two of her other friends. Lucky, the blinder has a cloth back and it slides smoothly across the floor. I grab the binder and race to the front door of the school. Outside, I run down the small hill that leads to the street. I see Shannon on the sidewalk. Her hand is holding a pink Razor phone to her ear.

"Shannon! I am HERE!" I scream on the top of my lungs. Shannon's face drops when she sees I am being chased by the group of cheerleaders.

"Run!" I yell. Shannon and I run beside each other.

"What the fuck Maria, what did you do?" Shannon asks while we run. "I can't get into another fight, I am in A.L.T.!" she shouts. A.L.T. This stands for 'Alternative Learning.' It is a school for kids who get in a lot of trouble and fights at the Danbury public high school. "We need to run down to the light and make a right." Shannon shouts. "Star is waiting for us at JK's Diner." Shannon shouts.

I nod my head, "Got it," I tell her. We cross the street. "They are far away, let's just walk," Shannon says, catching her breath. We approach the diner, 'JK's.'

Inside, I see Star at her favorite booth, beneath the glass ceiling and in the corner for privacy. "Hi, Star!" I smile. I place my binder in the booth and give her a tight hug.

"How have you been, my darling?" Star says. She gives me double Italian kisses on my cheeks.

"I am alright." I sit beside her. Shannon sits on the opposite side of Star and I.

"This girl just made me run the mile," she states.

"Shh." I shake my head at her.

"What, why?" Star drops her fork in her salad. She looks at me. "Maria, what did you do?" Star questions me with her Italian Brooklyn accent.

"Nothing." I shrug my shoulders and look at the menu. "I want a sandwich," I state.

Shannon shakes her head and looks at the menu. I pull out my cell phone and gasp. I have 9 missed phone calls from Tony. My heart sinks to my stomach. "I need to use the bathroom." I stand to my feet. I head into the diner bathroom. I quickly dial Tony's number. I prepare myself for the lecture he is going to give me.

"WHERE THE HELL HAVE YOU BEEN?" Tony shouts at the top of his lungs. I pull the phone slightly away from my ear. "I know that Shannon was on her way to get you, yet you did not tell me you are with her," he states.

"I am sorry, I forgot." I say.

"Where are you?" he asks.

"At JK's." I answer.

"You better be, I am on the highway," he says. "I will see you soon," he adds. Tony hangs the phone up. I sigh and walk out of the bathroom.

As I sit back down. I see Julie and a friend in their cheer outfits. They are waiting outside the front door of the diner.

"Shannon, they hunted us down." I sit back at the table.

"What?" Shannon says.

"The cheerleaders." I point to the front door.

"Oh my god, Maria…" Shannon shakes her head.

"What is going on?" Star asks.

"Please, please don't tell Tony!" I beg Star.

"What happened?!" Star slams her palm on the table.

"The cheerleaders bullied me about my highlights. I put gum in one of their hair," I add.

Star breaks out in laughter. "Oh, marona mia," Star yelps in Italian. "Maria, you always do outrageous things." She laughs.

"Well, I can go and push over that tall skinny one," Star states.

"I will go tell them to leave," Shannon says.

"Let me come with you," Star states. "No, no one is fighting them." She tosses her hands in the air. The vein in Shannon's forehead begins to pop out. Shannon shoos the girls away just in time before Tony arrives.

Tony enters the diner. He greets Star. "How is everyone?" he asks. He smiles and looks at Star. Star looks at me and then at Tony. I am hoping she doesn't mention anything.

"We are good, just about to put in food," Star says. "What do you want?"

She hands Tony a menu.

"How have things been now that you are living with Star?" Tony asks Shannon.

"I am happier," Shannon says.

"I want to enroll her in my church's school," Star states. "Grace Hope Academy," Star begins to explain.

Shannon holds up her hand. "No way," she says. "I am not going to a school where it is all about Jesus," Shannon scoffs.

"They also teach general studies, Shannon," Star laughs.

"I don't know about that," Shannon states. After we enjoy dinner, Shannon and I part ways.

"Have a good weekend." Shannon hugs me goodbye. I get in the car with Tony.

In bed at Tony's house. I pull out a book that I have been obsessively reading. I checked it out of the school library and plan on never returning it. The book is *The Biography of Mariah Carey*. I become fully engaged within the story of Mariah's life. I knew that she grew up poor and bi-racial, like me. Though, as a child she was bright and gifted with music. Her mother is an opera singer who taught her how to sing. As a young woman, she was married to a man named Tommy Mottola. The marriage revealed how he has emotionally abusive and controlling. I remember in 2001 there was a scandal of her 'having a breakdown' on TRL. It makes sense why she was calling out for help. Mr. Mottola was trying to destroy her career after she filed for divorce.

In the book, it has pictures of Tommy Mottola and Mariah on the red carpet. Instantly, an eerie feeling comes across me. I stare at the photos. It feels like my eyes are playing tricks on me. My brain is comparing Tommy to the way Tony looks. The man and Tony look very similar. Off the bat, I can tell Tommy is an Italian man. He has dark slicked back hair, goatee hair, a round nose, and small eyes. Just like Tony. He even wears a suit and tie just like Tony on Sundays. I shake my head as I ponder. I begin to relate to Mariah being by his side. Just as Tommy roams the red carpet with Mariah, I roam the church by Tony's side. Tony always makes sure my hair is done and I am dressed up. The comparison is uncanny. I continue the book. It explains that eventually Mariah grew the strength to break free from Tommy back in 2001.

On Sunday, Tony wakes me up by screaming, "Get your fucking ass out of bed!" He snatches the blanket off me. There are different levels of Tony's anger. After he gives two warnings, his rage of an Italian New York man comes out. I sit up in fear. I hop out of the bed and begin to search for clothing. "I set an outfit out for you," Tony shouts. He points to the top of the long dresser with the mirror.

"I am sorry." I look up at him.

He begins to slam things around the room. I place my clothing on the bed and begin to change. All of a sudden, Tony picks up a plastic toy Barbie horse. He chucks it at me, I duck and the horse's foot makes a hole in the wall above the bed. "I am the main leader for the church band now!" Tony shouts at me. "I am not allowed to be late to sound check." He storms out of the room.

"Ma, I am going to either wrap my hands around her throat or have a heart attack," Tony shouts.

Anna steps into the room. She is wearing a cream-colored robe. "Are you alright?" she asks. I nod my head. "Come here." Anna pulls me up by my arms. She smiles and brushes my hair behind my ear. I look into her dark eyes. "You should know by now, never make him angry," she states plainly. "He has worked hard to become the lead pianist at church. Do not ruin it for him," she explains. Her eyes are deceiving. I sit there and deeply ponder Anna's actions towards me. At first she was caring, then it seemed like she hated me.

"What are you still doing on the bed!" Tony scrunches his face in a low rage. Tony charges into the bedroom, closing the door behind him. "You little fucker!" he snaps.

"I am sorry." I rush to get dressed.

Tony grabs the collar of my pajama shirt. Suddenly, I feel my feet hanging off the bed as Tony's hand smothers my face.

"Stop it!" I shout as Tony holds me down on the bed. I try to fight his grip. I wiggle and turn my body. I can't breathe. Tony presses my face deep into the pillows. I feel like I can't breathe. I panic. *Is this how I die?* I kick my feet, fighting for air.

"Now, are you going to do what I say?" he asks in an aggressive tone. Tony releases his grip. I try to catch my breath. "Stand up!" he demands.

"Yes, sir," I barely whisper. I stagger to stand to my feet. Tony's face is red and his jaw is clenched. His dark eyes are cold and empty. Silently and with fear, I get ready for church.

On the ride to church, I sit in the passenger seat. Tony has road rage. He is cursing out everyone and calling people the N-word. I sit tall, still, and silent. I keep my eyes wide and looking aware. I make sure my face doesn't come across like I am thinking too much. Truly, I am freaking out on the inside. Tony forced my face into the pillows. The memory of the situation haunts my mind, his cold eyes installed a new type of fear within me. I fear that Tony has the ability to actually kill me. Sometimes he likes to threaten death upon me. I never took him as seriously as I do today. We enter the church parking lot. Tony changes his attitude like a switch. I turn off my overthinking thoughts. I know that I need to keep it together as Tony and I venture into a group of church people. "You better not act out of line," he whispers.

"I won't," I answer him.

We make our way through the lobby. The welcome desk greets us. "God is good!" Tony shouts.

"All the time!" people reply.

I keep a smile on my face as we make it through the sea of churchgoers. Praise and worship begins. I watch over the balcony. I hear Tony's voice on the microphone. "Good morning!" he says to the crowd. "Who is ready to praise the Lord today?" he asks. "Give him a joyful shout!" he states.

The crowd claps their hands and shouts to the Lord. Linda and I sit at the small desk on the side out of the balcony. On a laptop, I watch her begin to put lyrics on the two big screens on each side of the stage. Tony plays the grand piano and sings while the choir follows his lead. I look down over the glass divider.

Below, I can see the entirety of the sanctuary. All the seats are filled, everyone has a smile or an emotional looking face while they lift their hands to God. I look at them and then back at Tony. I can see why people are quick to greet him. He is like a musician with fans. Tony's voice leads people into praising their God. Suddenly, the tempo changes becoming fast paced. Instantly, my eyes shoot to the side of the sanctuary below. Like clockwork, when the tempo changes, Pastor Phil will venture out from a side door that is connected to his office. He has a security guard following. Pastor Phil steps on the stage.

"Praise the Lord." He smiles at the crowd. Everyone remains standing. Pastor thinks he is famous. He claims that now is the best time to be at his church because the ratings of his preaching on the local Christian channel have 'skyrocketed.'

After church, I am tired. I stand by Tony's side and smile. It is torture to have to stand by him and listen to whoever approaches him to talk. In the car, Tony drives in silence. We are five red lights away from Tony's house. At this certain red light, I always watch Tony from the corner of my eye. This red light is near a popular playground. Like clockwork, Tony always stares at the playground. So much so, sometimes I have to tell him that the light is green. I have noticed that when we are in public, Tony likes to stare at other children. The first time I recognized this was at church. A mother let her daughter hug Tony once. After that, every time Tony would see the little girl, he would watch her from afar. Always being beside Tony, I can tell what areas he keeps an eye on the most.

At his house, I prepare myself for whatever mood he is in. "Go into the room and take out your Bible," Tony demands. "Maybe you will learn something about respect," he adds.

I drag myself down the hallway. He follows me. I sit at the desk and move the keyboard aside. Tony slams a Bible down in my face. He opens it to the New Testament. "I will check in on you soon," he states and shuts the door.

I roll my eyes at the Bible. Since getting older, I learned a trick on how to make Tony believe I did my Bible reading. I skim the passage for keywords to use when he asks me to describe what I read. It is so boring. I scan through the passages and write down key words.

Getting bored, I walk over to the mirror. I look at my reflection and begin to cry. A flashback of Tony's rage from this morning surrounds my mind. I finally have time to myself to analyze my thoughts. I feel like he is never going to forgive me. So, I begin to write him a letter.

Dear Tony,

I am sorry I made you late for church. I will get up on time. I will follow the rules. Please forgive me. I want to learn how to stop disobeying you. I am sorry for sinning. I love you so much!!

Love, Maria.

At bed time Tony reads my letter. "I will forgive you this time," he tells me. "However, you need to prove that you really want to obey me," he states.

"I promise, I will," I assure him. Tony cuddles next to me in bed. Slowly, he begins his routine of forcing me into horrid actions with him. After he is satisfied. I lay next to him, ashamed. I hate the way my body naturally reacts to his touch. My body acts like it likes it when my mind is having a horrible time. I am wide awake as I watch George Lopez at 3 a.m. The show helps me laugh after all the things I just performed. Though tonight, I am filled with hatred and anger.

Tony's big, hairy arm lays across my stomach. His arm is so heavy. I will have to use the bathroom soon because his arm is adding pressure on my bladder. I look at his face. He seems to be sleeping peacefully. I wave my hand around and touch his nose. He is fully asleep. It feels like Tony is, sometimes, my boyfriend. I have to always make sure he is happy and satisfied. I ponder about Mariah Carey. She must have loved her ex-husband. I wonder if Mariah stayed up late at night, lying next to him. Staring at him. Wishing she never met him? I slowly lift Tony's arm and wiggle my way to freedom. I lean my back against the wall.

I still can feel what it was like when he smothered me with a pillow. I wonder if he would like it if I did the same to him. Darkness fills my mind. I can't help but imagine what Tony would look like dead. I tilt my head and look at his sleeping body. I imagine him having knives stabbed in his chest and eyes. I stare at Tony's fat neck. There is so much fat if I were to stab him, I probably wouldn't miss. My thoughts are beginning to scare me. Tears, silently, roll down my face. I use my anxiety tool. I touch each of my fingertips on my thumb. But, my impulsive thoughts lead my feet to stand on the floor. Slowly, I turn the golden doorknob and head down the hallway.

I glance in Anna's bedroom. The door is open. I can see Anna sleeping, lying on her back like a vampire. I tiptoe into the kitchen. My mind feels foggy. I reach for a knife. I tiptoe back down the hallway. Tony is in the same spot I left him. I get close to his face and hold the knife up with my hand. I take a deep breath and hover the knife over him. Waving it back and forth with an indecisive mind. I had the guts to think about stabbing him. Now, standing here, I feel like a coward. I hold the knife down to my side. I shake my head with the feeling of defeat. I give up. I do not care what Tony does to me anymore. I do not care what he makes me do or say. Nothing will ever change.

Suddenly, I hear Anna's slippers being dragged across the wooden hallways. I panic, the bedroom door is open and right near the bathroom. I bend down and hide the knife underneath the bed. "What are you doing up?" She catches me awake.

"Coming back from the bathroom," I whisper.

"What is going on?" Tony growls.

"She is up, walking around," Anna states. She shakes her head and goes into the bathroom.

"I was coming back from the bathroom," I state again. I look at Tony. He stands up and looks around the room.

"You better not be doing anything sneaky," he barks.

"I'm not." I climb back into the bed. Tony closes the door and shuts the TV off. He climbs back into the bed. "Go to sleep," he demands. I stare into the darkness. Suddenly, I see a blue magical sparkle. I do not know why I see this blue sparkle. However, it always gives me hope that maybe things will turn out alright?

The next morning, I rise. It is early in the morning. Tony is getting ready for work. "I am going in the shower. Start getting ready," Tony demands. "I need to drop you off at school and get to my job. I might get a promotion, so do not make me late," he adds.

"Yes, sir." I sit up in bed. I feel like a zombie. My eyes feel heavy from silently crying all night. My soul feels like someone blew out my flame. I hear the shower turn on. Quickly, I look under the bed and grab the knife from last night. I walk down the hallway, being sure I do not run into Anna. As soon as I hit the dining room, I run into the kitchen. I put the knife back. I have chills recalling me standing here consumed with the thoughts of harming Tony. Do I still want to harm him? Yes. Will I? No, a small part of me believes I am a good kid. I do not want to be known as a murderer.

I return to the bedroom. I begin to brush my hair. Tony steps into the room and shuts the door behind him. He is dressed in a polo shirt and jeans. He sits down in the wooden chair. "Come here." He pats on the bed. I sit down. Tony begins to cry.

"Are you going to go home and hate me?" he questions. I want to roll my eyes so badly. However, I would get smacked if I showed any ounce of an attitude. Tony begins to sniffle. Every time I go home, he does this crying routine. It used to work when I was younger. However, now it is an annoying routine that I have to act in.

"No, I am not going to hate you," I assure him.

"I am a man of God," he tells me. "Every Sunday, God throws my sin in the sea of forgetfulness," he states. "I hope this is the way you see me, as well." He wipes a tear from his eye.

"Of course, I forgive you just as God forgives us for the sins that we commit," I assure him by placing my hand on his shoulder.

Tony, dramatically, has his smile slowly grow on his face. He is such a phony, I want to call him 'Tony Phony Baloney.' Tony grabs my waist and hugs me. I hear him 'cry' into my ear. "You are the greatest gift God has given me," he whispers.

CHAPTER 14

Enrollment

I am finally a pre-teen. I have been dreaming of being 12 years old. I want to be a teenager so I can wear makeup, hang out with friends, and feel grown. My pre-teenhood has treated me well so far. In middle school, I have realized that I am liked and noticed by others. I am the type of kid who doesn't belong to one friend group. I speak to everyone and create acquaintance relationships. Meaning, people know my name, ask me to sit with them or talk a little bit of gossip. However, I do not have a best friend or a group of friends I hang out with. Perhaps my friendship skills are stained by the amount of times Regina moves us and we switch schools. Also, it isn't helpful that Tony doesn't allow me to hang out with friends on the weekends. The only social time I have outside of school is at Escape to the Arts.

Escape to the Arts is an extension of the YMCA. It is an after-school program for middle school students. I take a bus to the program every day. It has become an actual escape for me. I do rock carving, oil painting, pottery, dance class, and acting! All the things that I always wanted to do bundled in one place. I shine being at this program. My photo has been in the newspaper for the dance program.

I helped paint a mural in the office space and I got the lead role as Dorothy in the program's play for *The Wiz*. My acting teacher, Mrs. Gorgeous, is also the dance teacher. She is an impeccably talented black woman who has professional music and acting experience, so every instruction Mrs. Gorgeous gives I take seriously. She is a tough coach, however, her advice gives me the good type of discipline. We have a close relationship because Shannon used to attend this program. Mrs. Gorgeous is aware of how hectic our household can be.

The school year transitions into summer. Of course, like every summer, I attended Camp Hummocks. Being back in New York full-time doesn't phase me. Why? Well, I am here on the weekends during the school year. Every weekend, Tony forces me to go to church and forces me to engage in horrid sexual acts. Then he sends me home so I can forget about it until the next weekend. This trend has become normal. Although, since the summer has started, every night feels like I am playing the board game, 'Battleship.' Tony is usually predictable on when he will touch me. However, since the beginning of the summer, he hasn't touched me or made me shower with him. I am not sure when he will strike my battleship grid. His routine is off. I am unsure if I did something wrong or if he is testing me to strike first?

At camp, I am a C.I.T., which stands for counselor in training. I feel that I am a good candidate for the job because I have been going to this camp for years. I would love to teach young kids all the camp activities and traditions. Each C.I.T is grouped with senior counselors. I am in the 1st grade girl group called 'The Daisies.' Socially, all my camp friends are C.I.T's as well. After camp, they all hang out. I have attended a few of their hang outs at the mall. However, Tony cut my social times short due to his anxiety of not trusting me in public and out of his sight. For the majority of the summer, I live within the four walls of the extra room at Tony's house. Although, there is one magical event that has happened this particular summer. Since

Tony has always been a fan of Mariah Carey, he took me along with him to 'The Emancipation Of Mimi' tour.

―――

Seeing Mariah Carey in concert, absolutely, was a dream come true. It felt so magical to hear her vocals live. As we know, Mariah Carey is a songwriter. She knows how to sentence together a piece of art. The opening of her concert was the best part of the concert because it opened my mind, yet again. A video of a rollercoaster was the opening. Then a recording of her voice began to speak. To summarize, she explained that life can feel like a rollercoaster ride. There are ups and downs. Twists and turns. Just when life seems to be at the scariest part and we are upside down, everything stops and there is a moment of peace. We realize that whatever doesn't kill us makes us stronger. She ends her speech with, 'If you don't get on the ride, you won't experience the adventure.' Hearing these words opened my mind to a newly founded sense of hope. Just because my life seems scary and jumbled, I have to stay on the ride to experience my adventure. I am 12 years old now. I have dreams of being an independent and sophisticated woman.

After camp, I meet Anna in the art room so I can catch a ride back to Tony's house. We walk up the hallway stairs. I open the door and I see Marcella standing in the living room talking with Tony.

"Marcella!" I smile and greet her with a hug.

"Hello, my love." She hugs me back.

Marcella is Anna's eldest daughter. She and I have bonded over the years. However, Tony warns me not to cling to her. He is very protective over Marcella, calling her his favorite sister. He claims that she has witnessed the pain that their father caused Tony. Marcella has long, thick hair, like Anna. She has light brown eyes, high cheek bones, and an olive skin tone. Adding her raspy New York accent, she reminds me of early Mariah Carey from the 90's.

"What are you doing here?" I say as I look around and do not see any of her children.

"I stopped by to give a late birthday gift to my favorite brother." Marcella smiles at Tony.

"I have heard you have become a woman." Marcella smiles at me. She does a small curtsy towards me. I laugh. She is referring to how I have begun having my period.

"Why, thank you." I smile.

Marcella wraps her arm around me. "How was the Mariah Carey concert?" she asks with excitement.

"Hey, we are gonna go make a pot of coffee?" Anna states.

"Yeah, Ma, I will meet you in there." Marcella smiles and then looks back at me. I love having her undivided attention.

"It was amazing." I smile. "She said life is like riding a roller coaster," I explain.

"That is true, I am so happy you got to see her." She holds her hand above her heart.

"How is camp?" she asks. "You find any boyfriends?" she questions. "Or girlfriends," she giggles. "Hey, you never know," she adds with her New York accent. I giggle and blush.

"No, no, I am just teaching the kids on how to do camp activities." I laugh.

At nighttime, Tony slides into bed next to me, which is normal. He sleeps next to me every night. It is just a matter of when he will strike to touch me. I am still left unsure. I have been facing the wall trying to fall asleep. I feel Tony moving around. I turn over and look at him. His eyes are still shut, there is a slight grin on his face. He seems to be acting like he is tossing and turning. I watch him. He slowly begins to rub and grab himself between the legs. He tugs on his pants. I shake my head. I recall this behavior from when I was younger. He used to pretend to be sleeping and make me touch him until he 'pretended' to wake up to act surprised. Perhaps this is the test I have been anticipating. I am curious as to why he hasn't touched me in a while. I give into what he is baiting for.

I lower my hand underneath his sweatpants. I begin to touch him the way he has trained me to do. Suddenly Tony's eyes shoot open. He grabs my hand and squeezes it hard. It feels like he could break my fingers.

"Ow," I say. Tony looks deep into my eyes.

"That is disgusting!" he growls and tosses my hand back. "You have become disgusting. Don't you ever do that to me again!" He waves his finger in my face. I am speechless. "What makes you think I want to do that with YOU!" He jabs his finger on my cheek. Tony stands to his feet. He leaves the room and shuts the door behind him. Instantly, I begin to cry. What a slap in my face. Him saying, 'Don't you ever do that again,' makes me feel as if I have been the one promoting the sexual acts between us. As if I started all of this. How dare he make me feel horrible. I shake my head in the pillow and squeeze it. I have so much anger built up in me. I want to scream and express myself. I do not have the space to do so.

For the rest of the summer, Tony has changed our sleeping arrangements. I sleep in the bed. He has brought up a twin mattress from the basement. The twin mattress leans against the closet door until nighttime. Watching Tony sleep on a mattress on the floor, then wake up to be a grown man is odd to observe. In his waking hours he walks around as if he floats on water and is favored by God. Tony has not touched me since calling me disgusting. Instead, the new pressure Tony puts over my head is a private school called Grace Hope academy. He wants me to attend the Christian private school that Star enrolled Shannon in. I am not sure about it because I like going to public school. That is where I get to curse and act like myself. I can't imagine the rules that come with going to a Christian school. It would be like going to church every single day.

I pack my bags to head back home for the school year.

"Hey." Tony steps into the bedroom. He pulls up the wooden desk chair. I look at him attentively. "I need to update you on what has been happening in Connecticut," he states. Tony crosses his feet while he sits back in the chair. I prepare myself. Talks like this never end with good news. I am prepared for whatever change is heading my way. "Presley has rented a house for Regina. When I drop you off, it will be at the new house," he states.

A smile comes across my face. "House?" I question.

"Yeah, like a real house. You will have your own room," he explains. "If you are good and make your choices wisely... maybe I will take you shopping to decorate your room," he adds.

Excitement flutters through me. I get to have my own bedroom! This is going to be great.

"Which, talking about choosing decisions wisely..." Tony says. "Have you decided if you want to go to Grace Hope Academy?" he questions.

I take a deep breath. I feel like Tony is giving me the opportunity to speak my truth. "I decided I do not want to go," I state.

Tony shakes his head and rolls his eyes. "Have you not learned nothing from me?" He stands to his feet. "You drive me crazy!" he yells. He begins jabbing his pointer finger on my head. "You are so stubborn," he rants. "You are too busy worried about kissing boys at school to see how Grace Hope can help you," he screams. "You aren't going anywhere until you make the correct decision. This school can help you get into a good college," he rants. "I am willing to pay for a quality education so you don't end up a whore like your fucking mother!!" He storms out of the room.

I take a deep breath. The door slams. I remain on the bed.

I have been here many times before, forced to figure out what exactly Tony wants me to choose. I sit on my bed thinking perhaps it sounds fun to wear uniforms. High quality learning does sound like a smart choice for my future. Tony knows that I desire to be the first in my family to have a career path. I can understand why he seems passionate about enrolling me. Could it be so harmful to switch school once more? I have been doing it all my life. So, I do what I always do to calm him down. I pull out a composition notebook and write him a letter.

Dear Tony,

I am sorry that I upset you. I am grateful about all the things that you do for me. I do want to be successful. I will go to the private school. I want help for my future.

Love, Maria.

I turn the golden doorknob and head into the dining room. Tony is sitting at the table underneath the low light chandelier. He looks up from reading a piece of mail.

"This is for you." I smile and hand him my letter. Tony opens the letter and reads it.

"You are wise to come to an answer quickly." He stands to his feet. "I am so proud of you, Maria." Tony smiles. "Maybe you won't end up spreading your legs around town like your mother... Perhaps, you will be educated enough to go to college and get a degree." He leans in and hugs me.

"Thank you, Tony." I smile back.

In Connecticut, Presley moved my family into a four-bedroom house near downtown Danbury. 8 Barnum Road. The house has four bedrooms and 2 full bathrooms. My sisters, Karina, Selena, and I have never lived in a house that is not shared with an apartment above or below. It is just us. Regina and Presley have a room with a bathroom in it. Karina and Selena share a room. I have my own room with a closet. The fourth room is also Karina and Selena's room.

However, Regina doesn't like the idea of the girls sleeping downstairs alone, so they have their beds in the small upstairs room. Presley gifts the girls with toys and uses the downstairs rooms as their play area.

Presley is a Dominican man. He is very kind and caring. I do not mind that he favors Karina and Selena. I noticed that they do not have someone to spoil them. Shannon has Star that buys her nice things. I have Tony who buys me nice things. Now, the girls have Presley. Presley really cares about his appearance. He wears shiny jewelry and always dresses in designer clothing. He is a man that is particular about his grooming habits, such as shaving his chest hair into different shapes. When Regina is not working, she is either sleeping due to her addiction to painkillers, or she is catering to Presley's every need. The whole house is catered around him. She cleans for him. She even boils live lobsters for him, while we have cereal for dinner. If I am watching TV and Presley wants to watch something, I must let him. I guess that is the sacrifice of the man providing a house for my family.

In my own room, I wake up and look around. I smile as I stand to my feet. I walk across the beige carpet and sit in the purple fuzzy round 90's chair. I have another in pink. Tony kept his word, gifting me with pink and purple room decor. I raise the blinds and look out of the window to look at the sky. I like when I catch the sky slowly transitioning into morning.

"Maria! Are you awake?!" Regina bangs on my door.

"Yes!" I shout. After looking at the sky, I check my phone. I realize I have about 10 more minutes until I actually have to start getting ready. I smile and slip back into my pink and purple sheets. I snuggle my Build-a-Bear teddy and rest my eyes. Moments later, Regina barges into my bedroom. She picks up my purple lamp on my dresser. She flings the lamp.

"Stop!" I shout.

"Get your uniform on Maria!" she yells. Suddenly, Regina slides everything off my dresser. She flips over the small wooden dresser with my Karaoke machine on it. "You are a fucking selfish bitch!" she screams. Regina bends and flips over the mattress I am laying on. "Now you get to clean all this shit up when you come home!" she laughs.

Arriving at Grace Hope Academy, the building is on a huge plot of land. It is a long beige building with three oversized crosses on the front of it. The left side of the building is the church and the right side is the academy. Attending Grace Hope has been interesting so far. It is a small school. Everyone knows everyone and everything about everyone. I have become acquainted with the 14 students in the only 7th grade class. I am slightly popular because I come from public school. However, I do not like how the girls in the class have petty drama. They all bully each other. Every week there is a new issue. I try my best to stay out of their drama but then they bullied me for ignoring them. I can never win within the social circles.

Walking into school, I am greeted by Mrs. Hudson.

"Good morning, Maria!" She smiles. "What a great day the Lord has made," she adds.

I fake smile, I am not a morning person. Especially after the morning I've had with Regina.

"Good Morning, Mrs. Hudson," I say in my natural monotoned voice. My teachers are Mrs. Druid and Mrs. Hudson. They both teach the 7th and 8th grade class because the student count is low. Mrs. Druid is my homeroom teacher. She teaches 7th & 8th grade Literature and History. Mrs. Hudson is the 8th grade homeroom teacher. She teaches 7th & 8th grade Math and Science. The school is very religious and run by a family. The main pastor of the church, Fred, married a woman named Lindsay Zubi. Lindsay and her family have invested into creating and directing the academy side of the building. Lindsay's mother, Mrs. Zubi, is the principal of the school. The school is family owned and dominated by a religion. What could go wrong?

"Alright, everyone!" Mrs. Druid says. She is a tall, fair skinned, German woman. She has short, blonde hair, blue eyes, and a kind smile. "Let's head to chapel early, there are important announcements today," she states.

I look around the classroom. I tend to flock around the three Brazilian girls in the classroom. We have common interests, and their culture is similar to Puerto Ricans'. They like to have fun, dance, be loud and gift people with yummy food. Caroline, Dani, and Mya. Everyone wants to be friends with them. I don't blame them, they are cool and very pretty. However, they like to start drama and watch it unfold between the other girls. That is where I keep my boundaries with them.

"Maria, walk with us," Mya demands.

"Alright." I smile. Mya has long, dark, wavy hair, a perfect button nose, and a gorgeous smile. I might have a slight crush on her. Mya links her arm with mine as we walk. The other girls tag along. Morning Chapel bell rings throughout the academy.

The morning bell rings. Which means 7th-12th graders must report to the church side of the building. In the church sanctuary, we listen to Mr. Z speak. Mr. Z is a tall, lanky man with a brilliant mind. He is the high school history and drama teacher. Also, he is Mrs. Zubi's oldest son. As we walk down the hallway to the church side, we cross over the white school tiles and step on the black marble church flooring.

"Are you a lesbian?" Mya asks me.

"Mya, don't," Tay laughs. Tay has dark skin, her hair curled, and she always smells like expensive perfume.

"It is what we all want to know," Dani laughs from behind us.

"Yeah, that is what everyone is calling you," Caroline says. I snap my head back and stop walking.

"Who started calling me this?" I question.

"Mariel," Mya says. Mariel is a strange girl in my class. Last week she tried to be my friend by following me around at lunch, recess, and gym class.

Entering the sanctuary, the situation with Regina and now news about a rumor fills my soul with anger. Mrs. Zubi is at the head of the podium. She is an old Greek woman from New Jersey. Mrs. Zubi is a wide woman, who wears elaborate 80's pantsuits and a lot of lipstick. We sit down in the theater-like seats.

Mrs. Zubi speaks "Before, my brilliant son begins his morning message, I would like to make everyone aware that there has been a thief among you," she states in her New Jersey accent.

Everyone gasps. "See, here at the academy, we do not have locks on our lockers because we are all Christians," she states. "Thou shall not steal is one of the ten commandments," she adds. "Unfortunately, someone does not abide by God's law." She laughs. "This person has been removed from the academy," she informs us. "That is all, please have a moment to yourself before Mr. Z speaks."

Afterwards, she walks to the back of the room. Students begin to chatter. I look around and see Shannon laughing with a group of her friends. It feels like old times when we used to go to elementary school together. Sometimes I feel like grabbing the microphone and yelling, 'Hi, sissy.' Just to embarrass her for fun.

Suddenly, I hear the laugh of Mariel. I remember Mya telling me that Mariel has been saying I am a lesbian. It upsets me that Mariel has been acting like my friend for the past few weeks. Yes, I did disclose to her that I might have a crush on Mya. However, this school is very religious. They are the type of people who crack jokes and hate on others for being gay. I didn't want to start this new school with a rumor going around about me. Listening to my impulses. I stand up and walk behind Mariel. I wrap her long ponytail around my fist and yank it.

"OW!" she yelps. People around gasp.

"Stop talking about me behind my back," I demand, pulling her hair harder while her back slides on the seat. "If not, I will give you a black eye next time!" I shout. I let go of her hair.

Mariel stands up and shakes her head at me while she holds her ponytail. "You're a bitch," she says and walks away.

As I sit down, everyone is talking about what just happened. Suddenly there is a tap on my shoulder. "Come with me, now!" Mrs. Druid demands. I roll my eyes and follow her. Mrs. Zubi suspends me from school for three days.

I lay on the bed. Wrapping myself in the pink and purple comforter, I hold the cell phone to my ear. Currently, Tony is giving me a lecture on how bad I am making him look to the people at Grace Hope Academy. "Do you know that Mrs. Zubi knows I am a leader at my church in New York?" Tony yells. "I told you not to go to school and make a scene," he shouts.

"I know, I am sorry," I say softly.

"You are lucky that my car broke down today," he informs me. "I want to ring your neck out, I want to make your face turn black and blue," he describes his anger towards me. "You deserve nothing," he shouts and then hangs the phone up. I take a breath of relief that I am off the phone with him. I feel drained. I look around my room. It is still a mess from Regina. I roll over in bed and fall asleep to leave the mess for a new day.

The next morning, I wake up to an empty house. I slept through the rush of everyone starting their day. I walk around the house and act as if I own it. I shower, I cook myself breakfast and watch TV. After relaxing, I roam the house. I like to rummage through Regina's room to read her journal and steal mascara. As I explore, I come across a hollow part of Regina's bathroom cabinet. I reach down and find a Nike shoe box full of small packets of cocaine. It begins to click that Presley is a drug dealer. Curious as to why adults love to do drugs, I take a few bumps. I place the box back where I find it. I begin to feel the effect of the cocaine. Nothing too scary, I just feel very hyper and overly confident. I walk around my room singing Mariah Carey songs as best I can. In my head, my confidence is cheering me on as I attempt to hit high notes. Catching my reflection in my mirror, I laugh at how silly I feel.

The next day, Tony arrives at my house to pick me up for the weekend. He took the train and then walked by foot to our home. I am sure that I have a bag packed and waiting for Tony at the kitchen table.

"Maria!" Regina shouts from the small front porch. I race over with my bag.

"Hi Tony," I say softly. He looks at me with slight anger.

"Let's go," he says.

"Bye, baby I love you." Regina blows her cigarette smoke in the air.

I flash a fake smile. She acts so innocent. As if I forgave her for destroying my room.

"I got my job promotion," Tony says while we sit side-by-side on the train.

"What kind of promotion?" I ask.

"A big one, if I save some money for a few months, I can have a brand-new car in no time," he states. "I am going to be working in New York City now," he says.

"Wow, that sounds very cool," I tell him.

Inside, I have an odd fear. Tony is too calm and acting too normal. I fear for what will happen when he gets me behind closed doors.

We take a cab to his house. Once we get inside, Tony begins giving the silent treatment. The only direction I was given is to 'immediately go to sleep without any TV or video games.' I lay in bed. Tony lays on the mattress on the floor. He turns the TV on.

"Turn over, you aren't allowed to watch the screen," he demands. I do as I am told. Staring at the wall and listening to the TV show. I begin to fall asleep. When suddenly, my eyes shoot open. Time has passed as I lay here. I see the TV is still on. I scan the room and see

Tony sitting at the desk in front of the computer. I gasp at the sight of his genitals being exposed as he touches himself.

"Go to bed," he shouts. I look at his face. He has headphones on. I put the blanket over my head and pretend to go back to sleep. Under the blanket, I panic. I hear Tony moaning and the rubbing noise of his genitals. I am disgusted at what I have discovered. I know what he is doing. However, I just do not understand why he needs to do it next to me while I am sleeping.

I stay still for a while. I peek out from underneath the blanket. Tony is completely focused on the screen. Slowly, I slide down the bed. I act as though I am just moving in my sleep. I lay underneath the covers and peek out from the blanket. I am in alignment with the computer screen. I feel my eyes sink into my head. I see a window open to a chat room with a live camera feed. On the camera I see two little girls and a boy completely naked. Tears rush down my face as I silently cry. I pull a pillow near me and bury my head into it. The noise of his low moans and rubbing of his genitals haunts my ears. Over and over, I can't fall back to sleep with the knowledge of what he is doing. I lay there with my fingers in my ears until he shuts down the computer and goes back to sleep. Whatever he is doing on that computer, I never want to see it again.

CHAPTER 15

Birthday Wishes

October 5th, 2008. The brisk fall evening has the sky looking blue and cold. My family and I continuing to live in the house Presley rents. The house is silent and empty looking. Unfortunately, we are moving again. I walk outside in the backyard. I am wearing a dark purple hoodie, black skinny jeans and stolen eyeliner from Regina's make up bag. I walk through the backyard which is mostly made up of parking lot gravel. Along the way I collect some rocks. I reach the small, sickly looking grass area. Sitting on an old tire, I begin to clear a patch of land from leaves with my Converse sneakers. A few months ago, I decided that I like the fashion within emo-punk girl. I like to act like I do not care about the world and the standards society puts upon us. I can never feel like I reach the standards anyway. So why be like everyone else? Since I am in-tune with my dark, bad chick style, I declared myself a witch. I even told my new therapist I may be a witch. Her response was 'You could be' then she kindly giggled.

I use the rocks to form a circle as if I am performing a spell. As I guide the rocks. I reflect on that there are four more days until my birthday. On October 9th, I will be 14 years old. A lot has changed since my 13th birthday, a year ago. I remember Regina was having a cookout with her and Presley's friends. She ended up having cake for me. It wasn't technically a celebration dedicated for me. I did feel special that she remembered and got me cake. Now this house is just a bunch of memories. Presley has been deported for stashing drugs within the house.

Shannon got informed about the drugs. To teach Regina a lesson, she called the authorities. Regina claims she was happy living in this house. She enjoyed the way Presley treated her.

Since Presley paid most of the rent, we have to move out of the house and into a shelter. I am a bit heartbroken because I enjoy having my own room. Though, I do not blame Shannon for anything. She was looking out for us. No one knows it, but I once did use Presley's drug stash. If I wasn't too careful on that day, I could have mishandled the drug and died. Or what if Karina and Selena found the stash?

I finish the rock circle. I sit back on the tire and begin to bounce my toes in and out of the circle. I begin to sing Happy Birthday to myself, as I do have a few wishes. I wish that I have a birthday cake this year with people who I care about around me. Secondly, I wish that being 14 years old, I can be a normal teenager with a best friend like I see the teenagers have on TV. What I look for in a friend is someone who can take a joke, inform me of interesting information and someone who knows how to just have fun. The evening becomes darker. I head inside the packed-up house. Due to going to the shelter, Regina threw out all my room decor. She claims that it is just extra items to carry. All I have left from my pink and purple room is my sheets and comforter.

Days later, we have moved into a shelter. Regina, Karina, Selena, and I all share a room. Regina and Selena have one set of bunkbeds. Karina and I have the other. I have the bottom bunk, Karina has the top. I lay on the bottom bunk. With the advice from my therapist,

Jess, I have created the space to be used in my favor. Meaning, with the flat sheet from my pink and purple bed set. I shoved the sheet between the wooden planks that hold the top bunk together. This has created for myself a curtain for privacy from Regina. Next, I use the bed set and have placed items like a sketch book under my pillow for easy access.

"Karina, if you weren't so fat, then these jeans would fit you," Regina whines from behind my sheet curtain. I hear Regina slap Karina.

"Hey, stop it!" I stick my head out from the sheet.

"Shut up," Regina snaps. I yank a part of the curtain back.

"No, you shouldn't speak to her like that!" I snap back. A part of my lounge wear is revealed. I am in a t-shirt and underwear. Regina gasps at the sight of my bare legs.

"I hope you don't hang out like that around Tony's house," Regina states.

I shake my head and laugh. "No, trust me Tony isn't like that." I stand to my feet and put on black leggings. *He likes little girls.* A small voice says in the back of my mind. I gasp and hold my mouth. I didn't mean to think that. Plus, Tony hasn't touched me in a year or so. I hate when my mind makes me think of the things he has done to me in the past. I shake off my thoughts.

"Is Shannon really coming to have dinner?" I ask Regina.

"Yeah, the shelter staff is allowing her to come for your birthday." "She should be here now," she explains. I head downstairs. Shannon is talking to one of the staff members in the dinning room.

"Hi, sissy!" I smile and give Shannon an aggressive hug. I miss her so much.

"Happy Birthday, Ria!" Shannon smiles and holds up a small cake. I gasp and examine it. The cake has my name on it and a small pink and purple flower. "I got this with the money I make at my Bed, Bath and Beyond job," Shannon explains.

"I love it, thank you!" I hug her once more.

Regina made a big pot of Puerto Rican style rice, beans, and chicken. She shares it with a few other families staying in the house. Regina suddenly flips the light switch off. Shannon turns into the dining room holding the cake with candle flames flickering. I smile as I hear Shannon, Regina, and the girls sing to me. I stare at my cake. The last time I recall having a cake was at my 10th birthday party that was SpongeBob themed. I shut my eyes. I begin to wish that my 14th year of life will teach me how to be a grown, sophisticated teenager. I blow out the candles. The lights turn back on. Shannon slides her finger across my name on the cake. She keeps our sisterly tradition of putting frosting on the birthday girl's nose. "Ahh, you got me!" I laugh with pink frosting on my nose. Shannon snaps a few photos of us. Perhaps I am a witch. I got to have my own birthday cake, gifted by my sister.

On the weekend, like always, I go over to Tony's house. Tony and I get along well. He checks in on my homework. For my birthday, he gifted me with new video games for my DS handheld gaming console. That is pretty much what life is like when I visit New York. I rot away in the room watching TV, playing video games and, when I am allowed, I research interesting things online. Tony has officially broken me into obeying his every command. Yet, he leaves me alone in this room so often. I have begun to drown in sorrow and unspoken pain. I feel like I live a lonely life. At school, I don't fit in. At home, well, I have no home currently. Karina and Selena like to play Barbies with me. That is about as much social interaction as I get. This is why I yearn for a best friend.

It is Saturday morning, and Tony leaves a note on the dresser mirror. *At church band practice, eat the rest of the cereal in the cabinet.* The note reads. Being a teenager, Tony allows me to choose to stay or go to band practice. I always say no because I like sleeping in. I shower and begin my day. I keep my hair wrapped in a towel as I pour myself a bowl of cereal. I sit at the desk in the bedroom. I check to see if Tony left the internet wire plugged in. Sometimes when he leaves me home alone, he will take the internet cord. Luckily, he left it today. To distract myself, I go online and check my secret Myspace and Facebook account. Unfortunately, everyone is on Facebook now. I liked Myspace. As I scan the desktop for the internet, I see an icon of a cartoon donkey. The icon is always deleted but then appears again. It is called Donkey Mule. The only other person who uses this computer is Tony. I think it is the platform he uses to find inappropriate things of little kids.

I scoff at the icon. Though curiosity leads me into clicking the item, not to look at nasty photos. I wonder if Tony is on the dark web. I click to investigate like a spy looking for an answer. The screen pops up to a layout of files and search bars. I click the search bar. Recent searches pop up below. The horrid things that I read about finding children doing horrid acts. Immediately, I exit the platform. However pop ups begin appearing everywhere on the screen. I shut down the computer tower manually. I never want to investigate any further. It seems that I have my answer. Tony uses a peer-to-peer file sharing platform. I stand up with anger. Sometimes when my thoughts are too quiet I am haunted by the memories of Tony's abuse. However, it is over now. Tony doesn't hurt me anymore. I turn the TV on. I am feeling an overwhelming need to distract myself. I let the TV play as background noise as I plug into my DS gaming device.

Tony comes back from band practice. "Hey," he says walking into the room. He takes his shoes off and sits at the computer.

"Hey." I say mindlessly playing my video game.

"Whoa, what the fuck?" Tony begins to freak. I look up from my game and see the computer screen has pop-up windows everywhere. "Shit, did you go on the computer?" Tony questions.

"What? No," I lie. I did check my social media, however, I am smart enough to erase my internet history. Tony pulls out his blackberry cell phone.

"Hey, Sandra." He smiles. "I am well, remember how I said I might need your expertise on computers?" He chuckles. Sandra is a woman who works in the media ministry at church. She is an older lady who is one of Tony's 'Yes men.' Anything he asks, she is one of the women that will do it. Her and other church women think Tony is handsome and charming. I watch as Tony puts Sandra on speaker. She walks him through on how to reset the system with holding down a few buttons.

After fixing the computer, Tony turns the wooden desk chair towards me. "Are you sure you weren't snooping on the computer?" he asks.

"Yes, sir. I am sure," I state.

"I don't believe you." He chuckles. Tony walks over and flips the light switch off. The room is a bit darker, though daylight slightly shines through. "Tell me the truth," he says. I begin to panic.

"You want me to say something," I state.

"Yeah, tell me," he demands.

"I know what you do on the computer!" I point my finger back at him. He stares at me through the darkness of the room.

"What do I do?" he asks.

"You masturbate," I tell him. Tony nods his head and looks down at his hands. "I do and it is a sin," he states. "At night I sin and watch naked woman," he says. I hold my tongue in fear of triggering Tony to lash out at me.

In the back of my mind, I know my truth. I know what I witnessed that night I saw the computer screen. I know what I just saw on that dark web platform. "God is trying to heal me. I do not need you making fun of me." He sniffles. I stay silent. "Pastor Phil is my counselor," he explains. Every Tuesday, I got to his office at the church," Tony explains. "Just like you have a therapist, I have a pastor to listen to me," he states. "Can I trust you that we can move past this?" Tony asks. I stay silent. "Can we move on from this or do I have to convince you in another way?" he threatens.

"I promise, I throw it into the sea of forgiveness," I lie to him.

"Come, give me a hug," he cries. "Thank you for understanding me." He hugs me. I pat his shoulder and stare blankly in the air.

At church the next morning, I stand in the hallway greeting people by the sanctuary doors. I was offered to help pass out pamphlets to arriving church goers.

"Good Morning, Faith." I smile. Faith is a girl around the same age as me. We briefly hang out during youth group events.

"Good Morning, Maria." Faith smiles. Faith has dark Italian hair, long eyelashes and dark wide eyes. I hand her my last pamphlet.

"Hope you enjoy the service," I tell her.

"Do you ever want to hang out?" she asks me.

"Yeah, that sound fun," I say.

"You know, I always wanted to be your friend. Growing up, I would see you hang out with the deacon's kids," she explains. "I thought you were too cool to approach." She chuckles.

I shake my head, "Oh, please, I am just like you, a normal teenager," I state.

"Hey girls." Lauren, Faith's mom approaches us.

"Mom, can Maria come over and hang out one day after church?" Faith asks.

Lauren smiles at me. She has olive skin, dark hair and eyes.

"You will have to speak with Tony," I inform Lauren.

"Yes, of course." She smiles at me. "He is Italian, like me, perhaps he can come over as well. I would love to make him an espresso." Lauren smiles. I flash a fake smile at her. By the sound of it, she seems pretty eager to have a sit down with Tony.

After church service, Lauren approaches Tony about hanging out after church. Oddly enough, Tony agrees. Lauren and Tony enjoy coffee in her sitting room, while Faith and I hang out learning about each other. Faith says she admires how I am funny and outgoing. Turns out she wasn't lying, she really wanted to be my friend. Faith's house is filled with high quality living decor. She has a silver double-door refrigerator. I was amazed at how the refrigerator could also produce ice and water at the push of a button. I enjoy learning how middle-class families live. However, I was taken aback when Faith's father appeared from the basement. Apparently, he lives down there. He and Lauren secretly aren't on good terms. I acknowledged and observed that no matter what type of income bracket people live in, there are always some type of family issues going on behind closed doors. For the rest of the hang out, we sat on her couch playing guitar hero with her little brother.

I go back to the shelter for school on Monday. I wake up and wait to be next for the shared shelter bathroom. After, I get dressed in my uniform.

"Oh my god!" Regina says, flipping her phone shut. Seems like she just got some type of news. She shakes her head and adjusts her glasses.

"Julian just got arrested for touching Shannon and giving her weed," she states.

"What?!" I am shocked. I sit on my bed trying to comprehend the news. Regina moves on from the moment. She acts as if she didn't just shake my world view on my father. This whole time Shannon has been going to boxing with Julian and visiting his apartment, he was abusing her and giving her drugs.

At school, my morning has been rough. I have been snippy with everyone that even looks at me. The chapel bell rings. Students begin to pile into the hallway.

"Maria, can I speak with you?" Mrs. Hudson asks. Being in 8th grade, she is my homeroom teacher.

"What's up?" I ask her.

"Why are you being really mean today?" she asks.

I look her up and down. "I am not being mean, everyone here is just dumb," I state.

Mrs. Hudson chuckles. "Come on, I know you too well," she says. Mrs. Hudson and my relationship has been crossing boundaries lately. It all began when she wrote me a letter after noticing I have been acting emo. After her first letter, we just kept exchanging letters talking about depression, how to help cure it and also I tell her how much I cannot stand living with my mother in a shelter. I open up to Mrs. Hudson about the news of my father.

"Oh, sweetheart," Mrs. Hudson pulls me into her arms. She kisses the top of my forehead. Her embrace feels so safe. Though, I know it isn't healthy for me to hold on to her for too long. She isn't a family member nor my mother. Just a woman who has empathy for what I am going through.

Mrs. Hudson reaches for a sticky note on her desk. She writes, *"For the joy of the Lord is my strength.* "Here, this is something that helps me through a tough day." She smiles. I look at the note that is written in perfect script.

"Thank you." I smile and begin to head out of the classroom. Instead of going to chapel, I have been hiding in the bathroom. The last stall to the left is the big handicap bathroom. I like to sit in the furthest corner of the stall. I sit in the corner and look at the sticky note. I place it beside me on the floor. I dig in my bright red cardigan pocket and pull out a handheld pencil sharpener. I open the sharpener and pull out the loose razor. I roll up my sleeve and begin to cut my arm. I take a deep breath with relief. Cutting myself is a secret I have been carrying. It feels so refreshing to feel something. I walk around so numb. I feel like a smoker who finally gets their 15-minute smoke break. A small slice of pain. I like to admire the blood as it drips out of the cut. This is becoming addictive.

As the small amount of blood drips out, I glance at the sticky note. I roll my eyes and use it to soak my blood. I roll my eyes. If the Lord wanted to give me joy, wouldn't he have already done it? I hate how everyone tells me to trust and believe in God. If God exists then why am I experiencing such a horrible life? I feel hated by the people who are supposed to love me the most. How could my father hurt Shannon the way that he did? I hope she is alright. I know that Star will always protect her no matter what.

CHAPTER 16

In Plain Sight

The day before Christmas Break, I receive a letter back from Mrs. Hudson.

Dear Maria,

I hope you have a great Christmas. I used to be depressed because I had a daughter who died when she was young. It made me think God hated me. I really wanted to kill myself. I tried to throw myself out of a window. If you ever need to speak about anything please feel free to come to me. I have learned that speaking about it is the best way to heal from depression. I seek out my own friends, families or pastors if I need to speak with someone.

Merry Christmas! If you need anything over Christmas break, my email is below.

Love, Mrs. Hudson

I lay in bed reading this letter over again. Mrs. Hudson has a son and daughter that go to Grace Hope. It is interesting to hear that she had another child. I stare at the white ceiling. A few months ago, the last shelter we were in told us our contract was up. During the time at the shelter, Regina has been saving her money. Instead of saving up for a new apartment, Regina has been saving all her dollars and coins so she can move us to the Dominican Republic. She claims she is deeply in love with Presley and cannot stand being so far apart from him. So Regina moves us into another shelter around town. This shelter is called the Amos House. Fun fact about this place. This shelter is the place where Regina was living when I was born. Apparently, I slept in a dresser drawer padded with sheets and blankets.

Living at the Amos house has actually been a bit better than the last shelter. The only rooms that were available were the single resident rooms. The Amos house goes above and beyond to help families in need, so, they gifted us with being able to live within two of the small rooms. Regina, Selena and Karina share a room. I have my own room. Having my own room comes with a perk. The shelter has also given me a rule. They said that I must reside on the premises since I am taking up one of the single bedrooms. They declared that I can only go to New York every OTHER weekend. They claim it doesn't look good to other residents if I am allowed to only live here during the weekdays. Having a break from Tony's house seems like a blessing. I do not have to go to church nor listen to all his overwhelming rules. The only thing I miss is my DS gaming device. Tony only allows me to have my iPod touch. Wi-fi isn't a normal thing to have yet, so I can barely connect to the internet. I enjoy wasting away in the room while listening to music or playing an app game.

In this room, I have no mirror, no TV, no computer. Just the four white walls, a dresser, a bed and a big wooden wardrobe. I have all my Mariah Carey songs on my iPod. I even use the wardrobe as a fake 'recording studio' when I want to sing along to Mariah Carey and try to hit her notes. I bring my blanket and pillow inside it to add 'sound proofing.' Singing, for me, helps release tension built up in my throat. If I am feeling really angry or sad, I use the wardrobe to hide. I like to put my music on blast and scream into my pillow.

———

The shelter has ordered me to stay home for Christmas break. So far break has been going well. Regina works. I watch Karina and Selena. I like to play with them, either Barbies or pretend acting school. I even give them singing lessons. Presley's family gifted Regina with a used computer. Regina keeps it in her room to watch DVDs on. They also gave her a small video camera. I used the camera and wrote a small horror film with Karina and Selena for their 'acting school' requirement. We then rallied up the other children in the shelter to be in it. They are on Christmas break too. I filmed the movie. A boy named, Jaylen, was the ghost that haunts the shelter. Karina, Selena and Mecca were the residents that the ghost haunts. I used the movie editing program on the computer. I realized that from all those years of watching Linda edit film for the church service, I understand how to edit video clips.

The holidays at shelters always meant an overload of donations. The staff lets us rummage through the donations. The book donations really caught my attention. I came across a few that I enjoy. One book is about witchcraft and spirituality. The other is a book called *Twilight*. In my room at the shelter, the fluorescent lighting bouncing on the white walls hurts my eyes, so I hide in the wardrobe with my pillow and blanket. I leave the door cracked open for light to guide as I read the book on witchcraft and spirituality. This book has opened my mind in so many ways. It shines light that the world is full of energy and it is not ruled by just one God. In fact, many believe in various other Gods and Goddesses. This book reminds me of when my Abuela would talk about good and evil energy, which makes me reflect on the question, am I good or am I evil? I have convinced myself that the Devil is my friend. I mean, I cut myself. Sometimes when I cut myself I ask the Devil to just take me while he can.

After the New Year, 2009 is off to a weird start. I begin it with a therapy session with my A.P.R.N. I sit at a round table across from Jess. "How was your Christmas break?" Jess asks.

I look up at her soft blue eyes and long, black, blown out hair. Jess is so pretty, I am aware that I have a slight crush on her.

"I created a movie with the kids in the shelter." I smile.

"Oh, that is great, I know you always have a lot of ideas that float around in your mind." She smiles.

"Yeah, maybe one day when I am older, I can be a filmmaker," I say.

"Well, look at that!" Jess quickly stands to her feet. She grabs a purple hand mirror and hands it to me.

"Not the mirror." I roll my eyes.

"Look at it," she giggles. I pick the mirror up and look at myself. It is an exercise Jess has taught me. To look at myself when I feel sad or happy. "I look...kind of happy." I tell her.

"You were excited about a dream and goals," she states.

I place the mirror down on the table. "I am surprised I still have those." I laugh and push a piece of hair behind my ear.

"Hey, can I see your arm?" Jess looks startled.

"Why?" I panic.

"I thought I saw something," she says.

Jess stares at me with her beauty. Her gorgeous energy comforts me into opening up to her. I pull up my sleeve and show her my arm.

"Oh my." She examines my scabs. "You even carved words?" Jess says holding my hand.

Quickly, I pull my hand away and cover up my mess. "Now, you have to report me...huh?" I cross my arms and look away from her.

"Well, I am concerned," she states. "I am going to have to tell your mother and Tony," she states.

A tear rolls down my eye. I feel so stupid for that moment of feeling safe with Jess.

"Speaking of, I had a talk with Tony," Jess states. "He told me that you don't want to come back to therapy with me," she explains.

I sit up straight in my chair, shocked. "What, that is not true!" I exclaim.

"Maybe he had a misunderstanding?" Jess asks.

"Yes, for sure," I say.

Jess tilts her head at me, she leans in and places her hand under her chin. "Is there anything that you want to speak about?" she asks.

"No, I did enough speaking for today," I pout and fold my arms.

"Alright, well let's go rip the band aid off." Jess stands to her feet. The band-aid is breaking my cutting news to Tony.

I follow Jess downstairs, and she whispers as we walk. "I will tell Tony that you want to continue seeing me." She smiles.

I nod my head in agreement. We reach the staircase to the waiting room.

"Hi, Tony." Jess smiles while she greets him in the waiting room. "Maria is all set and I spoke with her. She would like to continue working with me," she adds.

Tony smiles, "Alright, great, she will see you next time." He stands to his feet and shakes her hand.

"Actually, could I speak with you?" Jess pulls him aside.

"Thank you for bringing this to our attention, I will be sure to let Regina know," Tony states. "Come on, love." Tony wraps his arm around me. He pats my back as we walk out of the building.

Tony and I walk to his new SUV, a black Ford Edge. I get in the passenger's seat. Tony begins to drive, his silence keeps me on edge.

"So, you are hurting yourself?" Tony questions.

"Yeah," I state plainly.

"You are just so dumb." He shakes his head. "How much attention do you need?" he asks. "You are lucky Jess doesn't report your mother to the authorities," he informs me. "You are fine, you are not depressed, you are just acting to piss me off." Tony continues to rant.

"I know, I am sorry, Tony," I say softly.

"If you continue this behavior, I will be sure you get locked up in the mental ward," he warns me. "And I will not help you out," he adds.

"No, please don't do that," I beg.

"Show me your arm!" he demands. I reveal my scabby arm to him. As he drives he glances at my arm with disgust. He flicks my arms away. "I swear you are going to end up giving me a heart attack," he scoffs. "I am tired of living every day in fear of what you will do next," he sighs. I stay silent. I sulk in my own shame and pit of despair.

At church, I am dressed in a dark pink shirt with skinny black jeans and a purple schoolboy flat hat. I follow Tony to the back offices. As I walk, I scan the church members looking for a girl named Gia. She is one of the church worker's daughters. She is widely known within the church. All the youth group girls look up to her because she is so popular. There have been rumors going around about a church helper sexually assaulting Gia. Apparently, He became friends with Gia's mother. She trusted him to be Gia's guardian on a field trip. The rumor is that on the field trip he was taking inappropriate pictures of Gia and her friends. Gia hasn't come to church since the rumors. All the youth group gossip is claiming that it is the church helper that has big ears. Walking through the church, I see a man with big ears. He enters the sanctuary.

"That is him!" I state.

"Huh?" Tony looks down at me.

I am horrified at why he thinks he can show his face around here. I turn to Tony. "What's wrong?" he asks.

"That is the guy who hurt Gia." I point.

"Stop it." Tony widens his eyes with anger.

"Tell him to leave!" I demand of Tony.

"Do not point at people when you are standing next to me," he states. "You leave that man alone," he warns me.

"Why is he here?" I ask.

"He is here because Pastor asked him to be," Tony states.

"So he is the one that hurt Gia?" I ask.

"He didn't hurt her, he is just misguided," Tony whispers. "Enough of this, go to youth group and do not think about telling anyone about this," he states. "If I begin hearing people talk about this man, I will know it came directly from you," he explains. "I will ground you from everything if you start any trouble," he adds.

"Yes sir," I say.

I step into the youth group room with a mean mug. I secretly hate coming to youth group.

"Hello Maria." Serenity smiles and hugs me.

Serenity is a fair skinned woman with light brown curly hair and green eyes. She and I have begun to bond. Tony, of course, painted my story to Serenity as soon as he noticed us becoming close. It seems that he painted me as having behavior issues because I grew up in the projects. Just like he tells everyone, he told her he has been trying to raise me to follow Jesus. "

Hey, Serenity." I smile and hug her back.

"OO, I love this purple hat." She smiles. "Miss Diva always looks so fashionable." She laughs. I faintly smile and then keep my mean mug.

"Ut oh, what is wrong..." she questions.

"Everyone is dumb," I state.

Serenity laughs. "That is your favorite line to say," she giggles. I press my lips together to hold in a giggle. "Listen, we are gonna be playing a Bible game today. Try not to crush them too hard." She jokes but is also serious at the same time. Every time we play a Bible game, I know every answer. This is because the Bible has been shoved down my throat at school and with Tony.

"I'll try to play fair." I smile.

"Maria, sit with me!" I hear Faith in the middle of the room.

After youth group, Faith and I stand in the hallway with our other friends we've made, Diamond and Kalisha. Diamond and I have been friends since we were in children's church. Diamond has big brown eyes, dark skin and her hair is in a ponytail with side bangs. Diamond is very skilled in dancing. She and I are actually working with Serenity on a dance routine for an upcoming performance for the youth group. Kalisha has almond brown eyes, dark skin and her hair is always in a fun style. Today she has short box braids. I have a secret crush on Kalisha. She has an African accent. Her parents are the first generation from Rwanda. I love when she jokes with me or debates my ideas in her accent. Although, her mother is very stern so I try not to be a trouble maker around her. I want her mother to like me.

"Are we going out to Dunkin?" Faith asks Kalisha.

"Yes, I want to," Kalisha answers.

"Maria, can you please come this time?" Faith asks.

"Listen, if your mother asks Tony... maybe he will say yes."

Faith and the other girls all hang at a close-by Dunkin Donuts. Franky, Faith's younger brother joins us. I feel very aware and excited to be finally having social time with teens my age. We sit at a separate table from Lauren and Tony.

"They seem to be very happy over there." Kalisha giggles. The girls start pointing out that Tony and Lauren seem to have a spark. They are laughing and glaring into each other's eyes.

"Oh stop, my mother is married," Faith says.

"Daddy sleeps in the basement," Franky reveals.

"Franky, stop." Faith rolls her eyes. I press my lips together. I look at Diamond and Kalisha. We did not want to open that can of worms. They move on from the subject. I sneak a peek at Tony. He does seem to be having a good time. *How can he be into Lauren if he is into little kids?* I question in my mind. I shake my head, again the small voice in my head. Always bringing up this subject.

CHAPTER 17

Suffering in Silence

The spring of 9th grade has been tough. Jess, my therapist, has prescribed me with anti-depressant pills. I take my anti-depressant with my Ritalin. The two medications make me feel foggy. I wake up and begin to walk to the bathroom. Regina moved us into a one-bedroom apartment. Within the last months, we overstayed our welcoming at the Amos house shelter. So, with the money Regina has been saving, she decided to use some of it. We got a cheap apartment in Waterbury, CT.

As I walk through the small living room, there are suitcases and bags of new clothing all around. Regina is preparing to leave in a few weeks. I have yet to decide if I am going with her. A part of me wants to go and live in a new land. However, I hate for it to be with Regina. I cannot imagine living with her anymore. I have reached the stress level of how Shannon felt before she moved out at 16. Regina has an impossible cycle of ignoring her children and using all her love, attention, and money on having a boyfriend. I am at a peak of realization. Why would I follow Regina?

I enter the bathroom and watch myself brush my teeth. I try and smile at myself, however, a spark in me is dim. I look like myself, yet, I can't recognize myself. I feel disgusting and worthless.

"Did you take your medicine?" Regina asks as she steps into the dingy bathroom. She opens the small washer and dryer set.

"I will." I roll my eyes.

"Stop with your damn attitude," she says as she switches out the laundry. I finish brushing my teeth and walk beside her.

"Just shut up, I hate looking at your fucking face," I scoff. Suddenly, I hear Regina's footsteps behind me.

"Come here you little bitch," she yells.

I run into the bedroom. Regina tries to squeeze through the door, I push back causing her to stay on the outside. In the car, Regina hotboxes us with her cigarette. Karina and Selena sit in the back seat. They still attend school in Danbury because Regina used a friend's Danbury address. I sit in the front seat and cover my nose with my red school uniform shirt.

"Can you roll the windows down?" I demand.

Regina turns up the Spanish music volume. I scoff and try to roll the window down, but she locked them.

"Come on, that isn't funny," I snap.

"It isn't funny that I am always late to work because you have to start with your attitude every morning," she rants.

I aggressively tap the window button.

"You are going to break the button!" Regina cries.

"It doesn't matter, this car is cheap," I say.

"I am going to try to sell it before I leave the States," Regina says as she drives on the highway. I look back at Karina and Selena in the backseat. They sit quietly and listen to the radio.

"Good, go be happy with your boyfriend," I say. "You can leave but I am not going with your crazy ass." I fold my arms and lean over towards the window.

"Fuck you, then," Regina scoffs. The rest of the car ride is silent.

I walk into my 9th grade homeroom. There are only four classrooms that make up the whole high school. Each teacher teaches a subject while 9th-12th grade classes rotate throughout the day. Dr. Green is the high school math teacher. He has fair skin, white hair, and always dresses like a 90's dentist. He is annoying because he brags about his degrees and side inventions that he is creating. He always bores me, and I try my best to not fall asleep when he teaches. High school is a blur. Every day, I try my best to ignore everyone. I only speak to my peers if I am trying to crack a joke. By now I am conditioned to not feel hopeful that I will fit in with everyone. I do not care if they accept me or not. What I care about is making it through the day so I can go home and lay down. I would rather disappear within my mind than interact.

After school, Star picks me up. Star moved recently. Her new apartment is near Grace Hope Academy. She lives in a one level condo complex. She has two bedrooms at the end of the hallway. Star is getting a bit older, and it is easier for her to not have to climb up stairs.

"Shannon, we are home!" Star shouts as she sits at the kitchen table. I sit on the bench side of the table. She begins to shuffle through the mail.

"Oh hi, Maria!" Shannon smiles. I greet her with a big hug. Since I found out about Julian's abuse towards Shannon, every chance I see her, I try to make it memorable. Though, I avoid bringing it up. I am not sure how to speak on the issue. I am glad she is safe with Star and doing better. Shannon dropped out of High school and is working at Star's family's country club in New York.

I change out of my uniform. We begin to take pictures on a digital camera. After, Shannon and I catch up.

"So, have you been getting my texts?" Shannon asks. I tilt my head and roll my eyes.

"You haven't texted me in forever," I say.

"Um, I know that isn't true. I tried to text you last night and then these other two days." Shannon holds up her phone as she scrolls through her texts to my contact. "Does Tony go on your phone?" she questions.

"Well, he has the password to my Facebook," I randomly state. I am beginning to get nervous. I am trying to figure out the correct words to perhaps alarm Shannon that she is on the right track.

"Yeah, I heard you post inappropriate photos on there," she states.

"Well, no, I just feel confident in them." I defend myself.

Shannon chuckles. "Well, next time, answer my text," she demands. I grab Shannon by the arm.

"Seriously Shannon, I didn't know that you texted me," I stare into her eyes. There is a knock on the door.

"Come in!" Shannon hollers.

Tony steps into the bedroom. "Hey, I brought some Chinese food," he informs us. "I am starving, I had to work all day." Shannon stands to her feet. I follow her to the dinner table.

As we eat, Star and Tony are discussing how he will drive Regina to the airport on the 1st of April. "Ha, almost seems like an April fools joke." I laugh.

"So, are you going to tag along with Mommy Dearest?" Star asks. I look up from my food. Everyone has been waiting for my answer.

"Yeah, she finally decided," Tony comments, putting me on the spot. He has done this on purpose. Tony has been begging me to come live with him in New York. He has been repeating the same three promises to me over and over again. He has been pressuring me with the following list of *convincing* ideas.

Idea 1: "If you stay, I will let you join the high school drama club. I know you want to be in the school play."

Idea 2: "With all your built up anger, do you think it is

healthy to live in another country with your mother? You can't escape her by coming to my house."

Idea 3: "In a few years, you will graduate. Maria, if you stay I will help pay for your college. You can get a part time job, live at my house and go to college here in New York."

The mixture of these ideas play around in my head. I know how angry Tony can get if I do not comply with his demands. I look up at Star. "I will be staying here in the states with Tony," I answer.

"Ain't it a shame." Star shakes her head. "Maybe time away from her will bring healing," Star adds.

"That is what I have been telling her," Tony adds. I keep a smile on my face, although Tony has never stated that time apart will bring healing. He is just trying to kiss Star's ass. "Now Maria will be able to join the drama club." Tony winks at me.

Shannon smiles in my direction. "I always heard the drama club was fun," Shannon states. She no longer attends Grace Hope due to a group of rich girls bringing booze in the prom, them blaming it on Shannon.

"Me too. I want to be in the plays," I state.

"Well, now you can be." Star smiles.

April 1st. It is 6:30 in the morning. Tony drives Regina to the airport. I sit in the back seat with Karina and Selena. I watch them sleep. I am going to miss living with them. I begin to pray that they have protection for a safe flight. Regina says that once she can call me, she will. With all the hate that I feel towards my mother, I have realized that it stems from a passion of waiting to be seen and loved by her. In the book, I read about witchcraft. It taught me that we are all connected through energy. Having an intention can fill energy with specific meaning. Today, I do not want to send my mother off with anger and hatred. What if she never comes back? To hold the energy of my mother, I brought along my teddy bear. I want to capture her energy and hold it within my bear.

Standing in the JFK airport parking garage, Regina hugs me goodbye. "I will miss you," she tells me.

"Me too," I whisper.

"Don't cry, Tony will take good care of you. He always has," she says. I look over to Tony watching our interaction. I make sure I smile in agreement to Regina's statement. Deep inside, I wish Regina would just grab my arm and demand I go with her. Why isn't she saying, 'This is my daughter, wherever I live she is coming.' She is completely content to be walking away from me.

"Wait, can you hug my bear?" I ask, holding out my bear dressed as a cheerleader. Regina nods her head. She grabs the bear and gives it a tight hug.

"Bye, Mommy." I wave. I hug Karina and Selena goodbye as well. Suddenly, Selena grabs the bear and hugs it. Karina copies her. I hold my tears in as I say goodbye to the last of my family.

On the ride back to Tony's house, I sit in the front seat.

"Well, it is official…You are living with me," he says. "If your school asks, tell them that Regina left me with temporarily guardianship," he explains. "I have the papers signed," he adds.

I nod my head, I could care less about what he has. I just want to be at the house so I can lay down. I look at Tony. I raise my flag. Tony has won. Living with him full-time means I have no more privacy. I need to always be alert on following the rules.

"Can I recline the seat?" I ask Tony.

"Yeah, it's fine," Tony says. I relax on the tilted seat. I pull my teddy bear close to me and rest my eyes.

Living with Tony has become a blur. I am on robot mode. I live the day numb. My coping mechanism is disassociation. At school lunch period, I usually sit alone. For the past few days two 10th grade boys, Chad and Sean, have been joining me. Sean has fair skin and a long nose. He is obsessed with talking about investing his family money into fishing. Chad is a mixed boy. White and Puerto Rican, like me. Chad used to date one of the girls I am kind of friendly with. Though, he has been giving me compliments every time I see him. I think Chad is cute. He has a button nose, blue eyes and flat brown hair.

"Chad, Jennifer keeps Facebooking me," Sean says. "She wants to fuck, real bad," he adds. "Might take her in the locker room." He laughs. I widen my eyes as I eat my chicken nuggets.

"Is that what all those girls be doing?" I laugh. I have learned to distance myself from girl drama. They are all bullies.

"Are you gonna add her to your list?" Chad asks.

"List?" I question.

"We have a sex list." Chad smirks.

"Chad said you are the hardest girl to be put on the list," Sean blurts out.

I do a double take at him. "You and that bubble butt." Chad licks his lips. I laugh. I can't deny it, I like the attention I am getting from Chad

"Well, you are kind of ugly," I joke with him.

"I have Spanish flavoring, you wouldn't be able to say no to me." He smiles.

I roll my eyes, "You ego is too big." I laugh.

"Yeah, it is as big as my dick." He high fives Sean.

I laugh at his dumb joke. "Who is on your list?" I ask Chad.

"I got a few people from this school," he says. "No one with a butt like yours." He laughs and places his hand on my thigh. His hand is light and gentle as he runs it up my leg. I get a chill.

"Do you have play practice today?" Chad asks.

"How do you know I go to play practice?" I question. I move his hand away.

"I am around after school. My baby brother goes to the church daycare," he explains. "I peek into the sanctuary and see you practicing," he admits.

"Yeah, I have play practice," I tell him.

"You should meet me in the hallway, then." He winks at me. I smirk.

I meet Chad in the hallway. Why? Well, I only tried to have sex with a boy one other time. Regina was working at a dentist next to a Burlington Coat Factory. Since I used to go to her job after school, I told a boy to meet me at the clothing store. We tried sexual things in the dressing room. Though, I chickened out due to flashbacks of Tony. I am ready to try again. Chad wraps his arm around me.

"Let's go chill in this space." Chad smiles, opening a door in the hallway.

"This is the children's church room," I state.

"Yeah, but it's empty and dark," he says.

"Oh." I pick up on what he is trying to say. We enter the dark room. The children's church has colorful set pieces around. We find a spot and begin to make out. Chad lays me on the floor. I pull down my pants and take a deep breath.

"You are so hot." Chad hovers over me. I feel him inside me. I am calm until I begin fighting my mind. In the dark room, Chad begins to remind me of how Tony used to hover over me to grab my body.

"Wait," I say and wiggle around. "Hold on, stop." I try to pull back.

Chad begins adding pressure on my arms. I yank my body and turn over. "Oh yeah, turn over!" Chad shouts. He holds down my lower back and continues. I use my forearms to drag myself away from him.

"I said wait!" I stand to my feet and pull my pants up.

"That was about 50 seconds." Chad laughs. "Consider yourself on my list," he states and heads out of the room. I stand there in shock and embarrassment. I just can't seem to make the right decisions.

Tony is right, I am stupid. I am going to end up a whore, just like my mother. I rush out of the room and run down the hallway. In the bathroom, I hide in my favorite stall to cry. This is all my fault. I should have foreseen him just waiting for me to be on his sex list. I wipe my tears and head into play practice.

After practice, Sandra from Tony's church picks me up. Sandra is an older woman with short red hair and wrinkly fair skin. She works in the media ministry at church. Basically, she is the new Linda because Linda left the church. Sandra works near my school, so she offered to help Tony out by picking me up from my play practice.

"How was practice?" Sandra asks as I get in her car.

"Great." I fake smile.

As we drive, Sandra does not stop talking. "You know that I work at a school for children with behavioral diagnosis?" she asks.

"Yeah," I say. "Well, it is a great school, a few celebrities bring their children," she adds. For the rest of the trip, I remain silent. I am too focused on what happened between Chad and me.

The next day, I sit in Jess's office after school. "What is going on with you today?" she asks me.

"Nothing," I say. Jess pressed her lips together.

"You aren't usually this quiet." Jess nervously laughs. "Your stare is a bit scary today," she adds.

"I had sex with a boy at school," I tell her.

"How did that go?" she asks.

"He added me to his list," I say plainly. "He has a sex list, I foolishly fell for him," I state.

"Did you say stop?" she asks.

"Yeah..." I say softly. "He stopped after I dragged myself away from him." I state.

"That is rape," she states. "You could tell your school or report him to the police," she says.

"No, that will cause too many problems," I say.

"Maria, if he is going around saying he has a list imagine who could be next?" Jess states.

I agree for Jess to invite Tony up to her office. She explains everything that I just told her. In the meeting, Tony keeps a concerned look on his face. In the car, he is silent. I predict he will erupt soon.

Which is exactly what happens as soon as we step into the bedroom. "Crying rape, this is extreme," Tony whines. He shuts the door behind him. "Are you trying to make a statement?" he asks.

"No" I say.

"I swear, you are really going to make me drop dead one day," he screams. Tony begins to shake me by the shoulders. "Why can't you just be normal, Maria?" he yells in my face.

"Stop it," I shout, trying to break free from his grip.

Tony shoves me backward on the bed. "Oh, I could just kill you right now!" Tony grabs my face between his fat fingers. He squeezes my face, and I can feel my jaw tightened by his pressure. "Let me just snap your neck right now." He begins turning my face.

"NO!!" I scream and hit his hands. I turn my body and pull myself up the bed. "I hate you!" Tony screams.

Tony takes a step back. "Why? Why do you hate me?" I ask him.

"You bring out the worst in me," he huffs. "Sometimes I can't even stand looking at your face!" he adds.

I look down at my hands. I have nothing left to say. "You are going to fix this before any of your family members find out," Tony demands. "You really are trying to challenge me," he laughs. I have no clue of what he means. "You aren't going to win," he adds. "I am taking you to the police station, you will give a statement but will NOT press any charges," he explains. "Then we will bring a copy to your little therapist so she knows I handled it," he adds.

"Yes sir," I say softly.

"If you know what is good for you.... do not come near me for the rest of the night," Tony warns. I feel like Tony wants to kill me so badly. It seems like he lacks courage to do so. However, I am going to assume that one day he could snap and really take me out.

Before school the following day, Tony takes me down to the

police station in New Milford, Connecticut. Tony sits next to me as I explain what happened between Chad and I. The policeman wrote everything down. I sign my statement and assure the police officer I do not want to press charges.

CHAPTER 18

It's Just a Shirt

I survived my sophomore year of high school. This past year, I made sure I did not cause Tony any stress. I accomplished this by detaching myself from the people around me. I figured this way, I won't get in any type of situation that may cause me to misbehave. It has been working.

I live in-between reality, depression and Tony's brainwashing. It is a Saturday afternoon. I am in the living room with Anna and her granddaughter, Molly. Molly is three years old. She has a cute babyface, big brown eyes, and she loves to sing. Anna encourages her to scream around the apartment. I play with Molly in the living room. Under Anna's couches are her children's 80's child toys. Most are wooden block toys of communities. Molly and I build a community with the wooden trees and buildings. Molly begins to sing and belt her singing notes. *Here we go...* I think to myself and look up at Anna. Anna is knitting while she relaxes in the recliner.

"Isn't she good?" Anna asks.

"Very." I smile.

"She reminds me of when Tony was little. He would walk around singing and playing his guitar," she explains. "Then, of course, his prick of a father would shut him down for being too loud." She rolls her eyes.

I tilt my head as I receive the information Anna is giving. I recall Tony telling me he hates his father. He claimed that his father was abusive towards him. In the detective part of my mind, I begin to open the case file of Tony. I know a lot of things about him. I am adding that, his father truly was a prick, to the list.

"Now look at my son, singing on stage at a popular church," Anna says. "He can get discovered and become the next Michael W. Smith," she adds while she talks and knits. I nod my head as I listen to Anna. Now I understand why Anna is obsessed with watching Tony sing at church. To her perspective, she is seeing her son's dream coming true, which explains why Tony is obsessed with keeping his image clean. He thinks he has stardom.

After the weekend, I head back to school. My 11th grade teacher is named Mrs. Milano. Fun fact, she is an ex-marine. Mrs. Milano has fair skin, dark red thick hair and green eyes. Mrs. Milano and I have made a connection. I have a habit of clinging to grown women that give me attention. Who could blame me, we are all looking to be witnessed someway in life. Mrs. Milano encouraged me to join her cooking class during our extracurricular block. Since joining her class, I have seen more of a softer side of Mrs. Milano. She is funny, charming, and wise. I even opened up to her about Regina moving away. She has a very hands-on approach when we cook. I find it calming to dig my hands in a recipe and watch it turn into a dish. Also, her daughter, Angelina, is in her cooking class. I love watching their mother-daughter dynamic. They both have a sarcastic flare to their relationship. Random thought; when I have children, I want to be close with my child like they are.

Today is dress down day. Dress down day is a special event here at Grace Hope Academy. If you pay the school $1, you are allowed to wear regular clothing to school. As if parents don't give the school enough money. All the girls in my class have been planning for this day by discussing outfits. I am wearing light jeans. I was wearing a blue shirt. However, I have changed into my new shirt that Shannon got me. It is a cream color shirt with a white tiger on it. The shoulders have slits in them with a small flare on the end of the seams. Lately, I have noticed that I have gained weight because it is a side effect of my new anti-depressants. Tony told me I could not wear this shirt because of the shoulders. The shirt is loose, and I am comfortable in it. Everyone chatters before class.

The bell rings for morning chapel with Mr. Z. "Maria, can you stay behind for a moment?" I hear Mrs. Milano call.

I turn around and look at her desk. "What's up?" I ask.

She takes a deep breath and looks at her computer. "You know, almost every day I receive an email from Tony..." she says. "I try my best to respond. I have even asked your previous homeroom teachers if he expects me to email him this much," she states. I stand tall as I listen.

"This email is just..." She shakes her head and scoffs.

"It's what?" I ask. Mrs. Milano plays with her mouse and then looks up at me.

"You need to change your shirt," she states.

"Why?" I ask. "In his email, he is explaining that you left with the shirt you weren't allowed to wear.... He described it as being revealing and not appropriate for school," she says.

"Did you tell him I am wearing it?" I begin to panic.

"Well, no I haven't responded yet," she sighs with her Texas accent.

"What are you going to tell him?" I ask.

"Well, I can't lie to him," she sighs.

"Yes you can...." I roll my eyes and run out of the room. I turn into the small gym hallway. I sit on the floor and lean my back on the wall. I try to hold my tears in, I can only imagine what life is going to be like when I get home. Tony is going to punish me.

"Maria," I hear Mrs. Milano call as she makes her way to me. "Oh, there you are." She smiles. Her thick, red, curly hair bounces. "I thought you were going to make me chase you around the building," she chuckles with her accent.

I look up at her with a small grin. "I don't want you to be upset with me." She sits next to me on the floor. "I am sorry," she adds.

"It's fine, it's just that... Tony controls my life," I tell her.

Mrs. Milano tilts her head at me. "Well, I think he cares about you and wants to be sure you are dressing your age," she states.

I scoff, rolling my eyes. "No, listen to my words carefully," I state. "Tony controls me. He makes everyone think I am like this horrible bad kid," I state. "You will be convinced that I am bad, just watch," I state and stand to my feet. Respectfully, I hold my hand out to help Mrs. Milano up.

"I do not think I can be convinced into believing anything like that. I am a trained US Marine." She smiles proudly. We stand at eye level.

"You know what... just wear the damn shirt," Mrs. Milano states. I smile and give her a hug.

"Thank you," I whisper in her ear. "I am 17 years old now, I can wear what I want," I tell her as we walk down the hallway.

At Tony's house, I disappear in the room. I toss my shirt into the abyss of the closet. That way, if Tony searches for it, I can hide my crime. I sit at the desk and begin doing my homework.

"Watch out," Tony demands, barging into the room. He unplugs the computer hard drive tower. Tony lifts the device and walks out of the room. I continue finishing my assignment.

"Tony?" I shout into the hallway. "Can I get a snack?" I ask.

"Yeah," he shouts back. I walk to the kitchen and pick out a pop-tart. Walking back to the room, I see Tony sitting in the recliner with a TV dinner tray in front of him. On the tray sits the computer tower.

"What are you doing?" I ask, walking into the living room. The tower panel is open. Tony is unscrewing random parts and placing them into a trash bag.

"This thing is broken, I need to take it apart," he states. "Then maybe dip it in water...," he thinks aloud.

"Can't you just throw it away?" I ask.

Tony sucks his teeth. "Is your homework finished?" he asks.

"Yes." I take a bite of my snack. I look at the TV. He is watching *Law and Order: SVU*. I sit down on the couch and tune into the show. I remember when I was younger this show would freak me out. Though as I got older, it really started making a lot of sense to me.

"Is there a marathon going on?" I ask Tony.

"Yeah, on the USA Network," he says.

I watch him devote his time to unscrewing each green hard drive board. A light switch begins to go off in my head. I look at the TV and then back at Tony. Perhaps he is breaking the computer tower because he has been on the dark web? Seems like something I would see on *Law and Order*. Tilting my head as I think, I make a connection. Does Tony watch *Law and Order SVU* to learn how to get away with being a pedophile? Or does the show turn him on in some way? "

"Oh my god!" I gasp. The little voice in my head is causing me to think of bizarre ideas.

"What?" Tony looks up.

"Nothing, I just really have to use the bathroom," I lie.

I rush into my bedroom and sit on the bed. My mind begins to analyze how Tony does have a dedication to watching Toddlers and Tiaras. Could he actually be a pedophile. I stand to my feet as the thoughts get heavier.

I have noticed that Tony likes to leave me home alone more often. He claims to go to bowling night or to Pastor Phil's office for counseling. Could he still actively be a pedophile?

Since Tony is occupied, I use my secret agent skills. I investigate the room. I listen to the small voice in my head telling me to search the tall wooden dresser he uses. I gently rummage through his personal belongings. I am careful not to misplace anything. I hope to find evidence. Suddenly, between his white t-shirts I find my clue. A brand-new package of little girl's underwear.

Underneath the package I see prints of photos. I shuffle through photos of two little blonde girls. They seem like sisters. In one photo, they are in a playroom. The next, they are posing with Tony by a river. Seems like someone else took the photo. Who are these girls? Are they who Tony leaves the house to see? The last photo is of the girls climbing a small familiar tree. "That is his sister Jen's house," I gasp aloud. The tree sits on Jen's front lawn. I am confused. There is no way for these little girls to have recently been to Jen's house. I would know because Tony takes me over when he visits. I would have heard about these little girls. I sit there and ponder.

I revisit each photo in hand. The girls are dressed like they are in the early 90's. Tony looks younger in the photo. What if these girls are from his past? Did he touch them like he did me? My chest becomes tight, I hear Tony's bare feet slapping the wooden floors.

I place the photos back and shut the dresser drawer. I toss myself on the bed and look up at the small TV. Tony is a pedophile. How have I never realized this? Or have I just been ignoring it this whole time? I see the episodes on Law and Order talking about pedophiles. Tony fits all the signs. Though, I feel like I have it better than most of the victims on that show. Tony doesn't seem to have the courage to kill me. Even though he has tried to, he can never finish the task. I sit on my bed and turn the Wii gaming console on. Tony doesn't know that I can access the internet on the Wii.

I open to my secret twitter page. I made an online friend named Tamika. We are the same age. She is from Australia. She knows about my life and has sent me photos and videos of what life is like in her country. I open Tamika and my private messages.

"I am ready to tell you about the secret I have," I type using the

Wii remote. I begin typing out, admitting to Tamika the abuse Tony has forced upon me. Instantly, she responded.

Tamika: I am so sorry to hear about your pain. Have you tried telling anyone? I watch *Law and Order SVU*. You live in America, can't you call those types of police?

Maria: That is funny, I watch that show too. No, in America there is no Olivia Benson type of phone number to call. Besides, it happened when I was little. I do not think anyone would believe me.

Tamika: I believe you. I am always here if you need a friend.

Maria: You are the only person I ever told. Thank you for listening to me.

Tamika: Anytime. One day we will meet and go to New York City. Then we can meet Mariska Hargitay and maybe go dancing at a club or see a Broadway show!

Maria: I can't wait for that!! I love our friendship. One day we will meet!

In the morning, Tony is at music practice. I get to start my day how I want. I take a shower and cry. Then I wipe my tears and have breakfast at the computer desk. I am watching the USA Network. I am intensely watching an episode called 911. Detective Olivia Benson is on the phone with a little girl named Maria. Instantly, I am drawn in. The little girl got ahold of her abuser's cell phone. The SVU team tries to figure out where the little girl is. All the while Olivia is keeping the little girl company on the phone, asking her questions on familiar things in her surroundings. Eventually, the abuser finds the girl on the phone and taunts Olivia, telling her she will never find the girl. In the end, Olivia goes on a search for the girl with the clues she collected from speaking on the phone. My heart breaks at the end when Olivia finds the girl buried alive. She digs her out of the ground and holds her in her arms. She says Maria's name over and over. I can't help but shed a tear. I want Olivia to rush in and save me.

I need to run away. I can't keep staying locked up in this room. I look myself in the mirror. I am ready to step out of Tony's house without his permission. I get my Converse sneakers on. I empty out a bag and pack a few clothes. I wish I could pack a snack. I fear Anna catching me. I pack my iPod but I leave my phone so Tony can't track me. With the bag on my back, I tiptoe around the hallway. I am trying to find out where Anna is. No sign of her. I take this moment to race to the kitchen, an opportunity to get a snack. I grab a few granola bars. I open the brown apartment door and walk down the dark blue hallway carpeting.

"Oh, you startled me!" Anna laughs as she carries up a laundry basket. "Where are you going?" She tilts her head and looks at the bag I am carrying. "Is that a bag of dirty clothing?" she asks.

I stay silent and race towards the front door. "Wait, you can't leave," Anna says as she reaches towards me. I run as fast as I can down the sidewalk. She is old, she won't chase me. This is my first time stepping out of the house without any permission from Tony. Feels like I am walking on the moon. I run down to the end of the street near the main road. I begin to walk forward, I know that the train station is this way. As I walk, I realize that I have no real plan on where I am going to go. Perhaps this is why I never left?

I have nowhere to go and no money. I walk past the highway. A man walks past me. I shriek back. "Ah, please don't kidnap me!" I shout. He, respectfully, passes by. Suddenly, I hear a horn from a car pulling alongside me. I begin to panic. I look at the car and instantly recognize Lauren's face and dark hair in the driver's seat. She rolls down her window as she pulls over.

"Where are you going?" she asks.

"How did you find me?" I ask.

"Tony called me. I was down the road getting my brakes checked," she adds. I look down at my feet. Anna must have called him when I left.

"Get in, I will bring you back to the house," she tells me.

"No," I state to Lauren. "You know, this is why Tony doesn't let you do anything fun. You act out of control," she states. I shake my head. In defeat, I get in the front seat of Lauren's vehicle. I know that I have no plan on where to go.

"If you are feeling sad, maybe I can talk to Tony... and see if you can have another sleepover with Faith," Lauren suggests. She pulls onto Tony's street.

"Yeah, maybe," I say softly. "Let me call Tony and tell him I have you." She smiles.

"Hey Tony, I am dropping her off at your front door now," Lauren says. Her phone is on speaker.

"Thank you, Lauren, so sorry for all the trouble," Tony says. "Please tell Maria to call me when she gets inside," he demands. Lauren hangs up as I get out of the car.

"See you at church," she shouts. I step back into the front door.

"You need to go straight into the bedroom," Anna says from the living room recliner.

"Yeah, I know!" I snap.

"Do not get pissy with me, you are the one causing problems for yourself," she scoffs. What a waste, now I have to hear Tony lecture me. In the room, I call Tony on the cell phone.

"Yes, I am in the bedroom," I state.

"You better stay there. I will be home soon," he says. I throw the phone aside.

Tony barges into the bedroom. He has a new looking computer tower in his hands.

"Where did that come from?" I ask.

"The church gave it to me," Tony states. He kneels on the floor to install it underneath the wooden desk. "You have fun trying to cause another scene?" he asks, plugging in wires. I stay silent. "You think you can outsmart me, Maria," Tony says. "Just remember, I am always five steps ahead of you," he smirks.

"Yes sir," I speak. I turn over in bed and begin to reflect. My life could be worse. I guess I do not need saving. I get to go to school and have an iPod. I am convinced that my life could be worse. If anything, *Law and Order* has taught me that girls around the world get human trafficked. I am lucky that I am allowed to go to school and church. I just need to stay committed on not breaking any of Tony's rules. I need to stay here so he can pay for my college. I can get a degree in something I enjoy doing. Maybe that is when my life will begin?

After church the next day, Tony is on the computer. "Hey, I need to go get something I forgot at church." Tony looks over at me. I am playing my DS gaming console.

"Alright," I say.

Tony stands from the desk. "Don't touch the computer, I will be right back," he demands.

"I won't," I assure him. Tony grabs his keys and leaves. I sit up in bed and look at the computer desk. Him telling me not to touch the computer is making me want to go on it. Especially since he has a new hard drive. I wonder if something is on the hard drive he was given? Or is this his clean slate of not sinning? What is he even doing on this new tower? I move the mouse. It reveals an open screen to Tony's email. I sit at the computer desk, intrigued. I scroll, I see lots of emails relating to the church band. Suddenly, I come across an email thread between Sandra and Tony.

The email thread reads:

Tony: She is turning 18 soon, I do not know how much longer I can help her. She tried to run away yesterday.

Sandra: Honestly Tony, if you feel that you have done all that you can do, maybe it is time to let her go. I know you care about her but it is just like with my daughter, Jane. Jane's depression was so bad she wouldn't stop harming herself, I sent her away for a little bit. Now she is better as an adult.

Tony: I think you might be right, God really wants me to move on from helping her. Do you have any suggestions?

Sandra: You have been more than a father to her, I know God is proud of you and the help you have extended to her. She has become ungrateful. I think you have to do what you fear. If she is not improving on her self-harm or depression... then she needs to placed in a mental facility before she turns 18 next year.

Tony: I think you may be right, can you help me find the best hospital fit for her?

The thread ends, my heart skips a beat. Tony wants me to go insane. He wants me to look like the mentally insane girl. This explains why he ignores the cuts on my arm. I shake my head. I have been letting him win this whole time. I reset the computer just as

Tony left it. I dive into the bed in a pit of despair. Tony is right, he is five steps ahead of me. I have no idea how to fix my life. No one is going to believe me. I waited too long to speak about the horrid actions he has done towards me. I shut my eyes and try to envision my happy place with the meadow, river, and treehouse. However, the meadow is now a wasteland. The river is dried up and the tree is failing apart. Every part of me feels dead.

CHAPTER 19

The Moving Finger Writes

By the end of the school year, I managed to gain Tony's trust back. I made sure to study to keep my grades up. I even ask teachers how I can get extra credit. I avoid confrontation. To my surprise, avoiding everyone has made peers want to talk to me. I became friends with two girls in the senior class. They thought it was cool that I spend time on YouTube looking up cheerleading dance moves. They both used to do cheerleading when they were younger. From there, we decided to sign up for the school talent show as a 'cheer squad.' It was Ally, Riley, and I. Though, Riley's boyfriend was on the team. He stood next to us and stepped in as an extra hand for our simple cheer stunt. I created a cheer routine and even taught them how to step dance.

Creating and performing a dance is a dream of mine. Letting Tony win seems like the best decision I have made. So much so that Tony is allowing me to join the high school camping trip. Mrs. Milano offered to be the chaperone that is in charge of me. I ride in Mrs. Milano's van with her and her youngest daughter, Henna. We venture to Bish Bash Falls in Massachusetts. Being in nature, I instantly realize that my phone has no service. So, I leave it in the tent. I feel a bit free because when Tony asks why I haven't messaged him, I can simply say there was no service.

Everyone cheers as we approach the 59-foot waterfall. There is a small pool that flows into another pool that leads to the river we have been following. It is a really beautiful sight to see. To everyone on this trip, they see a view of nature. To me, I see it as the perfect place to jump off and kill myself. Maybe this is how my story ends? 'She jumped off the waterfall and fell into a peaceful death.' I take a deep breath. My mind likes to create fake causes of death, sometimes I have to just get through the thought and then ignore it. I observe everyone having fun, taking pictures. I begin to think that they would be the witnesses to my death. Or witness to my *attempt* at death. What if I land into the water and come out fine? How embarrassing. That would really get me into the mental ward. Either way, I recognize that I would be traumatizing others if I were to toss myself over the waterfall.

"Alright, let's start climbing up!" Angelina, Mrs. Milano's eldest daughter, shouts to everyone. She points to the path leading to the top of the falls. I watch everyone cross the big rocks to the other side.

"Are you coming?" Mrs. Milano asks.

"No," I say. In the pit of my stomach, I have an aching fear that something bad would happen if I were to go.

"Why?" Mrs. Milano asks. I sit on the first rock between the two water pools. "I just don't want to, I am afraid of heights," I lie to her.

"Well, at least climb these few rocks." She smiles and walks deeper on the rock path. "I will stay with you, I have been up there a few times in my life," she states. I look at her, I feel relieved to have her at my side. We sit on the big rocks below the waterfall. "Everyone should be up there by now." She smiles pointing up to the top. "Oh, there she is!" Mrs. Milano waves.

"Mom!" Angelina shouts down. The group waves down to us.

"I am sorry you are stuck down here with me," I tell Mrs. Milano.

"No worries," she says. "This trip was Angelina's idea, she wanted to show all of her friends the waterfall," she explains.

After the waterfall, we head back down. Mrs. Milano pulls her younger daughter, Henna, and I aside. We stop at a hidden opening to the flowing river. We skip rocks. I watch Mrs. Milano walk, fully clothed, into the river and jump off of a rock. "Come on, Maria!" Mrs. Milano calls, her red hair glows in the sunlight. I take my sneakers off and follow Henna into the river. We swim around the shallow river. I love looking up at the sunlight shining through the trees. It makes me want to build a small house on the side of the river and stay here forever. Afterwards, the three of us hike back down the path.

"Maria, come here," Mrs. Milano pulls me aside. We sit on a large tree log. "So, what is going with you?" she asks me. I look into her dark greenish eyes. I shrug my shoulders.

"My therapist tells me I am depressed," I say.

"Why are you depressed?" she asks. "Is it because of your mom?" she wonders.

"Yeah, kind of," I say.

"Anything else?" she questions.

I take a deep breath. Perhaps, this is my only chance to finally be strong. I am tired of hiding my truth. "Tony makes me depressed," I tell her. "He always controls what I do. I want to kill myself because of him," I begin to talk fast. "That is why I didn't go up to the waterfall," I reveal. Mrs. Milano holds her hand on her heart. "I didn't want to traumatize everyone by witnessing my suicide," I add. I feel my chest get heavy with emotion as I break down in tears.

Mrs. Milano puts her arm around my shoulder. "He wants to lock me in a mental hospital," I cry. "I know all of his secrets," I add.

"What secrets?" she questions. I look at her and then look down at the ground. "His secret is he likes little girls. He used to touch me when I was younger. He acts like he didn't but I remember... I remember everything," I cry into her chest. "Every summer and weekend," I add.

"Oh honey, I am so sorry." She kisses my forehead. "I was beginning to feel something was off between you and him.... That day, when I almost made you change your shirt...." She sighs. "I felt that something wasn't right," she sighs. "You are safe right now, I want you to enjoy the rest of the camping trip." She tries to cheer me up. "We will figure out the rest when we get back home," she explains.

I back my head away. "What is there to figure out? You cannot tell anyone," I demand. "He will lock me away, he has temporarily guardianship over me!" I panic.

"Calm down, I won't tell anyone... alright?" She smiles gently. "Please, just do not hurt yourself on this trip," she begs. "Promise me?" she adds.

"I promise." I nod my head.

For the remainder of the trip, I try my best to act as if I didn't just spill my whole life's secret. Though, it is hard because deep inside I am counting down the hours until I will have to return to Tony's house. At night, I use my phone that has downloaded songs of my favorite artist, Katy Perry. I listen to Katy Perry's song 'Firework' through my headphones. Her voice relaxes me. The lyrics of the song make me feel strong and hopeful. I play the song on repeat until I fall asleep.

After the trip, Mrs. Milano drops me back off at Tony's house. I feel bittersweet inside. I enjoyed consistently being around Mrs. Milano. The next day, I go to church. It is a normal day. Everyone at church has given me a compliment. I smile and thank them as I walk along Tony's side. After church, we head back to the house. Tony sits on the recliner in the living room. He has his work laptop on his lap. I disappear into the room. I lay in bed, scrolling on my touch screen phone. I slide the keyboard up and open the Facebook app. Tony has forgotten he signed me onto my phone app. Since I do not have the password, I have stayed silent about being logged in. I am curious if anyone from the camping trip posted our group photo. As I scroll my timeline, I get a message from Mrs. Milano.

Mrs. Milano: Hey, what are you doing?

Maria: Nothing, just playing on my phone.

Mrs. Milano: Are you at Tony's house?

Maria: Yes.

Mrs. Milano: Delete these messages.

Maria: Why?

Mrs. Milano: Do not be afraid to call me.

I begin asking her what that means, there is no answer. I hear Tony's bare feet stomp across the wooden hallway floor.
"What are you talking about with Mrs. Milano?" he asks me.
"Huh?" I ask.
"Why did she tell you to delete messages?" he shouts.
"I don't know." I shrug my shoulders.
"Bullshit!" he yells and grabs the collar of my shirt. He shakes me. Tony snatches the phone out of my hands. "You think you are really so smart." He laughs. "I know you use Facebook on your phone," he explains. "I am on your account." Tony holds up his laptop. He shows me the computer screen on Facebook. I am not surprised. He is full of tricks.

Suddenly, there is a knock on the door. Tony looks at me and shakes his head. "Stay here!" he demands. I begin to panic, unsure about what is going on. Tony comes running into the room. He grabs my face.

"Why are the police here?" he shouts, showing his teeth. My heart instantly begins to pound.

"I don't know," I stutter.

"Stay in here and do not speak!" he demands, tossing my face aside.

Tony steps out of the room to answer the front door. I race over to the door and listen. I hear many footsteps enter the apartment.

"Is anyone else here with you?" a man with a deep voice asks.

"No," Tony says. "I live in this apartment level with my mother," Tony says.

He is so dumb to act like I am not here. What if they search the house?

"I was just doing work on my laptop," Tony says calmly. "I work for a company in the city, its call—" Tony explains but is cut off.

"Are you available to come talk with us at our office?" Another man asks.

"Sure, just let me change into a pair of jeans," Tony states. I hear his footsteps on the wooden floor once more. I step away from the door.

"Look at what you have done!" Tony gently shuts the door behind him. "I should have gotten rid of you when I had the chance," he rants while he grabs a pair of jeans from the dirty laundry pile. "You can say whatever you want about me," he declares. "You know why?" He stares at me. I shake my head, unsure why. "Pastor has told me I am forgiven," he whispers viciously.

"Pastor?" I question.

"Yeah, that's right, Pastor," he snaps. "He knows what I have done to you and God has forgiven me!" he barks.

I hear the golden doorknob jingle. "Hey! Who are you talking to?" a gentleman in a long black coat steps into the room. He looks directly at me. "She's in here," the man says.

"Escort him out, please," the gentlemen speaks to a cop dressed in police uniform. Tony is escorted out of the room. "I am Detective Harris," the gentlemen introduces himself.

I look him up and down. He isn't Olivia Benson, however, he will do just fine at saving me.

"What should I do, now?" I ask him.

"Get your shoes and jacket on," he states. I am silent and in shock. I stay strong. I begin to search for shoes and a sweater. I grab my phone in the process.

"Anything else you need?" Detective Harris asks.

I look at the closet. "He goes on the dark web and watches child porn," I state. "In the closet are his old computer parts," I add.

The Detective opens the wooden closet doors. "In that garbage bag!" I direct him. He grabs it.

"Hey, I am Detective Wilson." Another man comes in. He is wearing a short, slender shirt. "The street is filling up with civilians, we have to go." He looks at Detective Harris. The two men stand on each side of me. I walk between them. I look back at the bedroom door. Perhaps I will never see this room again.

"When we step outside, just keep walking," one of the men states. I step out of the front door. I can feel the warm summer night air hit my face. Police lights flash. I can hear chatter as the neighborhood gathers around to watch the scene. Suddenly, I feel the gentle hands of a woman. She is in a pantsuit. "I am here with child services, we need to walk and talk... alright?" She smiles at me. We walk past people on the street. They are staring at me. Under the streetlights, I get a glimpse of the woman. She has tan skin, big brown eyes, and tight curly hair.

"What is your name?" I ask.

"Melissa," she answers. She opens the back door to a car. I slide in. She is very stern, looking around and making sure things are secure. I look at Tony's family home. The police lights reflect off the white siding. I cannot believe that this is actually happening to me.

"Do you have family we can call?" the woman asks as we drive.

"My mother is in Dominican Republic." I state.

"You do not have anyone that can meet you at the station?" she asks. "I am warning you, love. The file says you are 17 years old, if no one claims you... you will be taken into the system," she explains.

"No, no...." I panic. I reach for my phone and remember what Mrs. Milano said. 'Do not be afraid to call me.' Quickly, I dial Mrs. Milano's number.

"Hello," she answers the phone.

"Mrs. Milano, the police took Tony and I am alone," I panic. "I don't want to be taken into the system," I cry.

"I know, I called them. I couldn't live with myself if I kept silent," she states. "I am on my way Sweetie, just take deep breaths... I will be there soon," Mrs. Milano tells me. She hangs up the phone.

At the police station, I am escorted to a bright room. There is a long countertop that is decorated like a desk. It has an old printer, a few desk chairs, and stacks of paper everywhere. The gentlemen look at me as I stare back at them. I am always a bit awkward when it comes to talking to grown men. Detective Harries has fair skin, a pointy nose, and kind eyes. Detective Wilson has fair skin, green eyes, and he is taller than Harris.

"Do you want water?" Detective Harris asks.

"Why, do you want my DNA?" I ask.

The two detectives look at each other and laugh.

"No, you aren't the criminal," Detective Wilson chuckles. Suddenly there is a knock at the door.

"Mrs. Milano!" I stand to my feet. She comes over to me and hugs me. I feel calm now that she is by my side. Mrs. Milano introduces herself to the detectives.

"We need to get her statement," Detective Harris says.

Mrs. Milano turns to me. "Are you comfortable talking to them?" she asks. I nod my head, yes.

"So, have you ever filed a police report before?" Detective Harris asks.

"Yes, actually," I answer honestly. "I filed a statement about a guy from my school, his name is Chad," I state.

The detectives look at each other. "Hold on, we need to read that report before we go any further," Detective Wilson demands.

"When and where did you put in a statement," Detective Harris asks.

"Like, last year... in New Milford, Connecticut," I state. I look at Mrs. Milano.

"What the hell?" I say. "They just need to be sure nothing is tainted when they take your statement," she explains.

"Tainted?" I question. "You mean to see if I am a consistent liar," I scoff. "If you do not believe me about Chad, then why don't you contact the New Milford police department in Connecticut," I snap at the detectives. The men leave the room.

We wait for the detectives to come back in the room. "Good news, we just got a fax of your report from Connecticut," Detective Harris waves a paper in the air. "We are sorry that it seemed like we doubted you, we are trying to do our jobs correctly," he explains.

I nod my head. "Plus, we are a smalltown station... we have never gotten a case like this before," Detective Wilson states.

I begin to give my testimonial about how everything started with Tony, all the way to the very end.

"Do you have any proof of the sexual abuse?" Detective Wilson asks.

"No, like I said... he stopped touching me when I was 12." I sigh.

"Well, lucky for you the state of New York has updated their laws on statute of limitations. You fit the bracket of being able to file a charge against Tony," Detective Harris explains. "We have to go and speak with him now." Detective Wilson stands to his feet. "We will be back shortly." Detective Harris walks out of the room.

As time passes, Mrs. Milano tries to come up with a plan. "Can you reach out to any of your family members?" she asks.

"No," I say in despair. I explain how my mother and father's family barely have any relationship with me. I did think of Star. However, she is a bit older now. I do not want to call her in the middle of the night. I fear it could lead her into a heart attack.

The detectives return to the room. "That man is very cocky," Detective Wilson states.

I nod my head in agreement.

"He is claiming all the accusations are false," Detective Harris says.

"He says that you have a history of lying and self-harm," Detective Wilson adds.

"I am not lying!" I shout.

Mrs. Milano pats my back.

"Trust us, we believe you." Detective Harris holds his hands up.

"We are going to keep him overnight and book him in the morning," Detective Wilson explains.

"His record isn't coming up squeaky clean," Detective Harris scoffs.

"What is on the record?" Mrs. Milano asks.

"For right now, I cannot disclose this information," Detective Harris answers.

"Before you write your final statement... we do have one last question," Detective Wilson says.

"Is there anything about his body you can describe?" Detective Wilson asks. "Any marks?" he adds.

I close my eyes and instantly I envision myself in the bed with Tony. I open my eyes, "The little balls of skin on his thighs." I state out loud. I look up at everyone. "He has these small skin things that look like little balls," I explain.

"Like warts?" Detective Harris asks.

"No, they are like little balloons." I explain.

"Skin tags!" Mrs. Milano states.

Detective Wilson nods his head. "Where on his body?" Detective Wilson asks.

"On his inner thigh, near his private area," I state.

Detective Wilson stands up. "Perfect. Harris, get the camera," Detective Wilson stands to his feet.

A moment later, Detective Harris steps into the room. Wilson walks behind him. "I want this man out of my interrogation room!" he shouts.

"Wilson, take five...." Detective Harris shoos him out of the room.

"Sorry, he has children and we haven't had a case like this before," Harris states. I write my statement, sign it, and agree to press charges against Tony.

Mrs. Milano brings me back to her house. She has informed me that I can't stay for too long because she is actually moving to Texas. Her father has early stages of dementia. Plus, Angelina is beginning college down there. I cried in her arms at the news, though she reassured me she will do whatever it takes to help me before she leaves at the end of the summer. I have been staying at her house for a week. There are about twelve cats and two dogs. Her house smells fresh, you can barely tell cats live there. I sleep in the extra bedroom. It has been very therapeutic to fall asleep and wake up to a group of five cats around the bed. I wake up today feeling a bit low.

Yesterday, Mrs. Milano and I received permission to go back to Tony's house. She helped me grab what is important to me. I grabbed my baby photos, my yearbooks, and clothing. Anything that meant something to me, we stuffed in Mrs. Milano's minivan. It was so strange to be back at the house. I have until the end of August to find someone to take me in.

Regina has been hard to reach. She has no idea of what has been going on here in the states. I know I need to leave Mrs. Milano's house soon. I am beginning to feel like her husband hates that I am here. Probably because at nighttime I become suicidal.

I have spoken to a few family members, like Shannon and Star. Though, Shannon has revealed that throughout the years Regina has been in and out of America. She has been visiting New Jersey, staying in homeless shelters while she works, then she takes the money she earns and flies back to Dominican Republic.

I haven't spoken to my mother since New Years. It was a video chat. I remember Tony stood behind the bedroom door to monitor our conversations. I remember how blah Regina was over the video. She then handed the conversation over to Karina and Selena. They were so happy to see me. They were listening to my old iPod that I sent them. The only future that I see for myself is turning 18 in the fall and living in a homeless shelter. There is no one who wants to take me in.

As the summer comes to an end. Staying at Mrs. Milano's house for the summer has brought me to a small place of healing. Every time I needed her, she would hug me. She told me that I am worth living, explaining that the worst part of my life is officially over. Henna and I have become close. We would go on walks and watch, *Doctor Who*. I am grateful. Grateful for the energy Mrs. Milano and her family have given me. I sit on the couch. We are about to go to a Goodbye cookout that Mrs. Milano's friends are throwing for her. I pet the cats that flock to me as I sit. Mrs. Milano is on the living room computer.

"Maria!" She turns in the computer chair. "I have some news," she says. "Remember when we went back to Tony's house with your detectives and we packed all of your belongings?" she says.

"Yes," I nod.

"I believe we may have accidentally grabbed a box of Tony's things," she says. "I found a letter from someone named Anna," she explains.

"That's his mother!" I sit up straight. "The letter was dated from 1997, it is a letter to Tony while he was in jail in Georgia," she explains.

"In jail?" I say shocked. "Maybe that's why one of the Detectives mentioned his record not coming up clean...." I begin to place the puzzle pieces together.

"I have researched online that in the late 90's Tony worked at an airport. He was caught calling little boys and speaking sexually to them on the work phone," Mrs. Milano reveals. "He did a few months in prison," she adds.

I shake in shock. "He has always been like this," I say. I take a deep breath.

I remember the very beginning of how Tony came into my life. I begin to explain how Tony used to be Star's roommate in the late 90s. "He must have fled to Connecticut when he got out of jail," Mrs. Milano states.

"You are a hero." She smiles at me.

I shake my head, no.

"Yes you are, think about how many other little girls you have saved by putting him behind bars," she explains.

"Before we leave, I have a few words I would like to tell you." She sits back in the computer chair. "There are two things I always want you to remember," Mrs. Milano smiles. She pulls out a small cardboard box. "First, remember the O.O.D.A. Loop that I have taught you," she says. The O.O.D.A. Loop is Observe, Orient, Decide and Act then repeat. "As you become an adult this cycle will help you delegate through situations," she explains. I nod my head and smile.

Henna enters the living room and sits beside me. Mrs. Milano hands me the cardboard box. I open it, revealing a pink leather bracelet with writing burned into it. "It has the quote that I believe can help you move on from your pain." She smiles. I smile, Mrs. Milano and I always bonded over literature. I read the bracelet.

"The Moving Finger writes; and, having writ,
Moves on: nor all thy Piety nor Wit

Shall lure it back to cancel half a Line,
Nor all thy Tears wash out a Word of it."

—*Omar Khayyám*

She begins to repeat the quote as she wraps the bracelet around my wrist.

"I have one too!" Henna smiles holding up her green bracelet. "Mine has a different quote," she adds.

I grin, "Thank you so much, Mrs. Milano."

I stand to my feet and give her a hug. I feel like she considers me close to her heart like her daughters. I know there is only so much she can do. It pains me to have to say goodbye to her soon.

At the cookout, I am having a good time. We all hang out in the backyard of Mrs. Milano's friend's house. The grass is green, the sky is blue, and they have a big blow-up obstacle course. However, an eerie feeling comes over me. I think it is unfair that I have to say goodbye to Mrs. Milano. A part of me wishes she would give me a chance, letting me run away to Texas with her. I want to convince her that if she takes me with her, I will get a job and try to get accepted into college. I look around at everyone chatting. I sneak away and step into the front yard. The woman's house is on a freeway. I watch all the cars pass by while they go 50 miles per hour in both directions. I stand here for a while as my mind fully convinces myself to step into the road. I walk closer to the edge of the road.

"Maria!" Mrs. Milano yanks me backward. "What are you doing?" she asks.

I can tell there is concern in her eyes. "I do not want to live anymore," I cry. I look around and notice everyone at the party is gathered. I see people are even watching me from inside the house.

"Well, I'm glad to give you all a show!" I loudly shout with tears. I toss my arms up into the air.

Suddenly, police sirens appear. A police car pulls up on the lawn. "Please be gentle with her." Mrs. Milano begs as a police officer handcuffs me.

"You should have just let me continue walking!" I scream at Mrs. Milano. "You're a bitch! I hate you!" I shout at her. I am put in the back of a police car. I watch as the crowd on the front lawn disappear from looking out of the window. The police drive until we show up at a hospital.

"Why are we not at the police station?" I ask.

The man driving laughs. "Did you commit a crime?" he asks.

I wiggle my hands in the hand cuffs. "No...." I say.

"Hopefully, you get the help you need," the young officer looks through the plexiglass.

I am pulled out and put in the mental wing of the hospital. I am free from the hand cuffs as I pace around the room.

"It is procedure that you wear the robe," the young woman nurse explains to me.

"I am not wearing that ugly thing," I stomp my foot at her. My cell phone has been in my back pocket. However, it is not connected to any cell service.

"Let me make a phone call!" I demand.

The doctor steps into the room. "I can't let you do that," he states.

"I need to talk to Mrs. Milano," I shout.

"I spoke to her. The police gave me her information," he explains. "She doesn't want to speak to you." He shakes his head.

"You are a fucking liar!" I scream. I lift up a chair in the corner of the room. I toss it at the doctor.

"If you keep acting this way, I am going to have to sedate you," he warns. "Please put the robe on," he asks. I agree to put the robe on over my clothing. He then asks for my sneakers in fear of me using the shoelaces. I walk around with blue hospital socks on. I am left alone with the young nurse.

"Listen, you need to go and tell that fucking doctor to let me make a phone call," I demand.

She is silent. The whole time she is leaning on the door frame. "What, are you afraid to step into the room?" I ask her.

"No," she says. Suddenly, I jolt my body and stomp my foot towards her. She jumps back. I step out into the hallway.

"Hello! I need a doctor!" I shout. I turn into another room. To my surprise I see the doctor sitting on the desk talking to someone on speaker.

"Is that her?" I ask. "Hello! Mrs. Milano!" I scream.

"She doesn't want to talk to you, I said!" the doctor raises his voice to me. "Let her go!" he adds.

"You are a fucking prick!" I begin tossing things off his desk. The person on speaker hangs up the phone.

Suddenly, the nurse tries to guide me back into the room. I push her off and begin to grab her hair. "Don't you fucking touch me!" I shake her. A group of nurses rush over and pull me into the room. I watch them prepare a syringe and stick it in my arm. The nurses shut the light off.

"Wait!" I force my voice to speak. I begin to feel like I can't move. I hate this restricted feeling. My legs start to feel like they have ants crawling inside my skin. I try to move my shoulders. It feels like I am moving. I can't tell. I feel my cheek hit the cold hospital floor.

"She fell down!" I hear someone say. I am lifted back onto the bed and left to fade into a deep sleep.

Fourteen-year-old Maria visiting Shannon at Star's apartment

Karina and Selena living in the Dominican Republic

Maria after Shannon wiped icing on her face for her fourteenth birthday living at Hope House Shelter

Teenage Maria hangng out and sneaking on the computer while living in the room at Tony's house.

CHAPTER 20

New Beginning

After being sedated, the hospital put me on a 72-hour hold. I felt alone and numb. The doctor that watched my case deemed me violent and said that I have an unhealthy emotionally attachment to Mrs. Milano. Of course, that man was the person responsible for trying to contact family during my 72-hour hold. Since I am 17 years old and not able to contact any of my family members, it made him frustrated. The fact that my cellphone alone had about 7 contacts made him angry towards me. I tried to explain that Tony controls me, all the phone numbers I had were people from Tony's church. I didn't even have Shannon's number nor my Facebook password. As I laid on the hospital bed, sedated, staring at the white wall, my mind had a lot of time to think without anyone trying to manipulate my mind. Analyzing all the current events. I came to the realization that the doctor will hand me over to the state soon. Tony got what he wanted, for me to end up in the mental hospital and taken away.

In the end, I believe he had a hatred towards me because I was a reflection of his sickness or as he would say 'sin.' This whole time he lived in fear of me. He lived in fear of me finding the correct combination of words that would destroy his life. In the hospital, I attempt to eat a sandwich. Besides that, my body just lies down. I can't move my body. My mind stares at the white wall. Although, staring oddly has me in a silent, blissful state. Perhaps the drugs induced my visual, imaginative mind. The hospital wall formed into a view of a meadow with the very same treehouse I always escaped to. It is sunset with the tree in view, butterflies fly around tall sunflowers and daisies. The grass is gently swaying from a breeze I can't feel. I feel as if I had died and went to heaven. Free from Tony and this world. I am still and at peace.

However, that peace ended as soon as my staring caught the glimpse of Aunt Sophia. Recognizing her face snaps me into reality. I say her name, begging to confirm that it is truly her. I grab onto her as she explains she was contacted and here to take me to her house. The car ride to her house was silent. My cousins knew nothing about what had just happened to me. Aunt Sophia claimed she didn't want to freak them out. I didn't care, I do not need to explain myself to her children. I just needed to know if I will end up in the foster system. To my surprise, a day later, Regina showed up on Aunt Sophia's doorstep. It was so awkward to have her try to hug and kiss me and tell me 'sorry.' I have anger towards her and now all of a sudden she is back in my life. This whole time she was low-key living in New Jersey. Apparently, she and Presley broke up.

Living with Regina in New Jersey has been challenging. I am fully traumatized, hurting, and confused. Regina has been frustrated that I am not active around the house. Sometimes I can be kind, other times I am angry and distant. I feel like she expected me to be happy she was back in the States. Selena and Karina finally flew in from Dominican Republic. That was the first time I had seen Shannon since living with Mrs. Milano. We made welcome home posters for the girls. Seeing my younger sisters felt heartwarming.

Living with Regina is always going to be chaotic, though deep inside of me I am thankful to her for taking me in. I didn't end up in the foster system. Although, right next to that thought is, 'how in the hell do I get myself away from living with Regina?' I am going to be 18. I want go and be that sophisticated woman I always wanted to be. However, depression rules my confidence, self-worth, and hope. One day I want to be grown, the next day I want to die.

Regina wants me to find a job so I can start helping with bills. I can barely leave the house and speak with people. I did try to go to an interview at Dunkin Donuts. However, my social skills are currently poor, I am not ready to be out in the world.

Since I used my out of service touch-screen phone for wi-fi, I figured out how to reset my Facebook password and got my account back. Serenity, the youth pastor from Tony's church, has kept in contact with me through Facebook. She told me that she and her husband are against Tony's behavior. She encourages me to find healing, as well as keeps me updated with the church drama surrounding Tony.

Apparently, most of the church members are supportive of Tony. Many of them even go to his court hearings. Some church members are disgusted but are not vocal about it. They simply gossip with their disgust of the situation. Serenity reminded me that I always spoke about being the first in my family to go to college. So, I buckled down and went to high school. I didn't last long at the school because Regina began her habit of endless moving. We lived in about three different dingy apartments. We even squatted for a few weeks in her friends' apartment while they were away. Mrs. Milano gifted me with a laptop in hope for me to use it for school and applying to colleges, which I did. However at any chance of finding wi-fi I would check on my favorite celebrity's twitter and write sci-fi stories.

On my 18th birthday, Shannon visited us. After having cake, Regina revealed that she always thought another man was my father. Since she felt so sure, Shannon and I demanded that she contact him.

Shannon wasn't too sure because she and I look so alike. We must come from the same father. Though, she kind of hoped that the man was my father because maybe I could have a chance at having a dad.

The man, Gabriel, is Brazilian and Spanish. He has a wife, son and daughter. He agreed to meet me. Gabriel offered for me to go back to meet his family in Connecticut. I accepted his offer but under two conditions. One, he and I need to take a paternity test. Second, If he was my father he would have to stick around and get to know me. If he is not my father, then I would like to be dropped off anywhere that is not Regina's apartment. He agreed. I didn't know where I was going to go if he wasn't my father. At this point, I have no idea how to be an adult. I have just been going with the flow of life.

The paternity test came back negative. It was disappointing. I got along with Gabriel's children. They are around my age and we bonded over Xbox video games. Since I was staying on the man's couch, I was always on the wi-fi. Faith and I had been messaging on Facebook. I never got to say goodbye to her.

She claimed Lauren hasn't allowed her to reach out to me. I remember the last time I spoke to Lauren. She called me to find out my side of the story. She claimed that she doesn't think Tony could have done what I claimed. I shocked her with saying she should be disgusted with herself because she was in love with a pedophile, then hung up the phone. So Faith and I speak on the down low.

I told Faith about Gabriel not being my father. Quickly, she offered a solution. She claimed she had been speaking about me to her Aunt Paula. Paula offered to extend a hand, letting me sleep in her extra room. I knew this was all temporary until I figured out what to do next. I jumped at this chance.

Gabriel dropped me off in Killingworth, Connecticut, a place that is in the middle of nowhere. The small town that has huge houses and yards. Paula treated me well. She let me use the wi-fi. Mrs. Milano is an angel. She sends me toiletries from Amazon. I spend all my time on my computer, I am heavily invested as a fangirl for Katy Perry. On twitter, I have been talking to friends around the world that love Katy Perry. We call ourselves, 'the Katycats.' My social interactions have been fulfilled online. Besides that, I tried to get a job. However, everything is so far from the house. Paula didn't want to take the responsibility of driving me to work. Nor did she like how I was eating all of her food for free. One day, she changed her wi-fi password and told me to find another place to live. I panicked and got a hold of Shannon. She gave the advice of coming back to Connecticut. She said she could ask Star if I could come live with them.

Taking Shannon's advice, I moved into Star's extra room. However, being back at Star's house, I was embarrassed to be around Shannon and Star. The memories of being with Tony in Star's condo have me triggered. I was lashing out, unable to communicate why. I fought against Star's help. I decided to pack my bags and move three doors down from Star's condo.

Three doors down was the front door to my father's mother, Camilla. Camila raises my cousin, Nani. Star and Camila are also close friends. I was excited to live with my grandmother. Being around her made me feel like old times when we would visit Julian. I expected living with her would be calm, healing, and I would learn how to cook family Puerto Rican recipes. Maybe a chance at feeling like I belong to a family. However this was not the case. Camila quickly showed that she only ACTS like she cares about me.

She hyped me up about helping me enroll in the local High School. She dropped me off at the local public high school, told me to go to the front office and that it was not a far walk back to the condo complex. She then sped off with Nani for a dance competition. I enrolled myself into the local high school, though the walk back to Camila's condo was very scary. I thought I was going to be kidnapped. I asked the school to print out walking directions to the condo. I used them and walked alone. Arriving at the condo,

I was safe and overcame a fear. I saw this as a first step to becoming a sophisticated woman.

I only went to school part-time. I had most of my credits from going to a private school. The school guidance counselor, Jules helped me get a job. I worked at an appliance store and learned how to take the public bus. Everything seemed to be going fine. Most of the time I had the apartment to myself because Camila and Nani were always on the road. Nani does a lot of dance competitions and beauty pageants.

Close to my high school graduation, Camila didn't want me living in her house afterwards. She spit in my face and told me to get over feeling sorry for myself. She claims she was sorry because she always had a feeling about Tony but never spoke on it. However, she could not handle me living around her house any longer. She even had Julian come over to the house to give me a 'pep talk.' Julian told me if I remained depressed in bed I would get butt sores and I need to figure out my future. He was no help, he only proved to me that he doesn't care about what I am going through. I feel like my presence after a period of time disturbs people.

Regina was frustrated with me. Paula couldn't handle how helpless I was. Now, I am a disturbance to Camila. I swear all I want to do is feel happy and work to provide for myself. I am trying to quickly figure out how to be an adult. However, Tony kept me sheltered on how to be independent.

Serenity visited me in Connecticut for my high school graduation. She filmed me walking into the building and showing off that I have a cute picture of Katy Perry in my graduation cap. 'Firework' by Katy Perry was my anthem for reaching a goal of my first steps into being sophisticated. I graduate from high school with a bunch of students I don't know. However, I stood with them and became the first woman in my family to get her high school diploma. Regina, Shannon, Serenity, Grandma Leona and Aunt Sophia attended my graduation. I am thankful for those moments of having a group of people in the crowd that support me. After graduating, I packed my belongings and asked Star to let me try living with her again. I realized that if I were to live at someone's house, I need to show them I can provide for myself. I assured Star that I will work and pay rent for living in her extra room. Star agreed. She also giggled because I was the one who ran from her house. However, making my way back could mean I am ready to be free and independent. She held me tight and told me I was a hero and if she ever sees Tony again, she will chop his balls off. Alas, a comforting person who cares enough to just hug me. No judgement or yelling at me.

I moved into Star's extra room. She has a huge king-sized mattress and a big fancy dresser with a luxurious mirror. Moving across the hall from Shannon made me feel less alone. It feels like old times with Shannon and Star. Living at Star's house gives me a space to grow. Waking up every day to the big, fancy mirror in the room made me face myself. I began finding out how to take care of my health. I felt fat. I felt like maybe the reason no one let me live with them in the past was because I was fat. Did my weight scare people away from caring about me? I tried to starve myself to lose weight. It worked. However, I pick the pieces up on how to stray away from my eating disorder. I got scared after making myself puke for many weeks. It is just as bad as when I used to cut myself. Though, I feel as if I am coming into a spiritual awakening. I do not rely on God or Jesus to rescue me. I saved myself by speaking up about my situation. My words alerted Mrs. Milano. She helped rescue me.

I believe we are faced with challenges and I will never back down. I have come to find that my strength and passion for finding out what will happen in upcoming chapters in my life means I am worthy of a chance. I also believe I am worthy of Justice. That is what I got a few months after living with Star. My detectives on my case contacted me with new information on Tony. His sentencing was coming up. I have a chance to give a statement while he stands for his sentencing. Immediately, I agreed and began writing. At the hearing, Shannon and Serenity joined me for support. Detectives Harris and Wilson got me a bouquet of flowers while they sat in the back to watch. I gave my statement, it was a rush and a blur. After reading, the judge asked Tony if he would like to apologize to me. Tony declined. The judge slammed the gavel, gave him 6 years of prison time and then the guards took him away. Before the door shut behind Tony and the guard, I could hear a man scream at him. As the door shut, tears rolled down my cheeks. I felt like Olivia Benson, I put a pedophile behind bars.

At the age of 19, I sit by a small river behind the condo complex. I like to watch the river flow. It has been a whole year since Tony's sentencing and graduating high school. Still living with Star and Shannon, I have found a sense of who I am. I feel connected to my wants and dreams. I don't understand how applying for college works. I have tried but gave up for right now.

I work full-time at a daycare as a floater teacher. I enjoy going on walks, smoking weed with friends, working out, writing, and going to Katy Perry concerts. Weed has helped me find healing and self-connection. I love to mediate after smoking, I dig deep into the corner of my mind to clear out the gunk and clutter. I open up my backpack and smoke a small blunt. The sound of the river flowing puts me in a calm state of mind. I pull out my sketch book. I turn to an art piece I am working on. I sit on a rock and begin drawing in black pen. As I draw, I reflect on how free and grown I feel. Having my own money has been fun.

Besides rent and my phone bill, I have spent all my paychecks on a pit tickets for Katy Perry. As I draw, my mind reflects on the moment Katy grabbed my hand during the concert. I chuckle to myself as I draw. Shannon went to one of the concerts with me. She left the pit because she couldn't take all the Katy Perry fans pushing her in the pit. I saw Katy perform a new song that inspired me to have love for myself. It is called 'Unconditionally.' The song sounds like she is singing about having unconditional love for a lover. However, I interpreted the song as her singing the words to herself. "All your dirty laundry never made me blink one time." "I will love you unconditionally..." These words are things I love to tell myself. Finding healing began with facing emotions that I was ignoring. I tried to go to therapy, however, I re-traumatize myself when I have to explain my story to the therapist. I think therapists are great. I had many growing up. I know that I can sit on the therapist's couch and talk about my problems all day. However, I am the one who needs to put action to my wishes of overcoming my past. If I figure out a plan and goals then I can be excited for my future freedom.

From my backpack, I pull out a pink and white binder. This binder is a file I created that is all about me. I gained this idea from doing a project with the preschool class at my job. They all made a paper booklet about themselves. The project made me ponder on my favorite things and attributes about me. In my binder, I have a page on everything I like and dislike. From TV shows to songs and food. I describe how I want to change my name to just M. Why? Well, for me, Maria is sacred. I want her to live freely through the new version of myself, M. On another page, I wrote about how I view the universe and God. I believe there is an all-seeing creator. I do not believe he is a man looking down at us on a throne. In fact, I believe the all-seeing creator is just an energy source that we are all linked to. A gender-neutral source of life. I look up at the sunlight shining between the leaves of the trees. I feel connected to nature around me. I have cried to this river, I have sung songs to this river. I have even written my fears and pain then tossed it into this river. I take a deep breath and pick up the project I was working on.

I am not sure where life will lead me from this point on. I know that I have come too far to ever give up. I finally have my freedom. I must live to see where my life leads. I slide the finished piece into the plastic slot on my binder. Holding up it up, I admire my masterpiece with the swirls around the edges of the paper. On the masterpiece there is artsy handwriting. I write words of advice for myself.

"Nothing gets better until you find
the will inside you that makes you fight the battle
The battle for your life."

—M. Alexis.

These words have helped me realize if we don't find or advocate for ourselves, no one else will. I won the battle of Tony. Victory is mine. I do not have to live my life in fear of his reaction. I do not need to waste time writing letters to convince him I am sorry. The only thing that lingers is the side effects of his abuse. Tony haunts me in my dreams causing me to wake up every day feeling heavy. I have to remind myself that I am not in trouble. I am not at fault. I hate that I feel pain and underlying guilt. The river flows louder and I snap out of my thoughts. I continue to sit on the rock by the river. My mind is in movement with an idea. I open my binder to a clean page. If I had the motivation to always write an apology letter to Tony, who says I can't write one for myself? My moving hand begins to write.

Dear Maria,

I am sorry for the pain and suffering you have endured. Life always seems stacked against you. The path ahead seems unknown. It is alright to fear it. However, embrace it. I am not sure if I feel blessed, lucky or honored to survive the horrid things I experienced. Or perhaps I feel all of those things at once. Don't waste your freedom on locking yourself away. Live life the way you want to. Have fun and smile.

Love always, M.

I read the letter over and over again until my eyes are stuffed with tears. I let them flow. I rip the page out and let it dissolve in the river water as a declaration of my future and healing. I stand to my feet, climb the small hill and head back up to the path. Who knows what could happen next?

Maria becoming one of the first in her family to graduate high school

Maria and Serenity

Maria reconnecting with her sisters

Maria enjoying her freedom, dressing up for the Katy Perry concert

Katy Perry holding Maria's hand during the concert

The river and rock Maria sits on to write, draw, and meditate

Nineteen-year-old Maria free, healing, and excited for her future

The drawing Maria created by the river

About the Author

My name is M. Alexis. I am enjoying my freedom as a young sophisticated woman. Everyday I wake up grateful. I greet the day with joy no matter what life tosses my way. My passion is for writing. I hope to bring my ideas to life within the spirituality, sci-fi and comedic communities. I love spending time with my chihuahua, Jordan. My smile is something no one can take from me. I carry on in the happiness I have created for myself. As I evolve I will never give up on being an advocate for everyone who deserves equality.

www.ingramcontent.com/pod-product-compliance
Lightning Source LLC
Chambersburg PA
CBHW072040160426
43197CB00014B/2567